CAROL RC

THE LITTLE BOOK

of

COFFEE LAW

Cover design by ABA Publishing.

14 13 12 11   5 4 3 2

Library of Congress Cataloging-in-Publication Data

Robertson, Carol, 1948-
   The little book of coffee law / Carol Robertson.
      p. cm.
   Includes index.
   ISBN 978-1-60442-985-5
1. Coffee--Law and legislation--United States. I. Title.
   KF1984.C6R63 2010
   344.73'076373--dc22

                           2010025034

Dedication

*This book is dedicated
to Rochelle and Nabil,
with whom I have shared
many espressos in Milan.*

Table of Contents

Foreword

It may surprise some to learn how much coffee and law have in common. As lawyers, we spend hours pouring over details, ensuring that we understand reasoning and rationale behind case judgments and how these decisions impact our work. Similarly, we in the coffee industry give the utmost care and attention to detail on how our commodity is sourced, roasted and brewed into every cup.

What many don't often realize is that each coffee bean has a story to tell. Many components including the soil, sun, altitude, even the fragrance of nearby plants, can play a role in the unique flavors of each bean. From where the beans are picked in Africa, Asia and Latin America they travel to the places they are roasted and eventually find their way into your cup.

Similarly, the facts of every legal dispute are unique and have traveled a long journey to find their way into the casebooks and the law. All of the cases put before you in this book relate to coffee. As a commodity, coffee has long been the subject and basis of cases ranging from trademark, insurance and trading issues that have been addressed by our legal system. *The Little Book of Coffee Law* provides many examples of how these two delicate crafts intersect.

I hope you enjoy this book and the perspectives it offers—perhaps over a cup of coffee?

executive vice president,
general counsel and secretary,
Paula Boggs
Starbucks

The Origin of Coffee

Black gold. Devil's brew. Wine from Arabia. The Common Man's gold. A dark liqueur. A sinful pleasure. Inspirational. Addictive. Coffee. Coffee has been called all of this and more. First consumed in connection with religious rituals, coffee has been outlawed and restricted from time to time by religious as well as secular leaders who have been fearful not only of its potential harmful effects on those who drank it but also because of the power it seemed to hold and its ability to inspire thought and ultimately foment revolution.

Coffee is a ubiquitous beverage. However, for all the impact that it has had on customs, mores, and the law, unlike wine or beer, its entry into Western Europe and the Americas is relatively recent. Initially discovered in the mountains of what is now Ethiopia, it was first introduced into Yemen and from there into international trade sometime between the fifth and the fifteenth century. Coffee was originally consumed as part of religious rituals—to keep the celebrants awake during nocturnal prayers. But this limitation soon disappeared.

By the late fifteenth century, establishments in Mecca were serving this dark liqueur to pilgrims, and by the early sixteenth century, Cairo had become a center for coffee, establishing the first cafes. Soon coffee drinking had spread across the Middle East and the first cafes were opened in Constantinople (modern Istanbul) in the mid-1500s.[1] In the seventeenth century, the ambassador of the Turkish sultan served coffee to the French

---

1. Coffee beans were carried to Constantinople by Syrian traders in 1555, and soon numerous cafes were in operation. Bernstein, William J., *A Splendid Exchange: How Trade Shaped the World*, Atlantic Monthly Press, New York, NY 2008, p. 246; *See also*, Sonnenfeld, A., Ed., *Food: A Culinary History*, Penguin Books, New York, NY, 2000, translated from *Histoire de l'Alimentation*, Gius. Laterza & Figli, ed. Jean-Louis Flandrin and Massimo Montanari, pp. 386-389.

King Louis XIV.[2] By then, coffee had also become a popular beverage in Italy, Germany, and the Netherlands.[3]

From time to time, efforts were taken to regulate and even ban coffee, but with little or no success. In the sixteenth century, the Grand Vizier attempted to close the coffee houses in Istanbul, fearing that the free speech enjoyed by habitués of coffee houses would foment public opposition to his rule.[4] In Mecca, Khair Beg, its governor, actually put coffee on trial and forbade its sale or consumption. This ban was soon lifted by the coffee-loving sultan of Cairo.[5] In France, attempts were made to create royally sanctioned monopolies over the sale of coffee and then later to assess tariffs on its import.[6] In 1767, Frederick the Great attempted to put import limits on coffee in Prussia, but eventually was forced to give up the effort because his tax officers were ill-treated by the population, who had developed a thirst for coffee and could not bear to have it limited.[7]

From the start, trade in coffee has been restricted and regulated by those who wanted to be the sole beneficiaries of this desirable product, first in the Arab world where the export of coffee plants or of green coffee beans (from which plants could be grown) was banned.[8] This effort was successful for only a short time, as Dutch traders managed to smuggle out coffee plants that they then planted in their colonies in Java.[9] Others—

2. Bernstein, p. 247; *See also*, Allen, Stewart Lee, *The Devil's Cup: A History of the World According to Coffee*, Ballantine Books, 1999, 2003, p. 142.

3. Sonnenfeld, pp. 386-389.

4. Pendergrast, Mark, *Uncommon Grounds: The History of Coffee and How it Transformed Our World*, Basic Books, New York, NY 1999, p. 6.

5. Kolpas, N., *A Cup of Coffee: From Plantation to Pot, A Coffee Lover's Guide to the Perfect Brew*, New York, Grove Press, 1993, p. 17.

6. Lévêque, André, *Histoire de la civilisation française*, Troisième Édition, Holt, Rinehart and Winston, 1966, pp. 168-169.

7. Kolpas, pp. 19-20.

8. Pendergrast, p. 7.

9. Sonnenfeld, p. 388. *See also*, Bernstein, p. 250, and Allen, p. 154. According to Allen, at this point coffee's nickname changed from Mocha to Mocha Java.

French, Portuguese, English, and Brazilian—were able to obtain coffee tree cuttings despite the efforts of the Dutch to maintain its monopoly, and coffee plantations were established in far-ranging parts of the world, including the Americas.

The history and the business of coffee are the stories that this book will tell, through the lens of the law—that is, through legal cases involving the production, distribution, marketing, and sale of coffee in the Americas during a brief moment in coffee history—from the early days of the new Republic of the United States to the present. It is a tale of trade, of subterfuge, and of invention, but it is also the story of the importance that coffee has attained in our daily lives, becoming an essential part of Western European and American culture. This book is also the story of people—those who grow coffee, those who roast and sell it, those who brew it, and those who consume it. Coffee is a dynamic product, evoking mystery and passion, and these play out in the disputes this book narrates, such as the story of a man compelled to return again and again to coffee plantations in Africa against the wishes of his employer; the story of men lusting for power over markets and the profits from coffee to the disadvantage of growers, workers, and investors; the story of men compelled by the desire for profits to engage in smuggling coffee beans.

The book begins and ends with trade—how coffee, grown in subtropical climates, is transported to its ultimate destination. The first case is a tale of adventure on the high seas, as coffee is shipped from the Caribbean to other parts of the world in the late eighteenth century. The last two cases involve "fair trade" in coffee, of contracts that are disadvantageous to coffee growers in the global coffee economy and whether local governments have the ability to mandate fair trade in their own coffee purchases. Other cases involve the role that new investment products invented largely by the Dutch—such as insurance and commodities futures—played in the growth of coffee imports. A number of cases illustrate the growth and commercialization of the coffee business, particularly in the mid-twentieth century, as coffee marketers, ever eager to increase their market share in an increasingly competitive market, attempted to dominate the U.S. coffee market.

This is also the story of innovation in coffee products, including the invention of vacuum-sealed coffee, instant coffee, and of new ways of brewing coffee. And these cases also tell a story of changing and developing coffee tastes, particularly in the last part of the twentieth century, with the adoption of espresso drinks and other gourmet coffees into everyday life in the United States, the growth of, and competition among, coffee shops and their impact on coffee culture, and the importance of coffee brands and labels. Interspersed throughout the book will be coffee breaks—short pieces that provide a background into the world of coffee: coffee customs, coffee brewing methods, as well as the legal world in which coffee is grown, produced, shipped, marketed, sold, and consumed. So pour yourself a nice hot cup of coffee, sit back, breathe in the aroma, and enjoy.

The Abyssinian Goatherd

According to legend, coffee was first discovered over a thousand years ago by an Abyssinian goatherd. Alone, in the high hills above his village, he noticed that his goats frolicked happily whenever they nibbled the bright red berries that grew on glossy green trees. He decided to try these berries himself and was amazed to find himself so alert, so full of energy. He brought them back to the village but the village elders were fearful of their magic powers. They threw the berries into the fire to destroy them but then were enticed by the aroma that rose from the roasting berries. They quickly pulled the now roasted beans from the fire, ground them into a powder, and dissolved it in hot water to create the first cups of coffee.

If this tale seems too imaginative, there is nevertheless a truth behind the inventiveness: at some time during the first millennium, coffee was discovered growing wild in the mountainous areas of what is now Ethiopia and became a source of sustenance for early Arab traders, who brought the beans to Mecca. These first nomads used coffee as food—grinding the beans into a paste, mixing this with grains, and rolling the mixture into balls that they carried as rations, which were valued for their sustaining effect.

Early traders, who encountered coffee as they made their way up and down the Arab peninsula, brought the green beans to their villages and planted them, cultivating the first domestic coffee plants. They learned to roast the beans and made the first coffee beverage, not unlike the Turkish coffee now consumed in coffee houses throughout the Arab world. From Mecca and the southern port of Mocha in what is now Yemen, other traders discovered coffee and the beverage soon made its way to Turkey, and from there to Austria, Germany, and the rest of Western Europe. From this humble beginning, by the end of the twentieth century, coffee had become one of the most traded commodities (second only to petroleum) in the world[1] and a universal beverage.

---

1. Pendergrast, p. xv.

THE LITTLE BOOK

of

COFFEE LAW

Chapter One

It's a Pirate's Life for Him:
The "Flying Fish" Case

Little v. Barreme, 6 U.S. 170, 2 Cranch 170 (1804)

From the earliest days, trade in coffee has been viewed as a wellspring of profit. The history of coffee is filled with stories of those who sought to control that trade—from the early Arabs who prohibited the sale of green coffee beans to foreign merchants to the French and Prussians, who exacted high tariffs on coffee roasters—and those who found ways to circumvent those controls. This would include the Dutch who found a way to grow coffee trees in Java, and later the French who transplanted coffee to the New World island of Martinique in the Caribbean. And this would include Captain George Little, an officer in the nascent U.S. Navy, who intercepted many an errant, coffee-laden ship in the waters of the Caribbean. Captain Little was like many other sea captains of the late eighteenth century—a little bit buccaneer, a little bit adventurer, not much different from the pirates he pursued. Poorly paid, he derived additional income from bounties obtained from the capture of vessels on the high seas carrying illegal cargo, generally receiving as much as 50 percent of the total value of the forfeited commodities. He was the subject of a number of court cases involving disputes over cargoes that he captured. But he remained undeterred. The incentives were too high: a ship filled with coffee was a profitable find for Captain Little. And thus he must have thought himself lucky to have captured the Dutch vessel, named the "Flying Fish," off the coast of Martinique, in late 1799.

By the end of the eighteenth century, coffee shipments from the French colonies in the Caribbean—particularly from Hispaniola (Haiti and Santo Domingo)—provided the bulk of France's then supply of coffee.[1] According to one study, by the eve of the French Revolution in 1789, Haiti alone was supplying half of the coffee consumed in France.[2] The Revolution and the wars that followed created significant disruptions in trade. Because the countries of Europe were at war with France and at times with each other during the period after the French Revolution until the defeat of Napoleon at Waterloo, it was considered a legitimate practice for a government to declare open season on another country's vessels in the Caribbean, depending on the alliances that were formed at the time. This disrupted not just French trade but also that of the newly formed United States. It was a form of legalized piracy, and in fact it was often difficult to distinguish the real pirates from those who, theoretically at least, were in the employ of an official government. They all depended on booty to survive. British sea captains were particularly aggressive in attacking vessels bound from the Caribbean, carrying coffee, tea, and sugar, to U.S. ports, at least until 1796. That year, the United States negotiated a treaty with Britain that ended their attacks on U.S. flagged vessels, at least for a time.[3]

1. Sonnenfeld, p. 388.
2. Watkins, T., "The Political and Economic History of Haiti," San Jose State University Department of Economics, 2010, http://www.sjsu.edu/faculty/watkins/haiti.htm.
3. Palmer, Michael A., "History of early US trade in the Caribbean," A History of the US Navy: The Navy: The Continental Period, 1775-1890, DEPARTMENT OF THE NAVY—NAVAL HISTORICAL CENTER, http://www.history.navy.mil/history/history2.htm.

However, into this brief period of calm stepped the French, outraged that their long-time ally since the days of the U.S. War of Independence would enter into a treaty with their mutual enemy, Britain. In retaliation, the French began attacking U.S.-flagged ships on the high seas, particularly near French colonies in the Caribbean. When the United States sent envoys to France to negotiate with Talleyrand, France's foreign minister, he demanded bribes to even see them.[4] This conduct outraged President John Adams, who demanded legislation from Congress empowering U.S. ships to target French commerce in the Caribbean in retaliation. In response, Congress enacted the Act of 9th February 1799, which began the undeclared "Quasi-War" with France.[5]

If we thought that relations between the United States and France were tense after the 2003 invasion of Iraq when "Freedom Fries" appeared on restaurant menus, let's not forget other times in our history when the French have provoked the anger of the U.S. Congress. When President Adams sent word to members of Congress that U.S. envoys had been refused an audience with Monsieur Talleyrand, they were stirred into open animosity. The Act of 1799 suspended commerce between the United States and France and authorized the seizure of French or American ships heading to French colonies in the Caribbean. The penalty for any vessel violating the Act was forfeiture of the entire cargo. President Adams went further than the Act allowed, ordering commanders of U.S. ships to stop any French or U.S.-flagged ships that were sailing to or from French ports in the Caribbean.

This presidential order gave Captain Little his opportunity. He was from all accounts not one to shy away from a ship full of

---

4. The so-called "XYZ Affair." Zarzeczny, Matthew, "The Quasi War with France," FINS, http://www.tallshipformidable.com/html/quasi-war_with_france.html.

5. Zarzeczny.

valuable cargo, particularly because the Act also provided that any seized and forfeited goods were to be sold and the proceeds of sale were to be divided equally between the government and the captain who brought in the vessel—a lucrative opportunity for a sea captain with a little buccaneer in him. In December 1799, Little seized a ship, the Flying Fish, that was carrying a load of coffee to the Danish island of St. Thomas in the Caribbean from Jerême, part of the French Virgin Islands. He brought the ship into port in Boston.

Once in port, however, things started to go wrong for George Little. He had thought himself on firm ground (so to speak) with this seizure: the captain of the Flying Fish spoke perfect English, with an American accent, and Little was sure that he had grabbed an American ship (surreptitiously sailing under a foreign flag in order to smuggle its precious cargo, coffee, away from U.S. control). But Little was proven wrong. The captain of the Flying Fish may have spoken English but this was only because he had worked previously on some American ships. He was, in fact, Prussian by birth and at the time of the capture was an inhabitant of St. Thomas and claimed Danish citizenship. He sued Captain Little for damages for unlawful seizure and trespass.

Because the Flying Fish was sailing under the Danish flag, it was neither French nor American and was not subject to seizure under the Act, nor technically under President Adams's more expansive order. But George Little nevertheless claimed that his actions were justified and that no unlawful trespass had occurred because he could not have been expected to know that the ship was not American, particularly given the captain's facility in speaking English. It was true that he had not tried to verify the ship's identity before hauling it into Boston harbor. It was worth taking a chance that the full cargo of coffee—too tempting to ignore—was being smuggled. The odds of this being the case were in Captain Little's favor. If he had judged correctly, he would have been entitled to over $8,000 as his share of the bounty, an enormous sum at that time.

The case went to the U. S. Supreme Court in one of the court's first decisions, rendered by its first Chief Justice, John Marshall. The court ruled against Little, awarding to the Flying Fish's owner a judgment of $8,400. The Chief Justice stated that, even in a time of hostilities, a president could not take actions beyond what Congress had authorized. The congressional Act had only authorized the seizure of U.S. ships sailing *to* French ports, not coming *from* the French colonies. In this case, the Flying Fish had picked up its load of coffee in Jerême, a French

7

colony, and was returning to St. Thomas, that is, it was sailing *from* the French port. Little had tried to argue that he was only obeying a presidential order when he seized the ship. The Court rejected this argument, noting that commanders "act at their own peril" when they obey invalid orders. "The [presidential] instructions cannot change the nature of the transactions, or legalize an Act which without those instructions would have been a plain trespass."

As a footnote, this was not the first nor was it the last time that Little skirted the edges of the law on the high seas. In 1800, two weeks after the Treaty of Mortefontaine ended the Quasi-War hostilities with France, Little was court-martialed for looting the possessions of French officers when he seized their vessel. And in that same year, he was sued by a sea captain named Silas Talbot for refusing to split the bounty paid out from the seizure of a French vessel, "Les Deux Anges."[6] *Deux Anges*, indeed—neither Little nor Talbot nor any other seaman at this time would likely have been called an *ange* or an angel.

---

6. *Little v. Les Deux Anges* (D. Mass. June 2, 1800), aff'd sub nom *Talbot v. Little* (Cir. Ct. Mass. Oct. 21, 1800), appeal on writ of error dismissed, S. Ct. Docket No. 96 (Feb. 7, 1805), cited in Leiner, Frederick C., "Anatomy of a Prize Case: Dollars, Side-Deals, and *Les Deux Anges*," *The American Journal of Legal History*, Temple University, Vol. 39, No. 2 (Apr. 1995), pp. 214-232, found at http://www.jstor.org/stable/845901.

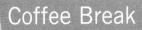

Coffee Break

The Coffee Trade: A Tale of Treachery and Smugglers

Coffee can be considered the first mass-marketed commodity. Trade in coffee is and has always been important because, from the first, coffee was more than just a beverage. Because the popularity of this drink demanded the availability of large quantities of coffee beans, Western European nations were early on interested in entering the coffee trade.

Until the seventeenth century, all coffee imported into Europe came from the Arabian Peninsula. It was illegal to export green coffee beans out of the Red Sea port of Mocha.[1] But the Dutch were up to the challenge. In 1616, Dutch traders successfully smuggled coffee plants from Mocha and set up coffee plantations in their newly captured colony in Sri Lanka.[2] By the eighteenth century, they had successfully transplanted coffee production to Java and had become the leading coffee trader into Europe. France soon followed, taking coffee trees to Guiana and starting coffee plantations in the Caribbean.

The Dutch were very protective of their coffee production, which had led to their trading success, and outlawed the import of any coffee trees out of their colonies. How did the French acquire the ability to produce coffee? The story of French coffee production is one of smuggling and espionage, and adventure on the high seas. In 1714, a Dutch diplomat gave a coffee tree from Java as a gift to King Louis XIV of France, who had it planted for display in the Jardin des Plantes in Paris.[3] From that point on, this special plant was guarded day and night and no one was allowed to take cuttings, as this was a royal tree.

In 1723, a young French naval officer, Mathieu Gabriel de Clieu, believed that coffee could be produced in the French colony of Martinique in the Caribbean. When he asked Louis XV for permission to take a cutting from the royal coffee plant, the king refused. Not daunted by this refusal, de Clieu entered the royal garden in the dark of night, using accomplices to distract

Coffee Break (continued)

the guards, and took a cutting from the precious plant. He then sailed for Martinique, with his special cargo encased in a glass cabinet.[4]

De Clieu's voyage to Martinique was not for the cowardly.[5] To successfully transport his plant, he had to overcome countless near calamities, any one of which should have destroyed the fragile coffee plant. Unknown to him, a Dutch spy was among his crew who tried to steal de Clieu's little sapling while de Clieu was giving it its daily sunbath on the ship's deck. De Clieu managed to rescue it, but in the course of the fight among the crew, a shoot was broken off the fragile plant. De Clieu next had to do battle with a corsair—pirates who attempted to steal his precious cargo. De Clieu's men managed to fight off the attackers during a daylong gun battle on the high seas.

Just when they thought themselves safe, a sudden Atlantic storm almost caused the vessel to capsize. The glass cabinet that held de Clieu's fragile plant fell and broke, but miraculously the plant survived. Just as suddenly, the seas calmed, the winds died down, and the vessel was stalled without making any progress for several days. During this time, provisions were depleted, including the ship's stores of potable water. The little that remained was rationed among the men. But de Clieu remained invincible, sharing his meager daily water ration with his little plant to ensure its survival. At last, the ship limped into shore in Martinique. De Clieu planted his coffee tree, which amazingly thrived. Within just a few years, there were successful coffee plantations in Martinique and elsewhere in the Caribbean. Coffee production had become so successful that King Louis forgave his disobedient officer, making him governor of the Antilles,[6] which unfortunately proves once again that it is better to beg for forgiveness after the fact than to ask first for permission.

Coffee trade in the Caribbean was not without risk. During much of the eighteenth and nineteenth centuries, Europe was in a perpetual state of war. Although much of the fighting took place in Europe, the "wars" were also carried out in the trade lanes of the Caribbean. Pirates, surrogate armies for the various European nations—especially France and Britain—roamed freely, acting loosely on behalf of one or other country. It was often difficult to distinguish between true buccaneers and legalized pirates: captains of British, French, and United States flagged vessels. These sailors were not so much patriotic as opportunistic. The promise of personal wealth and the freedom of the high seas were motivators for their activities.

Had pirates been able to continue their free activities, eventually trade would have been stymied. But, as the wars in Europe were gradually settled in the mid-nineteenth century, and because of the recognition of the great profit to be gained from lucrative trade in highly popular commodities such as coffee and sugar, global trade grew. It was facilitated, and indeed made possible, by the development and enforcement of property rights and the rule of law.

The French were not able to control the coffee market. In 1727, just a few years after de Clieu's arrival in Martinique, a Brazilian ambassador, invited to mediate a border dispute between French Guiana and Dutch Guiana, charmed the French governor's wife during his diplomatic mission. Once he had resolved the dispute, as he boarded his ship to return to Brazil, this lady gave him a present of a bouquet of flowers, into which she had concealed berries from a coffee plant.[7] From a small act of love and treachery, this Frenchwoman created the biggest competitive threat to French coffee interests in the Caribbean. Brazil eventually became the foremost producer of coffee until, by the start of the twentieth century, this country had a three-quarters share of the world's coffee production.[8]

---

1. Pendergrast, p. 7.

2. Sonnenfeld, p. 388. *See also*, Bernstein, p. 256.

3. Sonnenfeld, p. 388. Louis XIV died in 1715.

4. Allen, p. 161.

5. Stewart Lee Allen describes in detail de Clieu's various adventures during his voyage to Martinique. Allen, pp. 166-168, 170, 172.

6. Sonnenfeld, p. 388.

7. Sonnenfeld, p. 388.

8. Pendergrast, p. 29.

Chapter Two

The Wreck of the Mary W.:
Insuring Your Coffee

Orient Mutual Ins. Co. v. Wright, 68 U.S. 456 (1863)

There is an adage that insurance is cheap and plentiful in those times when you don't need it, but woe to anyone who actually has a claim. This was a hard-learned lesson for a coffee trader named Wright, who discovered after the ship carrying his shipment of coffee was lost at sea that the cargo insurance he had purchased had not actually covered that particular load of coffee, or so his insurers claimed.

It is an interesting factoid in the history of coffee that maritime and other insurance products, as we know them today, originated in a coffee shop. As early as the seventeenth century, the increase in global trade, particularly between London, France, and their colonies in the Americas, and the inherent risk in sea voyages in the eighteenth and nineteenth centuries, led to an increasing demand for ship and cargo insurance.[1] From the middle ages, sea loans—a loan that was to be repaid only fol-

---

1. Kingston, Christopher, "Maritime Insurance in Britain and America, 1720-1844: A Comparative Institutional Analysis," September 7, 2004, Dept. of Economics, Amherst College, Amherst, MA 01002, found at http://cniss.wustl.edu/workshoppapers/Kingston CNISS.pdf, p. 2.

lowing a successful voyage—had served as a type of cargo insurance.[2] These contracts depended upon wealthy individuals who could underwrite specific risks on a case-by-case basis. But the development of true maritime insurance became a crucial driver for the increase in global trade in the nineteenth century. The expanding need for these types of policies coincided with the growing popularity of coffee drinking, and Lloyd's of London met both these needs.

The first London coffee house was opened in 1652 and was instantly popular.[3] These coffee houses proliferated until, by the 1680s, they numbered in the hundreds.[4] Their popularity as meeting places where business transactions could be conducted was quickly established. Sometime around 1688, Edward Lloyd established his coffee house. From the first, Lloyd encouraged a clientele of merchants, sea captains, ship owners, and others with an interest in overseas trade, and those willing to underwrite cargo shipments, who came to enjoy his coffee and to share the latest shipping news.[5]

At first, maritime insurance transactions were fairly informal. A merchant with a ship to insure would request a "broker" to take the policy from one wealthy merchant to another until the risk was fully covered. The broker's skill was in ensuring that only persons with sufficient financial integrity covered the ships and their cargoes. Lloyd went further than most coffee house owners in amassing an incredible amount of shipping information to share with his customers. At a time before the Internet, before television or radio, before the telephone or teletype, when

---

2. Kingston, p. 3.
3. Sonnenfeld, p. 388. This café was established by a Greek named Pasqua Rosee and an Englishman named Daniel Edwards "in a shed in the churchyard in St. Michael Cornhill," Kolpas, p. 21.
4. Kolpas, p. 21.
5. Allen, p. 74.

most forms of communication were slow and unreliable, Lloyd's had a reputation for being a place where timely and trustworthy information could be had.[6]

This type of information was invaluable: there were numerous sources of uncertainty.[7] The underwriter needed to be able to assess the probability of a ship or its cargo being lost or damaged, and the appropriate premium to be charged depended on many risk factors, including the distance, the route, the season, and the characteristics of the ship—its age and seaworthiness—as well as the quality of its crew. In addition, in wartime, there was the possibility of capture by enemy privateers or cruisers, or seizure in a foreign port. And even during periods of relative peace, pirates always presented a threat. Add to that the lack of equilibrium between those who had and those who lacked critical intelligence. Merchants seeking insurance had a greater familiarity with the vessel as well as the cargo—in all, much better information than the insurer. There was a natural temptation for the insured to conceal information about a ship or the voyage and to take excessive risks once the policy was in place, such as sending the cargo in unseaworthy ships. Some were willing to commit outright fraud, such as insuring for more than the ship or the goods were worth and then deliberately sinking or running the ship aground, or seeking to insure a ship already known to be lost. In short, information was critical and painfully hard to obtain. Thus, many insurers were wary.[8]

To accurately assess the risk of a voyage, an underwriter had to have access to prompt and accurate intelligence on the movements and condition of particular ships, on political developments at home and abroad, and on the reliability and reputation

6. Pendergrast, p. 13.
7. Kingston, p. 3.
8. Kingston, p. 12.

of the merchant being insured, as well as the captain of the vessel in question. In a time without 24/7 information sources, a person with the networks and skills to assemble and disseminate information would win out in the risky world of maritime underwriting. Edward Lloyd was such an individual.

His coffee house served as a center of maritime information, and not just because his clientele possessed specialized knowledge and could bring in the latest news and gossip from the shipping world, although this was true. To meet his customers' needs, Lloyd made it his business to gather and disseminate the most accurate and up-to-date information. Besides relying on knowledgeable customers, Lloyd engaged runners who went along the docks gathering news of ship arrivals, departures, losses, and any relevant gossip and who brought it back daily to the coffee house. He built up a network of domestic and international correspondents who wrote to him regularly with shipping information from their home ports.[9] By 1740, over 90 percent of British maritime underwriting was done at Lloyd's.[10] Even though Lloyd's coffee shop did not outlive his death in 1715,[11] the business transacted in this central meeting place has lasted to this day. By the early 1760s, a committee of Lloyd's underwriters employed surveyors to assess the condition of ships and this information was placed in the Lloyd's Register, giving any underwriters information on the condition of any ships that they had an opportunity to insure.

In the American colonies, maritime insurance was carried out on an individual basis, much as in Britain. Merchants met in coffee houses and taverns "where they shared news and insured

---

9. Lloyd's was the first to use surveyors to assess the condition of ships. Kingston, p. 10.

10. History of Lloyd's of London, found at http://www.lloyds.com/About_Us/History/Chronology.htm.

11. Allen, p. 74.

each other's ventures."[12] But the security for such insurance could not match what was available in London at the time. Therefore, despite the inconvenience, colonial Americans frequently obtained insurance in London.[13] After the Napoleanic wars in the late eighteenth and early nineteenth centuries, Americans recognized the need for greater financial security for their growing trade. The first American maritime insurance corporation, The Insurance Company of North America, was formed in Philadelphia in 1792 and chartered in 1794.[14] By the mid-nineteenth century, there were insurance corporations in every important port in the United States, although the center of insurance activity was in New York.

These insurance companies employed the same methods as the early Lloyd's underwriters to determine probabilities and to fix premiums—they employed inspectors to verify the condition of ships, the reputations of ships' captains, and the integrity of the merchants to whom they issued insurance contracts. Each kept a register of ships in commerce in their home ports and the rating that each ship received at the time of its last inspection in that port. However, it was not until the end of the nineteenth century that a uniform rating system was available to all member insurance companies.[15] Until that time, each company kept its own register and relied upon the rating established for each ship in that register, based on ship inspections in the port where the insurance company did business. A ship that had not been rated by that insurance company could not be insured. The resulting lack of consistency was the source of Wright's problems.

---

12. Kingston, p. 16.
13. Kingston, p. 16.
14. Kingston, p. 18. The President and Directors of this new joint stock corporation were underwriters who had conducted business from City Tavern in Philadelphia. Two coffee houses in New York fulfilled a comparable function, pp. 17-18.
15. Kingston, p. 32.

17

Wright was a coffee trader. He bought coffee in South and Central America and shipped it to ports in the United States, in particular the port of New Orleans, which before the Civil War was the major port of entry for coffee into the United States. In the mid-1850s, Wright bought insurance policies from two New York-based companies, the Orient Mutual Insurance Company and the Sun Insurance Company. These were so-called "running policies," which allowed Wright to insure each shipment of coffee even though he had no way of knowing in advance which ship would be carrying the coffee. Under this type of policy, Wright paid a standard premium on a quarterly basis and was assured that, as long as he shipped his coffee in a "seaworthy" vessel, the coffee cargo would be insured under the policy for no additional premium. If the ship in which the coffee was shipped did not meet the required ranking for a "seaworthy" vessel (an A-2 ranking for Orient Mutual), then Wright's cargo was still insured as long as he paid an additional surcharge on the premium.

On July 12, 1856, 5,000 bags of coffee that Wright had purchased in Brazil were loaded onto a vessel called the Mary W. in Rio de Janeiro bound for the port of New Orleans. When Wright notified his insurance companies that the coffee had been shipped, they refused to insure the load because they claimed that the Mary W. was an inferior ship. Wright disagreed, attesting to the ship's seaworthiness, and demanded that the companies honor the insurance policies. They then agreed to insure the cargo but only if Wright paid a higher premium. Wright refused to pay.

As luck would have it, on July 29, the Mary W.'s captain steered the ship some 70 miles off course and then ran into some rocks. Unfortunately for Wright, the ship sank and its load of coffee was lost. Wright made a claim for the value of the lost cargo. Of course, the insurance companies both denied his claim, stating that the coffee shipment was not insured under the policies. Wright sued.

At trial, everyone agreed that the Mary W. did not meet the A-2 rating required by the policy to be considered "seaworthy." The trial court then held that, because Wright had refused to pay the increased premium demanded by the insurance companies at the time the Mary W. sailed, there was no insurance coverage for that particular shipment of coffee. The appellate court ordered a new trial.

At the second trial, Wright refused to concede that the Mary W. did not meet the A-2 standard required by the policy. The Mary W. had last been rated in New York during a stopover in 1849, and had received a below A-2 rating, but a rating that was seven years old was regarded by all insurers as stale, and therefore no rating at all. Wright pointed out that even though the ship might not have met the New York rating criteria used by Orient Mutual, which were considered to be more rigorous than those used by companies in other port cities, the vessel might have rated even higher in Rio or in Baltimore (where it had last been inspected). At both Baltimore and Rio, the ship had received an A-2 rating, according to Wright. Moreover, the attorney for Orient Mutual had previously provided a statement that, by the time the Mary W. left Rio, because of extensive and thorough repairs, she "was in seaworthy condition, fit in any voyage, and especially for the transportation of coffee." He further had stated that the ship was "entitled to a rate, and did in fact rate, at A-2 there."

For its part, Orient Mutual wanted the contract terms to be interpreted by usage: the rating for a vessel in its policy can only be the reference for the vessel in the company's own register. This might have been a good argument for Orient Mutual except for an inconvenient fact: the Mary W. was not in the company's register and therefore had no rating. Orient Mutual had only been incorporated in 1854 and had very few ratings for vessels in its register. It accordingly frequently relied on other companies' ratings.

The trial court accepted the additional evidence of the Mary W.'s seaworthiness and found for Wright.

On appeal to the U.S. Supreme Court, Orient Mutual tried to show that the insurance policy always required an additional premium whether or not the ship was above or below an A-2 rating and that, because the parties could not agree on the amount of the increased premium, there was no contract.

The Court asked why they should believe that a trader would pay a premium for a "running policy" if an additional premium was always required. And, the Court asked, would any reasonable shipper pay premiums for an insurance policy on coffee cargoes to be shipped on an ongoing basis in any seaworthy vessel if he knew that he was only entitled to ship on a limited selection of vessels, which might not be available to him at the port of origin for months to come? What value would such a policy have where the insurance company's register was incomplete? To the Court, this seemed inconceivable.

Moreover, the Court noted that the policy did not call for an increased premium in all cases and, on prior shipments, Wright had not been asked to pay any such additional premium. By its own terms, the policy called for no increase in premium on some shipments, an increase for others, and some shipments were entitled to a premium decrease. Because the terms of the contract seemed clear that the policy would apply as long as the shipper selected a seaworthy vessel, the insurer could not deny coverage arbitrarily simply because the ship did not appear on a registry that only dated back two years.

Quit stalling and pay up, said the Court, in so many words. Joyful words to the ears of an insured, even if late in coming— seven years after the cargo was lost.

Coffee Break

The Sinister Side of Coffee Trade: Coffee and the Slave Trade

It is a fair statement to say that the growth of the coffee trade in the eighteenth and nineteenth centuries depended on the slave trade and that coffee's wealth was built on the backs of slaves. This is the sinister side of coffee.

Sugar and coffee go hand in hand and both of these commodities were produced in the Caribbean, as well as in Central and South America, by thousands of slaves imported into these areas annually from Africa.[1] The history of coffee—and the development of coffee plantations in the western hemisphere—is intrinsically tied to the history of the slave trade.[2] Between 1500 and 1900, Europeans (and Americans) uprooted millions of people throughout West Africa and West Central Africa and shipped them across the Atlantic under inhumane conditions to work on coffee plantations in the New World. Many died during the voyage; many others died from the brutal conditions in which they were forced to work and live.[3]

The transatlantic slave trade generally followed a triangular route. Traders set out from European ports, largely from Britain and the Netherlands, and sailed to West African ports carrying loads of woolen and cotton fabrics, weapons, and other goods manufactured in Europe. These products were exchanged with African traders for slaves, who were then loaded into ships. The voyage across the Atlantic, known as the Middle Passage, generally took six to eight weeks. Once in the Americas, those Africans who had survived the journey were sold as slaves—in Brazil, the Caribbean, and elsewhere in the Americas—and forced to work on sugar and coffee plantations. The ships then returned to Europe filled with goods such as sugar cane and bags of coffee, which had been produced by slave labor.[4]

While this was a basic model, the so-called "triangular route" was more complicated. Some of these ships, laden with coffee,

21

Coffee Break (continued)

might have traveled to other ports in the Caribbean where the coffee shipments would be exchanged for other products, or the coffee might be shipped from there to one or more ports in the southern United States where locally grown commodities, such as tobacco or cotton, would be loaded into the cargo holds for shipment back to Britain. Or the coffee might make its way to a northern American port, such as Boston, where it would be off-loaded and replaced with textiles. The colonists in the Americas also made direct slaving voyages to Africa. This trade increased after 1800, as Brazil in particular, due to its increasing role in the supply of coffee, sought larger and larger numbers of slaves to work under inhumane conditions in the coffee plantations.[5]

Britain banned the slave trade (but not slavery itself) in 1807.[6] Other countries followed suit. Brazil was the last Atlantic import nation to outlaw the slave trade in 1831. However, illegal trading continued for another 60 years. Much of this unauthorized trade was to sugar plantations in the Caribbean and to coffee plantations in Brazil. During the period between 1807 and 1869, Britain had a love-hate relationship with Brazil.[7] British ships carried a large share of Brazil's coffee and sugar, but British traders had to acquire these by indirect routes for fear of otherwise stimulating a slave-trade revival. While battles were waged between necessity, philanthropy, and well-disguised self-interest, half a million Africans were enslaved, shipped, and off-boarded in Brazil during the period between 1830 and 1850.[8] Brazil's economy was adversely affected by the suppression of the slave trade.[9]

On the surface, Britain was deeply opposed to the slave trade; however, many British merchants collaborated with Brazilian plantation owners, dealing in what they knew would be "slave goods" in Africa, and arranging for continued delivery of coffee into Britain. Much of the social life of Western Europe in the nineteenth century depended on the product of slave labor. In homes and coffee houses in Europe and in America, people met over coffee, sweetened with Caribbean sugar. They wore

22

clothes made from American cotton, and smoked pipes filled with Virginia tobacco.

The end of the slave trade, and eventually of slavery, did not bring an end to Brazil's dominance of global coffee production, however. Once slavery was outlawed, Brazil brought into its plantations a new form of labor—the *colonos*—Italian immigrants. Under the *colono* system, Brazilian coffee production grew until, by the end of the nineteenth century, it had flooded the world marketplace with coffee.[10]

1. Pendergrast, p. 17.

2. Mintz, Sidney W., *Tasting Food, Tasting Freedom: Excursions into Eating, Culture and the Past*, Beacon Press, Boston, 1996, p. 22.

3. Mintz, pp. 37-38. Mintz estimates that nine and one-half million enslaved Africans reached the Americas between 1503 and 1886, of which almost a third (2.6 million) were brought into the Caribbean islands.

4. Pendergrast, p. 18. Haiti, alone among the Caribbean islands where coffee production had been introduced, ceased to be a significant coffee-producing nation in 1791, when the slaves rioted and took over the government of the island. Most of the coffee plantations were burned during the uprising. Allen, p. 174.

5. Pendergrast, pp. 22-23. Per Allen, over a two hundred year peiod, three million Africans were brought to Brazil to work in coffee plantations, Allen, p. 174.

6. Pendergrast, p. 23.

7. Thomas, Hugh, *The Slave Trade: the Story of the Atlantic Slave Trade 1440-1870*, Simon & Schuster, 1999, p. 630.

8. Bethell, Leslie, *The Abolition of the Brazil Slave Trade: Britain, Brazil and the Slave Trade Question, 1807-69*, Cambridge Univ. Press, 1970, p. 395.

9. Eltis, David, *Economic Growth and the Ending of the Transatlantic Slave Trade*, Oxford University Press, 1987, p. 236.

10. Pendergrast, pp. 28-29.

Chapter Three

I Like My Coffee Fully Leaded:
Adulterated Coffee

Arbuckle v. Blackburn, 191 U.S. 405 (1903)

R eading an ingredient label on a can of prepared food products today seems to require a degree in chemistry. Consider the following ingredient list for Suisse Mocha® Coffee, produced by General Foods International Coffees:

> Sugar, Nondairy Creamer [Corn Syrup Solids, Partially Hydrogenated Coconut Oil, Sodium Caseinate, Dipotassium Phosphate, Mono- and Diglycerides, Artificial Flavor], Cocoa (Processed with Alkali), Instant Coffee, Contains Less Than 2% of Nonfat Milk, Natural and Artificial Flavor, Lactose, Xanthan Gum, Salt, Sodium Citrate.

But at least, this label tells us what we are consuming so we know that, compared to the levels of sugar and other flavorings, actual coffee—in the form of instant coffee—is low on the list. Nevertheless, if there are inaccuracies in a product label or if the raw material supplier deceived the food producer, some of the risks we face today from prepared foods are comparable to those faced by coffee consumers in the nineteenth century.

Recent headlines have informed us that some food products imported from China, for example, may contain lead, melamine, and other harmful substances.[1] This was shocking news for U.S. consumers who have been comfortable in the knowledge that food safety laws in place since the early twentieth century should prevent such adulteration. In the nineteenth century, few such protections existed. Coffee roasters, in order to improve the appearance of inferior beans, used various substances, including lead and arsenic, as coloring agents. By the end of the century, there was great concern about adulteration of coffee, which by then had become America's favorite beverage.

Part of these concerns were raised by the coffee trade itself—competitors attacking each other's products—as well as by Charles Post, the inventor of Postum, a beverage made of toasted bran and sugar. Not content with merely extolling the health benefits of his coffee substitute, Post was a master marketer who made aggressive claims against the coffee industry and the products then being sold as "coffee,"[2] but which had been doctored with other substances to make them seem fresher, to disguise the flavor of moldy or bitter beans, and to stretch the product (by adding chicory or other extenders) for the sake of profitability.

But Post was not alone. Long before political campaigns learned the value of negative advertising, many coffee roasters then in business produced advertisements attacking the low quality of their competitors' products, including charges of adulteration.[3] And to a great extent, these ads were accurate: much of what was then sold as "coffee" consisted of nothing more than toasted grains, or worse, a blend containing minimal amounts of coffee, mixed with ingredients of uncertain provenance.

To prevent the most egregious cases of food adulteration, a

1. *See*, for example, Yardley, Jim, "More Candy From China, Tainted, Is in U.S.", *The New York Times*, Oct. 1, 2008, A 14, http://www.nytimes.com/2008/10/02/world/asia/02milk.html?_r=1.
2. Pendergrast, p. 99.
3. Pendergrast, p. 104.

number of states—including the state of Ohio—passed laws outlawing the adulteration of food and drugs. Ohio's law, passed in 1884, provided that no person within the state could offer for sale any article of food that was adulterated. "Adulterated," as defined in the statute, was, among other things, the result of mixing any substance with a food product so as to "injuriously affect its quality, strength or purity" or if it was "colored, coated, polished or powdered, whereby damage or inferiority" was concealed, or "if by any means it is made to appear better or of greater value than it really is." This law apparently had little impact on the quality of coffee sold in the state at the time, but it was used in an attempt to ensnare a very successful coffee business, Arbuckle Brothers, and its owner, John Arbuckle.

Coffee, as it was brewed in America in the mid- to- late nineteenth century, must have been a pretty foul substance. Even without adulteration, coffee beans, most of which at the time were imported from Brazil, were of inconsistent quality. They were purchased green from the local general store, usually from bulk bins or boxes that were located near the pickle barrel, for example. It is easy to imagine the odors and flavors that these beans acquired. Once purchased, they were roasted in a frying pan over a wood-burning stove or open fire (acquiring at best an uneven roast and at worst a burnt flavor), then ground and boiled in water for 10 to 20 minutes. Once poured into a cup, the coffee was thick with grounds that had to be "clarified." The most popular medium for use in clarification was an egg—preferably just the shells but at times, the whites or even the whole egg. Eggshells have a very thin membrane that helped congeal or "clear" the grounds, making them easier to strain. (In times when no eggs were available, eel skins or other suspiciously odd items were recommended.)[4]

---

4. Pendergrast, pp. 46-47.

John Arbuckle found his niche in this uncertain milieu by producing a coffee that was superior to the commonly available fare. After the Civil War, most coffee was brought into the United States through the port of New York, where Arbuckle established his coffee business. There he developed a coffee product that he called "Ariosa," which quickly became one of the best-selling coffees in the United States, from the East Coast to as far as the western frontier, where cowboys boiled strong Ariosa coffee over their campfires, and the Southwest, where Navajos built dwellings out of empty Ariosa wooden crates.[5]

Ariosa's main selling point was that it had a consistent flavor of somewhat higher quality than most beans then available. Arbuckle sold roasted rather than green beans, and he packaged them in sealed one-pound bags rather than in bulk. Although green beans can stay fresh for months, once roasted, coffee quickly loses its fresh flavor. To keep Ariosa beans from going stale, and to help in "clarifying" the boiled coffee, Arbuckle applied an egg and sugar glaze to his coffee before packaging it.[6]

Arbuckle was a very successful entrepreneur, always seeking ways to cut unnecessary costs, usually by eliminating the middleman. Rather than pay distributors, he established his own coffee export business, with offices located in the three major Brazilian ports—Rio, São Paulo, and Santos. When challenged with high shipping costs, he bought his own fleet.

When he tried to enter the sugar market, however—by building his own sugar refinery rather than paying what he considered overly high markups—he met his competitive match in Henry O. Havemeyer, who then controlled most of the sugar production in the United States through the American Sugar Trust. This move

---

5. Pendergrast, p. 52.
6. "The History of Coffee, Part IV—The Commercialization of Coffee," from Galla Coffee website, found at http://www.gallacoffee.co.uk/acatalog/History_of_Coffee_Pt_I.html.

by Arbuckle eventually led to a series of legal actions. Unwilling to accept Arbuckle's entry into the sugar market, Havemeyer retaliated by entering the coffee business. He purchased a controlling interest in the Woolson Spice Company, located in Toledo, Ohio, which produced a competing brand of coffee, the Lion brand.

Havemeyer immediately cut prices for the Lion brand coffee, selling the coffee for less than Arbuckle's Ariosa blend. Arbuckle in turn lowered his prices for Ariosa, and before long the companies were engaged in a ruinous cutthroat price war. This practically destroyed the Woolson Spice Company (which, before Havemeyer's acquisition, had been a profitable company, paying out annual dividends to its shareholders), while only making minor inroads into Ariosa's sales.[7]

Arbuckle then bought shares in the Woolson Spice Company and brought a shareholder's suit against the company's officers (i.e., Havemeyer) to force the company to stop selling its coffee at a loss. It is believed that Havemeyer then retaliated against Arbuckle by using his political muscle in Ohio, where the Woolson Spice Company was headquartered, causing Ohio's regulators to enforce Ohio's food and drug law against Arbuckle and Ariosa brand coffee.[8]

When the Ohio law was passed, Arbuckle took certain steps to meet its labeling requirements for his Ariosa coffee sold in that state. Although the law prohibited selling food mixed with other products used to conceal its inferiority—that is, to make it appear to be a better product than it was—the law also contained an exemption and Arbuckle took measures to make Ariosa fit within that "safe harbor." The law provided that its provisions "would not apply to mixtures or compounds recognized

---

7. Pendergrast, pp. 69-73.
8. Pendergrast, pp. 69-73.

as ordinary articles or ingredients of articles of food, if each and every package sold or offered for sale" was "distinctly labeled as mixtures or compounds, with the name and percent, of each ingredient" as long as the ingredients were not "injurious to health." Arbuckle sold Ariosa coffee in a one-pound sealed package with a label which was printed: "Ariosa is a compound made from coffee, sugar and eggs." The label also provided the percentage of each ingredient contained in the package: coffee .98, egg .01, and sugar .01.

Despite these efforts, Arbuckle was soon the subject of an aggressive enforcement campaign by Ohio authorities. In Toledo, the home base of Havemeyer's Woolson Spice Company, Edward Beverstock, a local inspector of the state's Dairy and Food Commission, charged a retailer named James White with selling Ariosa coffee in violation of Ohio's law. Beverstock alleged that Ariosa's beans were adulterated with an egg and sugar glaze used to cover up low-quality beans, that is, that they were coated with the egg and sugar mixture in order "to conceal inferiority." White's trial was held in Toledo and the jury found him guilty of selling an adulterated product. White appealed to the Ohio Appellate Court.[9]

The appellate court noted first that Ariosa coffee had been sold for many years and consisted of roasted coffee, sugar, and eggs, "constituting a transparent and exceedingly thin film." The court also noted that Arbuckle's label on the Ariosa coffee package clearly stated these ingredients and also provided the percent of each ingredient. No one disputed these facts. Consequently, Ariosa should have been exempt from the law, based on the safe harbor provisions, unless it was not a mixture or compound within the meaning of this safe harbor.

---

9. *James A. White v. State of Ohio*, Lucas Common Pleas, Nov. 14, 1901.

Beverstock had argued that Ariosa was neither a mixture nor a compound because the eggs and sugar merely coated the coffee beans. In his argument, these ingredients—to form a compound or a mixture—had to be so united or mixed as to form a new and distinct substance. The court could see no authority for making this distinction. Relying on the justices' own common sense as well as recognized dictionary definitions of "mixed" and "compounds," the court determined that "food may fairly and properly be called simple, then it is not mixed or compound; but if it cannot be fairly designated as simple, then it is mixed or compound." The court concluded that "in view of the object to be accomplished—to protect public health and prevent deception"—it could see no point in prosecuting or in trying to find an adulteration in a product that was an article of food "composed of two or more ingredients which are recognized as ordinary articles of food, and no one of which is deleterious to health, whether singly or in combination."[10]

This court found that Ariosa was within the statute's exemption and that it was, therefore not unlawful to manufacture or sell it. Before the appellate court handed down its decision in November 1901, clearing White and, therefore, Arbuckle, of all charges, the head of the Dairy and Food Commission for the state, Joseph Blackburn, publicly singled Ariosa out as an adulterated coffee and threatened prosecution against Arbuckle. On February 5, 1901, while White's case was on appeal and without waiting for the appellate court's decision, Blackburn issued a circular letter to the grocery trade asserting that Ariosa failed to comply with Ohio law. These accusations, which were soon to be judged to be inaccurate by Ohio's own courts, injured Ariosa's reputation and hurt sales, even though Blackburn did not actual-

---

10. *James A. White v. State of Ohio*, Lucas Common Pleas, Nov. 14, 1901.

ly carry out his threats and ban Ariosa or bring charges against Arbuckle. Arbuckle was outraged by the continued harassment and innuendos.[11]

He brought suit against Blackburn in federal district court in Ohio, asking that Blackburn be required to cease his attacks on Ariosa, which Arbuckle maintained were damaging the goodwill of his business. In order to gain federal jurisdiction over his dispute with Blackburn, Arbuckle claimed that the state authorities were violating his constitutional rights. He argued that Blackburn's continued threats to use the Ohio law against him was a taking under the Fourteenth Amendment and a violation of the Commerce Clause.[12] The district court denied Arbuckle's request for an injunction against Blackburn and Arbuckle appealed. The Federal Court of Appeal confirmed the dismissal and he then filed an appeal to the U.S. Supreme Court.

In its decision, the Supreme Court failed to find any constitutional controversy that entitled Arbuckle to relief in the federal courts. The Dairy and Food Commission had been created by the state of Ohio to protect consumers from fraud and adulteration in the food industry. The act that Blackburn was threatening to use against Arbuckle provided for definitions of adulterated food and a product that fell within those definitions would violate that law. Arbuckle did not claim that the law was unconstitutional but only that Blackburn's attempts to label his Ariosa coffee as adulterated were wrong and Blackburn's attempts to enforce the law against Arbuckle were unconstitutional. The Court did not accept this argument. Whether or not Ariosa coffee was adulterated as defined in the Ohio law and whether or not it was a "mixture" or "compound" were simply questions of fact that could be determined under a valid law by the Ohio

11. Pendergrast, pp. 69-73.
12. Article One, Section 8 of the U.S. Constitution.

courts.[13] But these findings in themselves did not constitute a deprivation of property by the state of Ohio nor did they represent interference with interstate commerce.

Because Arbuckle had conceded that the Ohio law was constitutional, he then had no constitutional argument and essentially had no business in federal court. Because the federal courts had no jurisdiction over the matter, Arbuckle was not entitled to any injunction against Blackburn. In other words, the federal courts were not willing to interfere in a state regulatory matter where the state had a legitimate constitutional reason to regulate. The Justices also were not blind to the fact that the Ohio courts had already ruled in favor of Ariosa and that by the time the Supreme Court decision was rendered, Arbuckle had no further need for an injunction against Blackburn. Although Arbuckle lost his case in the Supreme Court, the Ohio court's decision in favor of Ariosa, giving it status as a legitimate, unadulterated food product, prevented the state from taking any further action against Arbuckle.

Despite this involved litigation, and the continued attacks against Arbuckle until the cases were resolved, Ariosa continued to thrive, even in Ohio. During this same period of time, the company's sales of Ariosa grew to such an extent that Ariosa reflected almost a quarter of all American coffee sales during the early twentieth century.[14] Eventually, Arbuckle and Havemeyer negotiated a "truce" in their competitive war, with Ariosa coming out of the fray barely damaged and leaving the Woolson Spice Company, which once had been a quiet but profitable business, on the verge of bankruptcy.[15]

---

13. In fact the Ohio courts had made that determination by the time of the Supreme Court's decision—something that certainly was not lost on the Justices.

14. Pendergrast, pp. 72-73.

15. Pendergrast, pp. 72-73.

Coffee Break

Coffee in the 19th Century: A Growing Taste and Brazil's Cartel

By the middle of the nineteenth century, coffee prices were low due to the larger quantities of beans grown in coffee-producing areas. Coffee gained popularity as a result of its ready availability, even among the lower classes. In urban areas of the United States, Germany, and the Netherlands, a coffee-roasting industry was developing.[1] The Civil War slowed this trend for a time. The Union government levied a duty on imported coffee and blockaded southern ports. New Orleans, which had been an important port of entry for South American coffee into the United States,[2] saw coffee imports dwindle. The result was two divergent coffee economies. In the North, although coffee consumption among the civilian population lessened, the Union Army became an important coffee buyer, making coffee the stimulant of choice within its regiments. Soldiers used coffee as barter.[3]

In the South, on the other hand, people sought out coffee extenders and substitutes. Residents of New Orleans made their coffee laced with chicory, at least until the fall of New Orleans in 1862.[4] Most others made do with roasted acorns or toasted rye or wheat. Even after the war ended, when coffee was again available, New Orleans' residents, having developed a taste for coffee blended with chicory, continued to favor it. Today, any visitor to New Orleans does not have to venture further than its airport to taste the city's famous café au lait (chicory-laced coffee with heated milk) and beignets—those delightful deep-fried, sugar-dusted pastries now synonymous with the Crescent City. Meanwhile, in the North, after the war, veterans returned home with a craving for coffee.

One reason why prices for coffee were low in the period between the late nineteenth and early twentieth centuries was that Brazilian coffee dominated the market, producing approximately three-quarters of all coffee sold in the world coffee markets. Increased demand for coffee in consuming countries led to larger and larger coffee plantations in Brazil, as the producers struggled to keep up with the ever-increasing demand. But coffee has always been a "boom-bust" industry: when an event such as a frost in Brazil or a war in Colombia depresses supplies, coffee prices rise, encouraging new plantings. When the beans from these new trees come onto the market three to four years later, creating a glut, prices fall, sometimes precipitously. When consumption goes up to match this increased supply, then prices rise accordingly, leading to another wave of increased production.

Coffee prices have always been extremely volatile. This has been a source of frustration not only for the coffee consumer in the United States who expects coffee to be a low-cost beverage but also for coffee traders and producers, who were never certain whether the coffee they were producing would be sufficient to satisfy the market while in low enough quantities to prevent the low prices resulting from a glut on the market. From time to time, coffee-growing countries had tried to control and stabilize the coffee trade.

The period between 1889 and 1896 was relatively calm for the coffee industry. Prices had remained stable for some time and Brazilian plantation owners, traders, and international bankers had become wealthy from the coffee trade. But in truth, even at this time, the coffee market was unstable. Overproduction, particularly in Brazil, had created a glut of coffee on the world market. The crisis began to unfold in 1896, when supply finally outstripped the growing demand.[5] The per-pound price of coffee fell. When the crisis did not resolve itself over the next few years, coffee-producing countries, with Brazil leading the way, began to look for ways to control and stabilize the market.

In 1906, when an abnormally large coffee crop proved ruinous to plantation owners, the government of Brazil invented a so-called "valorization" plan (from *valorizacao*, meaning to maintain the price of a commodity). Under this scheme, São Paulo, the

Coffee Break (continued)

largest Brazilian coffee-producing state, agreed to buy up surplus Brazilian coffee and store it until prices rose.

To effectuate the scheme, São Paulo borrowed 1 million British pounds from a German bank. When this sum proved to be inadequate, a consortium of London and Paris bankers stepped in with a much larger loan— 15 million British pounds. The deal was brokered by Theodor Wille & Co., the largest German coffee exporter, and Hermann Sielcken, a German-born coffee magnate who resided in the United States.[6] The loan was secured by the unsold coffee, amounting to approximately 7 million pounds, which was stored in warehouses around the world, including in New York. The coffee was placed under the control of a seven-member committee appointed by the bankers, with one of the members being the representative of the São Paulo government. Hermann Sielcken was the representative on the committee in the United States. Once the committee took over the coffee, the valorization scheme had its intended effect and coffee prices began to rise.

This, of course, provoked outrage in the United States. By 1910, the price of Rio No. 7 coffee was selling in New York for approximately 15 cents per pound, almost double the price it had sold for the prior year.[7] By 1912, President Taft and the U.S. Congress felt compelled to intervene. Sielcken was called before the House "Money Trust" committee to explain the workings of the valorization committee.[8] The Department of Justice was asked to investigate whether there was a monopoly in the coffee industry. Shortly after, in May 1912, the U.S. Attorney in the Southern District of New York brought a suit under the Sherman Antitrust Act against committee members, including Sielcken, Theodor Wille & Co., several European banking interests, the Brazilian committee member, Dr. Paolo de Silva Prado, and the New York Dock Company, alleging that they were members of an illegal coffee trust and asking that their combination in restraint of trade be dissolved.[9]

The U. S. Attorney obtained a temporary injunction against Sielcken and the New York Dock Company to prevent the

disposal of 950,000 bags of coffee allegedly stored in company warehouses in New York City. He also attempted to seize the coffee, but this motion was denied. At issue was whether the U.S. government had the power to confiscate property of a foreign state warehoused in New York on the grounds of antitrust law violations. The U.S. government argued that it had the right to enforce U. S. laws against acts that were in violation of those laws in the United States, regardless of whether the acts would be unlawful elsewhere or whether one of the participants in the illegal activity was a foreign state.[10]

Sielcken responded that the courts of the United States had no jurisdiction over the property of a foreign state simply because that property was warehoused in New York, in the custody of an agent of that foreign government. He also maintained that no act in violation of the Sherman Act had occurred in the United States. The economic policy of valorization was lawful in Brazil, where it had been enacted, and every act done under that policy was controlled by the laws of the countries in which it had been carried out, such as Brazil, Great Britain, Germany, and France.

Coffee Break (continued)

The only act that had occurred in the United States was the shipment of coffee for sale in New York. And, Sielcken argued, it was not unlawful to warehouse property until it could be sold at a more advantageous price.[11]

While the case was pending, high-level international negotiations were taking place, which resulted in a settlement of the controversy. By agreement, the warehoused coffee was put up for sale and the case against the consortium was dismissed.[12]

---

1. Pendergrast, p. 48.

2. Pendergrast, p. 52.

3. Schoenholt, Donald N., "Making more coffee with less: coping with hard times; the historic effort to make more with less, from adulteration, short-weigh," *Tea & Coffee Trade Journal*, August, 2009, Reprinted in Entrepreneur online, http://www.entrepreneur.com/tradejournals/article/print/205906545.html.

4. Schoenholt.

5. Pendergrast, p. 78.

6. Pendergrast, pp. 84-85.

7. "SUES TO BREAK THE COFFEE RING; Before Opening in Equity United States District Attorney Gets an Injunction," *The New York Times*, May 19, 1912, found at http://query.nytimes.com/mem/archive-free/pdf?res=9F01E2DC1E3CE63 3A2575AC1A9639C946396D6CF.

8. "Find Money Trust in Big Coffee Deal: Investigating Committee Learns New York Bankers' Share in Brazilian Scheme - 'Patriotic,' Says Sielcken," *The New York Times*, May 16, 1912, found at http://query.nytimes.com/mem/archive-free/pdf?res =9A06E0DA103AE633A25754C1A9639C946396D6CF.

9. *United States v. Herman Sielcken, et al.* Petition in Equity, filed May 18, 1912, in the U. S. District Court, Southern District of New York, cited and discussed in Ellery Cory Stowell and Henry Fraser Munro, "International Cases: Arbitrations and Incidents Illustrative of International Law as practiced by Independent States," *American Journal of International Law* [1912], Vol. VI, pp. 702-06, Houghton Mifflin Company, 1916, found at http://books.google.com.

10. *United States v. Herman Sielcken, et al.*

11. *United States v. Herman Sielcken, et al.*

12. "COFFE CORNER ENDS.; Brazil Assures US the 920,000 Bags Stored Here as Security Are Sold," *The New York Times*, Thursday, April 17, 1913, found at http://query.nytimes.com/mem/archive-free/pdf?res=9A00E3DB1F3AE633A25754 C1A9629C946296D6CF.

Chapter Four

"Quaff the Quality Cup"—Hills Bros. Recognized Standard:
Trying to Control the Coffee Market

Hills Bros. v. Federal Trade Commission,
9 F.2d 481 (9th Cir. 1926)

n 1924, the following banner advertisement ran in the May 23 issue of *The Deseret News* (Salt Lake City's main newspaper): "29 Years after the Gold Rush came Hills Bros. Red Can Coffee."

The half-page ad read:

"A generation following the Storied stampede of the Forty-niners (in 1878 to be exact) another event of importance took place in the West—the birth of Hills Bros. Red Can Coffee. The coffee *pot* became a serious contender for the laurels of the prospector's *pan*. In truth, the lure of the lode, though more spectacular, has not eclipsed the charm of the golden cup of Hills Bros. Red Can Coffee—the largest selling brand in the world, known everywhere as the Recognized Standard. Break the vacuum seal of a tin of "Red Can"; inhale that aroma. Brew a cup and lift it to your lips! Then you will understand the popularity of this wonderful coffee."

On the other side of the ad was a picture of a coffee can with the words: "In the Original vacuum Pack which keeps the coffee fresh."[1] Another ad from the same time in the Prescott, Arizona *Evening Courier* read: "Quaff the Quality Cup and know why Hills Bros. Red Can is the favored coffee of a coffee-ritual West."[2]

Certainly these ads seem quaint by today's more sophisticated marketing standards. However, their message was clear: there was only one brand of coffee in the Western United States for the discriminating coffee drinker and that coffee was Hills Bros. By the early 1920s, three coffee producers in the United States had established themselves as the dominant players in the new domain of direct consumer marketing—Hills Bros., Maxwell House, and Folgers. Two of these companies—Hills Bros. and Folgers—had been founded in San Francisco during the California Gold Rush years and were competing for dominance in California and other western states. With its popular Red Can Coffee, Hills Bros. had a strong market position.

At the time, advertising to consumers was new and exciting. Direct sale of branded merchandise was an innovative strategy in the 1920s. New advertising messages directed at the American housewife instead of retailers sold branded products as diverse as shaving creams and coffee. As one historian has described the moment, in the 1920s, "the jazzed up North Americans entered a golden age of hustle in which business, advertising and con-

---

1. Found at http://news.google.com/newspapers?nid=336&dat=19240523&id=4-MQAAAJ&sjid=PIYDAAAAIBAS&pg=3727,4551401.
2. Found at http://news.google.com/newspapers?nid=897&dat=19240522&id=NKE NAAAAIBAJ&sjid=k4DAAAAIBAJ&pg=3706,5205181.

sumption defined the decade."[3] A confluence of events had shaken up the coffee industry: the naissance of a bustling retail industry, changes in American beverage consumption habits, as well as new legislation aimed at protecting the consumer and limiting monopolistic behaviors.

For most of the late nineteenth and early twentieth centuries, Americans shopped at a variety of small neighborhood stores: the meat market, the produce market, and, for the rest, a small general store that sold dry goods (tea, coffee, spices, sugar, flour, beans, and pickles) in bulk. Customers gave their orders to the white-aproned clerks behind the counters. Coffee was coffee, sold primarily in the form of green beans that were roasted and ground at the time the beverage was prepared. A few enterprising coffee roasters had started selling their product already roasted in one-pound packages, but the product was largely marketed to the storekeepers, not the consumers.

This model began to change at the turn of the twentieth century, when the modern self-service grocery store was born, where more than one brand of a product, whether coffee, flour, or canned goods, was displayed on open shelves for selection by the housewife. The first self-service grocery store opened in 1912 in California.[4] Branding took on a new importance. At the same time, the coffee industry was changing. During Prohibition,[5] coffee emerged as a substitute for alcohol in social settings. At the same time, changes in eating habits helped promote coffee as a drink to enjoy with the light sandwiches and soda fountain hot plate specials that became the midday staple of factory and

---

3. Pendergrast, p. 155.

4. Halper, Emanuel B., *Shopping Center and Store Leases*, Law Journal Press, New York, NY, 1979, 2003, §9.01[4], p. 9-36.94. Halper points out that the Alpha Beta name was chosen because its products were shelved in alphabetical order.

5. 1920-1933. *See* Robertson, C., *The Little Red Book of Wine Law*, American Bar Association Publishing, 2009, pp. 23-26.

office workers. Coffee was even promoted as a healthy drink because it made people feel more energetic.[6]

In 1914, Hills Bros. introduced its Red Can brand of coffee that it heavily promoted as a better quality coffee. It was not alone. As coffee consumption began to climb in the 1920s, several companies emerged as fierce competitors. In San Francisco alone, three major coffee companies—Hills Bros., Folgers and MJB—battled for market dominance, expanding their sales territories east. Newly developed packaging helped promote coffee sales for Hills Bros., giving the company a competitive edge. In 1900, R.W. Hills, a founder of Hills Bros., had obtained a one-year exclusive license for a process that removed the air from coffee packaging, resulting in fresher beans. This process was called "vacuum packaging."[7] By 1930, Hills Bros. coffee was sold as far east as Chicago and had become the number-one-selling coffee in the western United States, largely due to its heavy advertising promotions, relying on the "freshness" of its coffee packed in the vacuum-sealed can, a technology that its competitors were slow to adopt even after Hills' exclusive license expired. But Hills Bros.' success was also due to the company's aggressive sales tactics.

In this latter respect, Hills Bros. soon found itself in the spotlight of federal regulators at the newly created Federal Trade Commission (FTC). What had specifically caught the regulators' eyes were the company's pricing policies. Pricing was a sensitive topic at the time on many fronts. As competition in a variety of industries increased in the early twentieth century, a number of business and trade associations attempted to address what merchants perceived as a price-cutting problem that was leading to consolidation, driving smaller competitors out of business. In

---

6. Pendergrast, p. 158.
7. Hills Bros website chronology, found at http://hillsbros.com/coffee/history.html#.

1907, for example, the National Grocers' Association, at its conference in San Francisco, adopted a program to induce product manufacturers to adopt mandatory minimum resale prices. They also encouraged a boycott of any distributor who refused to cooperate with manufacturers' efforts to set resale prices. This was the first but not the last major price fixing movement in the California grocery trade.[8]

These efforts came up against new federal antitrust laws. The Sherman Antitrust Act, enacted in 1891, had outlawed "every contract, combination or conspiracy in restraint of trade."[9] Although various business groups in the early twentieth century saw price fixing as "benign" because it was done only to prevent "an endless downward price spiral" that was harming industry, courts generally condemned this type of collaboration among competitors.

The Federal Trade Commission Act was enacted in 1914[10] to eliminate "unfair methods of competition" under the Sherman Act. The Act empowered the FTC to prevent businesses from using unfair methods of competition in commerce and empowered it to issue cease and desist orders against such practices. Nevertheless, in the early days after its creation, the FTC took what some viewed as a "reasonable" view of business conduct and what others perceived as hesitation.[11] This approach was defined early on in an important U.S. Supreme Court case (the *Beech-Nut* case): a business person does not violate antitrust law "by simply refusing to sell his products or goods or by with-

---

8. McHenry, Lorenzo Alva, "Price Stabilization Attempts in the Grocery Trade in California," *The Journal of Marketing*, University of California, Vol. 2, No. 2 (Oct. 1937), pp. 121-128, found at http://www.jstor.org/stable/1245904.

9. 15 U.S.C. §1.

10. U.S. Comp Stat 8836e.

11. Kovacic, William E. & Shapiro, Carl, "Antitrust Policy: A Century of Economic and Legal Thinking," *Journal of Economic Perspectives*, Vol. 14, No. 1, Winter 2000, pp. 43-60, found at http://faculty.haas.berkeley.edu/SHAPIRO/century.pdf.

holding them from those who do not sell them at the resale prices he fixes, but he may *not* by contracts, or combinations . . . unduly hinder or obstruct the free and natural flows of interstate commerce."[12]

It was under this "reasonableness" standard that Hills Bros.' activities were scrutinized. By 1926, it had become a major coffee company. It generally sold its coffee direct to retailers for resale to consumers. More than 50 percent of its customers were located in California; the rest were in other states, most bordering California—Washington, Oregon, Nevada, Idaho, and Utah. By aggressive advertising in its primary markets, it had created a strong consumer demand for its Red Can brand of coffee. This enabled it to dictate terms to its retail customers.

Early on, Hills Bros. saw that price cutting by retailers tended to diminish the perceived value of the Red Can brand, which the company advertised as a "quality" coffee appreciated in "homes of wealth and discernment." In November 1920, under pressure from some of its customers, Hills Bros. adopted a minimum price policy, which mandated that the retail price of Red Can Coffee be 5 cents per pound above store cost (list price plus transportation). The purpose of this policy was to make the price of Red Can Coffee uniform wherever it was sold and to prevent price cutting by retailers. Under the policy, the store price could exceed the minimum 5 cents per pound but could not sell at a lower price. As a result of this policy, most retailers sold Hills Bros. Red Can Coffee at the established minimum price and no other. Hills Bros. advertised this minimum price and its customers and distributors knew about it. Whenever Hills Bros. changed its price for Red Can Coffee, it notified its sales force and they in turn notified retailers.

---

12. *FTC v. Beech-Nut Packing Co.*, 257 U.S. 441, 452 (1922).

Hills Bros. enforced its minimum price by refusing to sell to any retailer who discounted Red Can Coffee below the minimum resale price. Hills Bros.' salesmen reported instances of price cutting back to the home office. Retailers also were encouraged to report any cost cutting by competing stores, and voluntarily reported such failures by their competitors to observe minimum pricing. Whenever Hills Bros. learned that a customer was violating its pricing policy, future orders for Red Can Coffee were not filled unless the retailer agreed to restore the minimum price. Whenever a report of cost cutting was received, a Hills Bros. salesman would call on the offending customer and try to obtain a promise to restore the minimum price. If the retailer refused, the salesman would threaten to remove his name from Hills Bros.' customer list. If the retailer agreed, he was assured that Hills Bros. would continue to fill his orders. A "DO NOT FILL" notice was placed on the customer ledger next to the name of each noncompliant retailer. At the time the FTC intervened, Hills Bros. had refused to sell Red Can Coffee to approximately 100 retailers across the western states.

The FTC issued a cease and desist order against Hills Bros., ordering the company to stop enforcing the minimum pricing policy. At this time, the agency was still experimenting with its regulatory authority. Hills Bros. sued the FTC, asking the court to rule that its order was erroneous because the Commission had not made a finding that it was acting in the public interest when it issued its order. The trial court affirmed the FTC's order, holding that any finding that a method of competition used by a producer was anticompetitive was, by its nature, a finding that the activity was contrary to the public interest. Hills Bros. appealed.

The Ninth Circuit affirmed the lower court's decision, ruling that Hills Bros.' requirement of a minimum selling price violated unfair competition laws and was contrary to the public interest. According to the court, Hills Bros.' minimum resale price policy and practice as applied to its Red Can brand tended to constrain all retailers to uniformly sell coffee at the prices fixed by Hills Bros. in their geographic area and this practice tended to restrict competition among the stores that carried Red Can Coffee. In other words, Hills Bros.' policy obstructed competition in the sale and distribution of not just Hills Bros.' product, but all coffee.

Hills Bros.' main contention was that its practice was not against public policy because it was simply refusing to sell to retailers who did not maintain its minimum price. It claimed the right to do so under the Supreme Court ruling in the *Beech-Nut* case: any business person can withhold his goods from those who will not sell them at the price that he fixes for their sale. But the Ninth Circuit did not agree with this contention. This was not all that Hills Bros. was doing. Under *Beech-Nut*, the Supreme Court had also ruled that a party may not, by contract or other-wise, unduly obstruct free commerce. In other words, what a person may lawfully do as an individual is not permitted when done as a cooperative effort with others. The Ninth Circuit held that Hills Bros. had successfully fixed and controlled the retail price of its coffee in interstate trade not solely through its individual efforts, but through the cooperative efforts of its salesmen and its customers. This latter element rendered the competition unfair under the recently enacted antitrust laws.

Hills Bros. also argued that the FTC had no jurisdiction over the pricing policy because there was no restraint on interstate commerce with respect to its California sales, which represented more than 50 percent of its total sales. The court did not need to entertain this question of jurisdiction, however, since Hills Bros. enforced the same policy on a uniform basis both within the state of California and in interstate commerce. The distinction sought by Hills Bros., therefore, was not considered to be relevant.

Hills Bros. tried to show that other coffee sellers throughout the country were selling under agreements to maintain minimum prices and that these others refused to sell to retailers who failed to maintain the fixed prices. The court did not dispute this contention, but noted that Hills Bros. could not justify its own violations of law by proving that others were equally guilty. By its size and success, the company had drawn attention to itself and it alone had to bear the burdens and responsibilities that came with that success.

Coffee Break

The Commercialization of Coffee

By the twentieth century, coffee had become as much a staple at the American dinner table as milk or bread. This tied in with trends in food production and consumption in general. The mass food production and preservation industry that developed in the late nineteenth century had provided convenience to American cooks in the form of canned fruits, vegetables, meats, fish, and even prepared food such as stews and soups. Canning companies such as Campbell and Heinz were able to sell large quantities of products throughout the country by using advertising strategies.

Convenience in food preparation was valued over quality.[1] The introduction of new ways to preserve food, time-saving kitchen appliances, and the self-service supermarket all converged to enable Americans to put food on the table with minimal effort and in limited time. Concerns about eating well and "cooking from scratch" gave way to the convenience offered by these food production innovations.[2]

Coffee was a beneficiary of these new technologies, through the development of the vacuum pack, licensed to Hills Bros. as a means of preserving coffee, for example. The new electric percolator was another popular time-saving device. Instead of buying green coffee beans, roasting them in a frying pan, grinding them in a hand-cranked grinder, and boiling the grounds in a pot for 20 minutes, the housewife could buy pre-roasted, ground coffee in a vacuum-sealed can, put the grounds in the percolator, add water, plug it in, and watch as the boiling coffee cheerfully bubbled up and down in the little glass ball on the top, while she went about other food preparation tasks. However, for many coffee lovers, this invention is not viewed as a positive development. The period from the late nineteenth century to the late twentieth is considered by many to be a negative period for coffee. During this time, American coffee was commercialized and became standard, ordinary, and not very good.[3]

Boiling the coffee was not the best way to prepare it, but in the nineteenth century, when green coffee beans were roasted in small batches, at least the coffee was fresh. With the onset of mechanization, coffee was roasted in large commercial plants in large batches and packaged for transit to stores often many miles away. The popular Ariosa brand in the late 1860s was one of the first of these pre-roasted coffees to be sold. By the end of World War I, there were a large number of regional roasters, including Folgers, Hills Bros., and Maxwell House. These companies offered consistent quality and convenient packaging for home coffee preparation. But the tradeoff was freshness and taste. It could be several weeks and sometimes even months before the final product made its way into the home.

Hills Bros. introduced the vacuum-sealed can of mass-produced coffee and after several years, Folgers and Maxwell House followed suit. But the vacuum seal did not guarantee a rich fresh taste associated with a cup of newly ground coffee. Once ground, coffee quickly loses its flavor. The product placed in the can had already lost much of its flavor before it was even sealed. To compensate, the producers began adding a "coffee essence," which released its smell when the can was first opened.[4] But this only deceived the senses and was soon lost as the opened can was placed on the cupboard shelf. Once opened, the unused coffee in the one-pound can continued to lose flavor. However, consumers really did not seem to mind; they appeared to value consistency and convenience over flavor. They just wanted to put the heaping measure into the top of their percolator every morning and set it in motion. They wanted their coffee to taste the same—hot and not too strong.

There was another reason why coffee quality diminished as it was mass-produced. Large coffee production companies were at heart profit-making enterprises. And producing coffee was and is an expensive process. New technologies that reduced manpower requirements and increased efficiencies helped to reduce costs. But there was also another way to increase profit margins and that was in the blend. Traditionally, good coffee came from the "arabica" coffee plant. But in the late nineteenth century, French

51

Coffee Break (continued)

and Portuguese colonists began to cultivate a different variety, known as the "robusta."[5] Robusta beans were less expensive than arabica beans because they are easier to grow and the plants are more robust, but these beans also have a harsh, acid, less savory flavor. This harshness is less noticeable when the robusta beans are blended with arabica. Depending on the blend created—with a higher percentage of arabica coffee vis-a-vis the robusta—the coffee can still be a good-flavored product. Much espresso in Italy, for example, is an arabica-robusta blend.[6] But American coffee producers in the 1940s and 1950s, seeking to minimize their costs, began blending larger and larger quantities of robusta beans with smaller quantities of arabica beans to produce a less-expensive product.

They also used shorter roasting times. This reduced weight loss, which allowed them to use fewer beans per can of coffee produced. But it also diminished the flavor of the coffee, leaving a less-intense brew.[7] However, American consumers' tastes had gradually adapted to changes in their favorite brands of coffee, and they seemed to prefer this vapid, watery brew to the richer coffees favored by Europeans, for example. Americans who traveled abroad complained that they could not get a good cup of coffee and that European coffee was too strong, while Europeans traveling in the United States equated the liquid in their cup to dishwater.

1. Sonnenfeld, p. 524.

2. "In food, this meant that concerns of health or gastronomy took a back seat to 'convenience' or what food processors like to call 'built-in-service.'" Sonnenfeld, p. 524.

3. Pendergrast, p. 117.

4. Pendergrast, p. 262.

5. See Coffee Break, "Coffee Basics: The Bean and Beyond."

6. A robusta blend makes a better crema. See Kolpas, p. 75. It produces a thick, rich coffee with a touch of foam on top, known as the crema.

7. Shoenholt. This was called "High Yield Coffee." A patent was issued to Folgers in 1992 (US Patent 5322703) for a "flash-roasted" coffee to create, when blended with traditional ground coffee, "a less expensive high yield coffee, perceived as having richer, stronger flavors." www.patentstormm.us/patents/5322703/fulltext.html.

Chapter Five

Taking the Easy Way Out

*Marsalli's Blue Ribbon Coffee Company
v. Blue Ribbon Products Company,*
159 Cal. App. 2d 357 (1st Dist. 1958)

C harles Marsalli was a familiar figure in post-World War II San Francisco. A long-time resident of the Italian-American community in North Beach, he was considered a rising star in local politics, running for county supervisor in 1957.[1] He operated a well-known restaurant on Kearny Street, known as "Marsalli's."

Marsalli, like many restaurant owners, purchased a standard blend of coffee from a wholesale coffee supplier, which he featured in his restaurant. For more than five years, he had been a regular customer of a company that produced a brand of coffee called "Blue Ribbon Coffee." This was a high grade of coffee that Marsalli's customers enjoyed and he had been satisfied with the relationship. But the coffee, because of its high quality, commanded a higher price than some other coffees. Marsalli was torn between wanting to keep a coffee that satisfied his customers and wanting to pay less, or else he wanted to share in the profit margins from the sale of coffee.

---

1. Declaration of Charles Marsalli in support of his candidacy for San Francisco City and County Supervisor in the General Municipal Election of November 5, 1957, found at http://sfpl.org/pdf/main/gic/elections/November5_1957.pdf.

The supplier of Blue Ribbon Coffee, Blue Ribbon Products Company, was involved in what is known as the institutional business—it supplied coffee and teas to restaurants, hotels, and other businesses in the San Francisco Bay Area. Its coffee products, which made up 90 percent of its sales, had always been sold under the trade name, Blue Ribbon Coffee. The company had for some time engaged in an intensive marketing campaign to promote its coffee and by the late 1950s, it was selling between 1-½ and 2 million pounds of coffee per year under the "Blue Ribbon" brand.

As he watched from the sidelines, Marsalli saw profit potential in selling his own coffee in his restaurant, as well as to other restaurants in the area. He initially approached the Blue Ribbon Products Company seeking to invest in that business, but he was rebuffed. He then set about forming a competing business and, in 1957 (the same year he ran for city supervisor), he set up a corporation that he called "Marsalli's Blue Ribbon Coffee Company" for the business purpose of selling coffee to restaurants and hotels in Northern California.

He didn't wait for Blue Ribbon Products Company to take notice. Shortly after incorporating his business and before actually selling any coffee, Marsalli filed an action for declaratory relief in San Francisco Superior Court, requesting a ruling from the court that he had the right to use the words "Blue Ribbon" in a brand of coffee that he intended to sell. Blue Ribbon Products Company then cross-complained against Marsalli, asking the court for an injunction against Marsalli, to prevent him from using the term "Blue Ribbon" in any manner dealing with the sale of coffee in Northern California, or in Washington, Oregon, Nevada, or Arizona. The court granted Blue Ribbon Products the injunction. Marsalli was also ordered to destroy any materials, such as labels or packaging, that used the words "Blue Ribbon" or "Blue Ribbon Coffee." Marsalli appealed.

The thrust of Marsalli's argument was that the term "Blue Ribbon"—because it was a common phrase meaning "top grade" or "prize winner"—did not merit trademark protection. The appellate court acknowledged as much. However, it determined that, under California law, the term had acquired a secondary meaning for use as a trade name by Blue Ribbon Products Company. In other words, people in the restaurant and hotel business had grown accustomed to purchasing Blue Ribbon Coffee to serve in their establishments and they would assume that any coffee sold under that name would be the product of the Blue Ribbon Products Company, whether or not any other qualifier, such as "Marsalli's," appeared on the label to distinguish the product.

Moreover, the court found that, by taking the Blue Ribbon name—so closely identified with Blue Ribbon Products Company's coffee—Marsalli had engaged in unfair competition under California law. The main question to be considered to prove unfair competition is whether the public is likely to be deceived by the similar verbiage on the coffee label. In this case, the court found that there was not merely a *likelihood* of confusion; there was *actual* confusion. Blue Ribbon Products had provided witnesses in the trial who testified to this effect. But more importantly perhaps, the court noted that even Marsalli and his attorneys were confused because in the appellate brief they had filed, they had referred to the "Blue Ribbon Products Company" as the "Blue Ribbon Coffee Company."

The court expressed suspicions about Marsalli's motives in setting up his business. He had bought coffee under the "Blue Ribbon" brand for many years from the Blue Ribbon Products Company before striking out on his own. He testified that he had never heard of anyone other than Blue Ribbon Products Company using the term "Blue Ribbon" in the coffee business. He knew of the company's reputation for high-quality coffee and he also knew that Blue Ribbon Products Company had used the term "Blue Ribbon" to identify its coffee for more than 40 years. And he had unsuccessfully tried to buy into the business before setting up his own company. Moreover, soon after being rebuffed in his investment offer, he had decided to go into direct competition with the Blue Ribbon Products Company using the very two words in his brand—"Blue Ribbon"—that identified his competitor's coffee. The court found all this to be "highly suspect." In affirming the lower court decision, the appellate court noted that the choice of the words "Blue Ribbon" surely had to be attributable to something other than sheer coincidence.

Although the court acknowledged that an injunction prohibiting Marsalli's use of the name was "a drastic remedy," it did not think that Marsalli would be significantly harmed by such a ruling in this case because he had not actually engaged in any business using the 'Blue Ribbon" trade name. He had a wide choice of terms to identify his coffee that, according to the court, would be "equally as effective" for his use, except "perhaps for the unjustified purpose of confusing" the public, the coffee trade, and customers of the Blue Ribbon Products Company.

Marsalli ceased serving Blue Ribbon Coffee purchased from the Blue Ribbon Products Company in his restaurant once this case was decided. He changed the name of his coffee business to Royal Crown Coffee. One wonders if his customers noticed the difference in blends. Apart from the coffee served in North Beach cafes run by Italian-Americans, for the most part, in the 1950s, a cup of coffee served in a restaurant in San Francisco as elsewhere in the United States would more likely than not have been fairly mediocre.[2] It is certain, however, that Marsalli's political career was short-lived: he ran again—unsuccessfully—for supervisor in 1961 but then disappeared from the political scene.[3] In a city known for its more eccentric politicians, Marsalli was just a dot on the history timeline.

---

2. Duggan, Tara, "Exploring our love of the bean from the grounds up," *San Francisco Chronicle*, Thursday, March 12, 2009, Section E-1 (online version found at http://articles.sfgate.com/2009-03-12/entertainment/17211960_1_alfred-peet-hills-bros-coffee-culture), citing a February 18, 1963, San Francisco Chronicle front page story titled "A Great City's People Forced to Drink Swill," which highlighted poor restaurant coffee.

3. In his declaration in support of his candidacy for San Francisco Supervisor in 1961, Marsalli stated, "My wife and I successfully operate Royal Crown Coffee and Marsalli's Restaurant," found at http://sfpl.org/pdf/main/gic/elections/November7_1961.pdf.

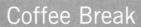

Coffee Break

Coffee Basics: The Bean and Beyond

Coffee requires a hot, humid climate, which means that it can only be grown in those parts of the world that are near the equator. But that leaves a large part of the world. Curiously, most of the world's coffee consumers today live in regions where coffee cannot be grown: the continental United States, Britain, and Western Europe. Most coffee drinkers do not know how the coffee beans they buy at the store or from their local coffee shop are produced.

It is important to understand that coffee is a labor-intensive commodity. The cherries (in which the beans are held) ripen at different times so they must be picked by hand. There are two beans in each cherry. There are about 4,000 coffee beans per pound of green coffee. Each tree is picked numerous times during the season.

Coffee beans are not even beans but rather a fruit—a little red berry that resembles a cherry. When the coffee tree blooms, it forms delicate jasmine-like blossoms that quickly morph into the red berries. These berries house the seeds that we know as coffee beans. Coffee is actually like a peanut, with several layers of pulp that protect the seed. The outer skin of the berry, the pulp, is very thick. Within this cherry is an inner layer, called the parchment, that protects the seed. Inside the parchment, there is yet another covering over the bean, called the "silver skin." Before coffee can be shipped, the pulp and parchment must be removed.

There are two basic ways to remove the fruit from the seeds: the dry process and the wet process. Dry processing is also known as the "natural" or "unwashed" process. Beans are spread out in the sun to dry for 15 to 20 days. During this time, they are regularly raked and re-spread several times a day to ensure even drying. The dried cherries are then hulled to remove the dried out pulp or parchment. This is the more traditional method of coffee processing, which has been used for centuries.

The wet process uses a soaking method to cause the pulp to come off: this produces a coffee sometimes called "washed coffee." A few hours after the cherries are harvested, the pulp is removed, leaving the sticky centers covering parchment protected beans. The beans are washed through a process that involves cycles of fermentation and rinsing, for 12 to 24 hours. The fermentation softens the pulp and the skin, making them easier to rinse off and, incidentally, developing their flavor. This causes less damage to the beans.

The green coffee beans are then dried, sorted by size, and graded for quality. Grading takes place on-site at large coffee plantations or in the exporters' warehouses for coffee grown by small producers. The final step is cup testing—roasting, grinding, and brewing a small sample of each batch of coffee—to assess the qualities of the beans and to rate the coffee (judging its aroma, flavor, and body) for pricing.

There are two types of coffee that are generally consumed in the world today: arabica and robusta. The species known as *Coffea Arabica*, after its region of origin, is the source of the best-tasting coffee. *Coffea robusta*, a species grown in poorer coffee-producing areas, but also in Brazil—one of the major sources of coffee in the U.S. market —matures more quickly, is heartier than arabica, and costs less to grow; it is therefore less expensive to buy. However, coffee from the robusta bean has less subtlety and, as a consequence, it is mainly used in commercial blends as background, rather than for better-tasting quality coffees.

Chapter Six

Dominating the Institutional Market:
The Fate of the Wagon Men

Cain's Coffee Company v. N.L.R.B.,
404 F.2d 1172 (10th Cir. 1968)

From the 1920s, coffee was sold at retail in the United States through several channels of trade: independent grocers, self-service supermarkets, mail order houses, specialty tea and coffee stores, drug stores, and wagon route distributors, so-called "wagon men." These latter traveled from door-to-door and, much like the milkman, delivered coffee on order direct to the consumer in the home and to businessmen in their offices. As an inducement for these regular deliveries, the house-to-house dealer offered a household article, as a premium to establish goodwill.[1] Some of the wagon men also developed relationships with, and provided their coffee to, independent grocers.

By 1921 there were approximately 600 wagon route coffee dealers.[2] The largest single wagon route supplier was the Jewel Tea Company based in Chicago.[3] Over the next decades, through consolidation and competition, the number of coffee distributors

---

1. Ukers, William Harrison, *All About Coffee*, New York: The Tea and Coffee Trade Journal Company, 1922, p. 415, found at http://www.gutenberg.org/etext/28500.
2. Ukers, p. 417.
3. Pendergrast, p. 161.

decreased, but the method of selling remained the same, particularly for the institutional dealers—those who supplied coffee to hotels, restaurants, and offices. As these companies evolved, the wagon men exchanged their wagons for delivery trucks and vans, but their task remained the same: make regular visits to customers, obtain orders, manage relationships, and deliver the coffee on a weekly or bi-weekly schedule.

By the 1950s, several companies dominated the institutional coffee market in the United States—Cain's Coffee Company, Blue Ribbon Products Company, Peerless Coffee, and Farmer Brothers Coffee.[4] Although some of the buyers sought quality, many simply wanted a consistent product to offer to their diners or office workers, who in turn only demanded that the coffee be plentiful (with free refills), hot, and black. Coffee purchases were treated the same as those for other commodities, such as table salt and ketchup. In the face of competition among suppliers, some superior blends were created for specific customers, which were marketed and sold for a higher price. But it was still, by today's standards, an average coffee.

By 1966, competition in the coffee business was fierce. Cain's Coffee Company was experiencing "financial difficulties" and was putting pressure on its salesmen to increase sales and maintain customer satisfaction, in the face of rising prices for raw coffee beans on the commodity markets.

Like the wagon men of old, the institutional coffee salesmen were assigned to specific routes and were expected to maintain ongoing relationships with their customers. They were generally paid a small salary plus commissions. Gordon Griffin was one of Cain's 32 salesmen employed in the Oklahoma City area. He was

---

4. "Changing coffee tastes brew trouble for Farmer Bros.," *Los Angeles Business Journal*, December 8, 2003, found at http://www.thefreelibrary.com/Changing+coffee+tastes+brew+trouble+for+Farmer+Bros.%28Up+Front%29-a0111404766.

not alone in feeling the pressure but he was the most outspoken in the group. After a company sales meeting, he and several other Cain's salesmen met in a local cafeteria to discuss their grievances. They decided to present these complaints to company management and asked Griffin to be their spokesman.

The following week, while on his route, Griffin encountered the company's general sales manager who asked him about the "secret meeting." Griffin told him that the men had some grievances that they wanted to discuss with management. The sales manager set up a meeting for the following Saturday, where the men were encouraged to discuss their issues. After that, however, nothing changed. Unhappy with this result, Griffin then called upon the local Teamsters Union representative to discuss the employees' problems. He signed a union authorization card and agreed to take the lead in organizing the men.

Sometime earlier, because he was having trouble earning enough from his salary and sales commissions, Griffin and his wife had purchased a motel. When the company president, Jack Durland, learned of this, he informed Griffin that the company had a policy against "moonlighting" and that he would have to sell it. Griffin agreed to put the motel on the market.

When Griffin reported on his meeting with the Teamsters, many of the salesmen agreed to sign on to the union and they filed an election petition with the National Labor Relations Board (NLRB). Three weeks before the election, Durland called the salesmen individually into his office to discuss the election. He told each of them that he could not "understand why a professional man earning $1,000 a month would want to turn his business over to someone else to represent him."

When Durland interviewed Griffin, he took a different stance, reminding Griffin about the company policy against moonlighting and asking him if he had sold his motel. Griffin told him honestly that he was trying to do so but that he had not had any offers.

When the election was held, the union was defeated by a vote of 12 to 22.

A few weeks later, Durland sent Griffin a letter officially restating the company's opposition to its employees' engaging in outside business activities. Griffin responded to the letter, telling Durland that he was trying but had so far been unsuccessful in selling the motel. The company then dismissed Griffin, ostensibly because his sales had drastically declined and some of his key customers had expressed dissatisfaction with him, and also because of his continued operation of the motel in violation of company policy.

The union filed a complaint with the NLRB alleging that Cain's had interfered with union activity. The trial examiner for the NLRB determined that Cain's had violated the National Labor Relations Act by coercively interrogating its employees about their union activity. But he did not find any violation in Griffin's dismissal because the company had other legitimate business reasons for the firing: Griffin's declining sales record, his interest in the motel, and his difficulties with his customers. These were all good and adequate grounds for a discharge "for cause." Certainly the timing of the discharge tended to link the dismissal with Griffin's union activity, but this could have been a coincidence because Griffin was discharged the day after Griffin's supervisor visited a key customer—representing over 35 percent of Griffin's sales—who complained of a "running feud" that he had with Griffin over delivery times.

The NLRB disagreed with the trial examiner's findings, concluding that the company's opposition to the union-organizing activities—as evidenced by its unlawful interrogations—and its knowledge of Griffin's leadership in union organizing, when combined with the timing of Griffin's dismissal, were more than mere coincidences. The Board concluded that the discharge was discriminatory.

Cain's appealed.

The appeals court disagreed with the NLRB in connection with Cain's dismissal of Griffin. The court noted that union-organizing activities are not a shield against discharge. Under the established law of at-will employment, an employee can be dismissed for any reason or no reason at all, as long as the union activity is not the basis for the discharge. Certainly, if the dismissal of an employee raises suspicion, the burden falls on the employer to show a legitimate reason for the discharge. But if the employer provides evidence that demonstrates such a legitimate motive, then the burden shifts back to the NLRB to show an improper motive behind the dismissal.

The court believed that the employer's evidence was strong enough to preclude any finding of discrimination. It mainly relied on the fact that when Griffin purchased his motel, his sales showed a drastic decline and at the time he was fired, he had had a 27 percent loss in coffee sales, which counted for 70 percent of his total sales. Of course, Griffin may have purchased the motel because his coffee sales were declining. And the other employees had expressed grievances: coffee sales were declining across the board for Cain's in 1966 and no salesman had performed well in that time period. In fact, on an annual comparison, Griffin ranked third in sales at the time he was fired in 1966. However, in 1966, at-will employment was the rule in Oklahoma City and Griffin had faced an uphill battle to overcome that tenet.

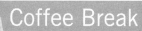

Coffee Break

The Coffee Break

The British call it their "elevenses"—that time of morning when a break from work is called for, between breakfast and the midday meal. They may drink tea at other times, but coffee is the beverage that generally accompanies elevenses.[1] It is usually served from the coffee cart, steaming hot, black, or white (half coffee and half milk, both poured into the cup at the same time). The Germans call it their Kaffeeklatsch, a time for a relaxing cup of coffee in the mid-afternoon, accompanied by delightful conversation with a good friend, either at home or in a Konditorei—more than a coffee shop, but serving coffee accompanied by delicious German pastries. The term originated in the nineteenth century when German men described how their wives got together to drink coffee while spreading gossip and scandal.[2] Now it is less a time for gossip than a moment to discuss the day's news and to philosophize in the best German tradition.

In America, the "coffee break" is a relatively new phenomenon. The term was invented in 1952 by the Pan American Coffee Bureau as part of an advertising campaign to encourage coffee consumption.[3] "Give Yourself a Coffee-Break—And Get What Coffee Gives to You" was their slogan, not the most innovative of ads, but the concept caught on quickly. It institutionalized a practice that had started during World War II when workers were given short periods of time off from the defense plant assembly lines to sit down, relax, and re-energize with a cup of coffee. Most American businesses followed the model until, by the mid-1950s, 80 percent of firms polled provided a coffee break to their workers.[4]

Today coffee breaks are as ubiquitous as the drink itself—a time to unwind, a time to rewind, a social time, and a time of repose: all of the contradictions of coffee within the coffee break.

---

1. Kolpas, p. 85.
2. Kolpas, p. 97.
3. Pendergrast, p. 242.
4. Pendergrast, p. 242.

MER DU

Is du Cap Ver
S.Yago

Pertorice
I. de la Guadeloupe
le Martinique
I. de la Grenade

OCÉAN

de Grenade
I. de la Trinité
S.te Fe de
Bego la S.Thomas
Surinam
Guyane Cayenne
R. des Amazones

Ligne Equ

I. de Rio
negre
S.t Luis
3 40
3 50
I. de Fernaõ de Noronha
36 o

AMER
Amazone
Para
Seara
OCEAN
M

I QUE
BRESIL
Francois
Fernambouc

MERIDION
S.t François
Xavier
St Salvador

La Pa
Chaco
PARAGUAY R.

Tucuman
Villa Rica

S.t Miguel
Cordova
Rio Janeiro

I. S.te Catherine

ILI
Rio de la
Buenos aires

de Mag

Chapter Seven

Having Your Coffee and Drinking It Too

Brown v. Comm'r, 446 F.2d 926 (8th Cir. 1971)

F or most people, the ideal job is one that combines work with one's passion or hobby. And for most people, having this is just a dream far removed from reality. But not for Dana Brown. He was able to combine his passion for coffee with his love of exotic travel, at least until he encountered Cain's Coffee Company.

Brown was employed as the president of Manhattan Coffee Company, a small supplier of coffee, some of which was sold under the "Manhattan Coffee" label and some of which was sold into the institutional market, especially hotels and restaurants, to be furnished to their customers under private labels. He was primarily engaged in sales and marketing for the company and was a key player in formulating Manhattan's advertising strategy. This was the era before the multimillionaire CEO, laden down with stock grants and stock options. Brown owned no stock in the Manhattan Coffee Company but, rather, received a fixed annual salary that was not tied to company sales. He also enjoyed a generous expense account for all authorized travel and entertainment expenses.

Dana Brown loved to travel to exotic locations. In the early 1950s, he began to take annual two-month-long trips to various coffee-growing countries, using his company expense account. When he first started taking these trips, the purpose was largely to visit coffee plantations in order to familiarize himself with all aspects of the product that he was marketing and selling. Later, he started to combine these investigative trips, especially to coffee-growing locations in Eastern Africa, with big-game-hunting safaris. During these trips, he would take many photos of both the coffee production and the wild game. Soon, he learned how to make motion pictures and began to produce films of these remote lands that showed a talent for capturing the landscape and the people. These films became a high point of Brown's sales meetings. Over the years, he edited his films into mini-documentaries recounting his experiences. They became a popular attraction at numerous dealer meetings. He accompanied his films with a lecture discussing coffee-growing practices, methods of coffee merchandising, and the art of blending beans of varied quality and from different locations in order to produce the high-quality private label coffees for which the Manhattan Coffee Company was noted.

As Brown's popularity and reputation—both as a big-game photographer and as a coffee expert—grew, so did the sales of Manhattan Coffee, and the renown of the brand. In 1956 and 1957, the company used some of Brown's films in its television commercials for Manhattan Coffee. By 1957, according to court records, Brown sold 6 million of the total 8 million pounds of Manhattan coffee reflected in the company's annual sales. That the bulk of these sales was in the private-label business indicated that Brown's reputation as a coffee expert—rather than the strength of the Manhattan Coffee brand or the high quality of the company's coffee—was primarily the reason for the company's profitability and growth in sales. Because of the link between Brown's travels (and the films he produced) and the company's sales growth, the company was more than willing to reimburse Brown for the cost of these trips.

Enter Cain's Coffee Company. In 1958, Cain's acquired the Manhattan Coffee Company and retained Brown as president. However, Cain's had an entirely different attitude toward Manhattan's sales strategy. Whereas, as an independent business, Manhattan had focused its sales and marketing efforts in developing its lucrative private-label business, Cain's saw tremendous value in the Manhattan Coffee brand due to its reputation for high-quality coffee blends. Cain's wanted to focus the company's sales and marketing efforts to building this brand and developing the Manhattan franchise. It foresaw a higher profit margin from sales of Manhattan-branded coffee than from the private label sales that Brown had previously promoted.

Given this strategy shift, Cain's changed the advertising program for the company, discontinuing the TV commercials that had shown off Brown's safaris, because Cain's did not believe that these films conveyed a message to consumers around the quality of Manhattan Coffee but, rather, promoted Brown as a big game hunter and coffee expert. Because of this shift away from Brown's expertise, Cain's saw no value in Brown continuing his safaris and refused to grant him the two months' paid leave that he had formerly enjoyed to take these extensive travels. Brown, wanting to continue this pleasurable aspect of his job, was forced to use his annual one-month paid vacation for this purpose. Cain's did humor him, by allowing him to combine his vacation with a one-month annual unpaid leave of absence so that he could continue his two-month safaris.

These trips cost Brown approximately $15,000 in 1960s' dollars, which Cain's refused to reimburse. The company did not ask Brown to take these safaris and, in fact, viewed them unfavorably. Instead of paying Brown $15,000 to travel to Africa to make a safari film, which was considered to have no value in promoting the Manhattan brand, the company preferred to spend the same $15,000 on media buys—television, newspaper, and radio ads.

Despite the company's lack of support for his passion, Brown continued to take his annual safaris and to make his coffee culture films which he paid for himself. He continued to use the films he made at sales meetings, which the company did not prohibit, even though it took no steps to promote them. Because he failed to obtain any reimbursement for the trips, Brown claimed a tax deduction for his expenses, claiming that these were an unreimbursed employee business expense.

The IRS disallowed the deduction, arguing that the expenses were incurred in relation to Brown's hobby, big game safaris. Brown then filed an action against the IRS in U.S. Tax Court. The Tax Court disagreed with the IRS position: these were not incurred purely to support Brown's hobby (and therefore personal) but also had a business purpose. Since Brown's employer would not reimburse them, the expenses could be viewed either as an unreimbursed expense of Brown's employment (as Brown had claimed) and therefore deductible, or as amounts spent to acquire a business capital asset (Brown's expertise as a coffee expert). Unfortunately for Brown, the Tax Court determined that they fell into the latter category because they were incurred primarily to build up Brown's personal reputation "as a coffee expert and only incidentally to increase sales of Manhattan's coffee." These expenses therefore were not deductible because the so-called "capital asset"—Brown's reputation—was still in the development stage and had not earned any separate income for Brown.

Brown appealed this decision. "Nonsense," said the appellate court, while still upholding the Tax Court's judgment, denying Brown his sought-after tax deduction. These were not expenses to acquire some intangible "capital asset." Brown's expenses were not deductible because they were not *necessary* to his employment. The appellate court noted that even though Brown, as an executive of the company, equated his personal interest—coffee plantation visits combined with safaris—with that of his company, they were not aligned. Cain's had made it clear to Brown that it did not view his safaris or films to be useful in promoting the Manhattan Coffee brand, that his continued employment did not depend on his taking the trips, and that he was not expected to spend his own money to make films for coffee advertising purposes. The Tax Court had used these facts to conclude that, since Cain's specifically refused to recognize the safari expenses as a corporate expense, this was prima facie evidence that the safari costs must be a personal expense. But the appellate court was more subtle in its analysis.

Simply because a corporation refuses to absorb an employee's expense does not legally render it outside the scope of a business expense. The cost of advertising is a corporate burden not customarily passed on to individual employees. In the past, Brown's coffee safaris had been viewed as instrumental in promoting the company's coffee. Both Cain's and Brown acknowledged this. If Cain's had elected to reimburse the safari expenses, there was no question that it could have deducted this cost as a business expense. It did not choose to do so. But an employee cannot incur an expense to promote a company's product and then try to convert the *company's* right to a deduction into his own. According to the court, the question to be asked was: even though Cain's did not reimburse the expense, was it nevertheless "necessary" to Brown's employment? If so, then the expense would be deductible. If not, then it would not be. In the case of Brown's safari expenses, the court answered "no."

Section 162 of the Internal Revenue Code allowed (and still allows) a deduction for all of the "ordinary and necessary" expenses incurred by the taxpayer in carrying out his trade or business. Brown's trade or business, whether he liked it or not, was to be a corporate employee. He was responsible for formulating the company's advertising programs, but not for payment of the expenses associated with such programs out of his own pocket. The Tax Code does not allow a taxpayer to deduct personal business expenses that are clearly those of the company for which he works, whether or not the corporation chooses to deduct them. The bottom line for Brown was this: the expenses were not ordinary or necessary. In the end, it is doubtful that Brown appreciated the appellate court's subtle analysis, because no matter how the expenses were treated, he still lost his deduction.

Coffee Break

The World of Coffee: Where Coffee is Grown

The United States has the world's largest number of coffee consumers. However, no coffee is produced in the continental United States.[1] Most of the world's coffee is grown along the equator and in subtropical areas north and south of the equator: the "middle of the world" where the climate is warm and humid, suitable for the sensitive coffee plants. Coffee is grown in more than 50 countries within this band, across the globe, including many developing countries. Coffee is the second largest export commodity for developing countries.[2] For many of these countries, coffee crops are critical to their economic well-being. Coffee is grown in such far-reaching areas as Central and South America, Indonesia, Africa, and India, as well as the Middle East.

Coffee originated in Africa, and today Africa produces some of the highest quality coffee, as well as some of the worst, some of the most rare and expensive as well as some of the cheapest. About half of the world's specialty coffees are produced in Africa, in what is known as the "coffee belt," which stretches along the eastern coast of Africa from Ethiopia to Zimbabwe.[3]

The primary coffee-producing countries in Africa's coffee belt are Ethiopia, Uganda, and Kenya. Ethiopia, on the northeastern Horn of Africa, is the birthplace of coffee, and this product remains essential to the Ethiopian economy. This country produces only arabica coffee beans. On the other hand, its neighbor, Uganda, largely produces robusta beans. In fact, while Ethiopia is considered the original source for arabica coffee, many believe that Uganda is the original source of robusta. Centuries ago, Ugandan warriors would chew the robusta bean before going into battle, making them feel strong, brave, and invincible,[4] much like the heavily caffeinated "warriors" of American high finance and trading today.

In the seventeenth century, the Dutch introduced coffee to

Coffee Break (continued)

Java, in Indonesia, and this country today remains a significant coffee producer. In the eighteenth century, the French and British brought coffee to their colonies in the Caribbean and from there production spread to Central and South America. Today coffee represents a major export for Costa Rica, Guatemala, Brazil, El Salvador, and Colombia, as well as to a lesser extent, Bolivia and Peru.

Areas of the world lesser known for coffee production are Vietnam and India. Vietnam is a relative newcomer into the international coffee market. Before 1990, this country had minimal involvement in global coffee trade. However, by 2000, Vietnam had displaced Colombia to become the world's second largest coffee-growing country, after Brazil.[5]

India has a long history of coffee production, even though Indian coffee has little to no recognition in the United States. Coffee was introduced into India in the late seventeenth century. It is the source of another coffee-smuggling legend. In the seventeenth century, Saint Baba Budan made a pilgrimage to Mecca, traveling through the port of Mocha, in Yemen. There he discovered coffee. At the time, it was illegal to take green coffee beans out of Arabia. On his return to India, again passing through Mocha, Baba Budan wrapped seven green coffee beans around his belly and brought them back to India. The number seven has great significance in the Muslim religion and in its rituals and therefore Baba Budan's act was of religious importance. On his return home, Baba Budan planted the seeds in the hills of Chikkamagaluru in Southern India.[6] Today most coffee produced in India is grown in the south, not far from where Baba Budan first planted his seven beans.[7]

Although most Americans are not familiar with them, Indian-produced coffees are well-regarded in Europe, which claims most of the production, commonly as a source of supply for espresso blends. Tata Coffee, one famous brand of Indian coffee, won three medals in the Grand Crus de Café competition in Paris in 2004.[8] Indian arabica coffees tend to be low-toned, subtle, and rounder than the brighter, more acid varieties produced in South

America and Africa, which traditionally have been preferred by many coffee distributors in the United States. But Europeans have a preference for the sweeter, less acidic, coffees produced in India.[9] Today, India is the third largest coffee exporter to Italy, after Brazil and Vietnam.[10]

---

1. Hawaii is the only U.S. state where coffee is grown.

2. Wasserman, Miriam, "Trouble in Coffee Lands," Federal Reserve Bank of Boston, Quarterly Review, Quarter 2, 2002, p. 4, found at http://www.bos.frb.org/economic/nerr/rr2002/Q2/coffee.pdf.

3. See Official website for EAFCA (East Africa Fine Coffee Association), found at http://eafca.org/index.asp.

4. "Uganda: The Origins of Robusta Coffee," EAFCA Official Website at http://eafca.org/chapter/uganda.asp.

5. Wasserman, p. 6.

6. Discussed at http://www.sweetmarias.com/coffee.asia.india.php.

7. Allen, p. 77.

8. "Gold Medal for Tata," The Times of India, June 2004, found at http://timesofindia.indiatimes.com/articleshow/755061.cms.

9. "Something for Everyone: Indian Coffees 2009," Kenneth Davids Coffee Review, October 2009, http://www.coffeereview.com/article.cfm.ID=164.

10. Punnathara, C. J., "Italy plans buying more coffee from India," The Hindu Business Line, Friday, Sept. 28, 2007, at http://thehindubusinessline.com/2007/09/28/stories/2007092851811300.htm.

Chapter Eight

The Importance of the Brand:
Private Label

Hills Bros. Coffee v. Hills Supermarkets, Inc.,
428 F.2d 379 (2nd Cir. 1970)

B y the late 1960s, most coffee sold to consumers in the United States was dominated by major brands: Maxwell House, Folgers, MJB, and Hills Bros. This was an era where branding and advertising, both in print and on television, had a major impact on consumer choices in stores. Maxwell House introduced ads featuring a percolator with coffee spouting into the glass knob on its lid, accompanied by hip music. And Folgers found Mrs. Olsen, a domineering Swedish busybody who was always inserting herself into others' coffee claches and who could always advise its participants which coffee brand was best (why, Folgers of course).[1] This was also an era where brand managers grew more and more aware of the importance of shelf space and product visibility in supermarkets, where most consumers now purchased their groceries.

The 1960s was also an era that saw the evolution of the grocery channel, where competition led to lowered profit margins

---

1. Pendergrast, p. 283.

for retailers, and market managers continually sought out products that they could buy for less and sell for more. One means to improved profit margins was through the placement of private label products in their stores. These are products, such as soap, detergent, milk, and coffee, which are sold under either the grocer's name or a generic brand. Private label was not a new concept in the coffee business. The A&P Stores, in fact, started out largely as a roaster selling its own brand of coffee and gradually expanded into other store-branded product offerings, while continuing to sell in its stores its predominant brand—Eight O'Clock Coffee—as it became a national grocery chain.

Private label goods are positioned generally as lower cost alternatives to national or regional brands, due to lower advertising costs. These are frequently produced by the same manufacturers of the products carrying major brand labels. To achieve sales, grocers often place these products on the shelf next to the nationally advertised brands. Sometimes, store-branded merchandise mimics the shape, packaging, and labeling of these national brands, closely resembling them, but not enough to create sufficient consumer confusion to be in violation of the national brand's trade dress.

It is irksome enough to see one's product mimicked on a shelf. It is another thing to have that lower cost product sold under a store brand with the same name. This was the situation faced by Hills Bros. coffee when Hills Supermarkets decided to introduce its private label coffee product, Hills Coffee, into its stores. Hills Supermarkets claimed that it was not trying to take advantage of an established brand. It was labeling its coffee product the same as its other store-branded products—Hills Dish Soap, Hills Flour, and Hills Coffee. It took the position that it had the right to use its store name on its store-branded products. Hills Bros. saw the situation quite differently.

Although originally a San Francisco-based coffee roaster, before World War II, Hills Bros. had already successfully expanded to the East Coast, commanding a large share of the national coffee market by the 1950s. Hills Bros. coffee had been a prominently featured, well-selling product in Hills Supermarkets stores in New York state for some years. However, by the 1960s, its sales were slipping, as its quality declined, and it suffered from an "old-fashioned" image.[2] Given its already low sales volume, the last straw was Hills Supermarkets' decision to bring a private label coffee—a coffee that would be lower priced but likely not much worse than Hills Bros. coffee was at the time—into its stores, carrying the "Hills" name.

Hills Bros. filed a lawsuit against Hills Supermarkets to prevent this use of the name "Hills" on the store label, arguing that this proposed use would infringe on Hills Bros.' trademark for its coffee. Its request for a preliminary injunction to stop the use was denied and Hills Bros. appealed. In order to obtain a preliminary injunction, the company had to demonstrate that it was likely to succeed in its trademark infringement suit against Hills Supermarkets, and also that it would suffer irreparable damage if the injunction were denied. In other words, it had to show that the use of the "Hills" mark on Hills Supermarket's coffee would in all likelihood cause confusion, which would lead consumers to mistakenly buy the private label coffee when they intended to purchase Hills Bros. coffee. This in turn could damage the "Hills Bros." brand because the store label coffee was undoubtedly inferior (or at least Hills Bros. argued) to the nationally branded coffee. Or worse, the consumer would not be able to detect a noticeable difference between the two coffees and would permanently switch to the lower-priced store brand, resulting in lost

---

2. Pendergrast, p. 284.

sales for Hills Bros. In short, Hills Bros. argued, allowing this use would endanger Hills Bros.' sales and reputation.

The appellate court agreed with Hills Bros.' contention, understanding that there was a strong likelihood of confusion between the "Hills" label and the "Hills Bros." label on cans and jars of coffee. The risk of confusion was particularly likely where the two brands of coffee would be located in the same area of the store, and possibly even on the same store shelf, next to each other. Because the word "Hills" would be prominently displayed on each can, even reasonably careful shoppers would be likely to mistake one brand for the other. Moreover, in its marketing campaigns, Hills Bros. at times shortened "Hills Bros." to just "Hills," making confusion virtually certain.

It was true that Hills Supermarkets may have only intended to put its own name on the cans of generic coffee that it intended to sell. But the court had no doubt that Hills Bros. had a prior right to the "Hills" trademark for coffee in the New York geographic area, having had a presence there since the 1920s. Moreover, the company had a federal trademark registration for both the "Hills Bros." and "Hills" trademarks.

The court agreed with Hills Bros. that allowing Hills Supermarkets to start using the "Hills" mark on its coffee, which it had not yet begun to do, until the trademark infringement case was concluded would cause severe dilution of the "Hills Bros." mark. The court weighed the equities, as it needed to do in a preliminary injunction case, and found that, on the one hand, Hills Supermarkets would suffer no harm if forced to change its store label for coffee before the trial on Hills Bros.' trademark infringement claim. On the other hand, Hills Bros. would potentially suffer significant harm to its coffee sales and to the reputation of its coffee if Hills Supermarkets were allowed to sell coffee under the "Hills" name until the conclusion of the trial. The equities therefore balanced in favor of Hills Bros., and the court accordingly ordered Hills Supermarkets to cease all use of the "Hills" mark on its coffee.

Ironically, this case probably did little to save the reputation of the "Hills Bros." brand. With or without competition from private label coffees, as Americans gradually came to prefer the fuller flavored specialty coffees that came into their own in the 1970s and 1980s, the Hills Bros. brand continued its slow decline, until the business was finally acquired by a Brazilian company in the 1980s.[3] Today, unfortunately for Hills Bros. when one thinks of a quality coffee, Hills Bros. does not often come to mind.

---

3. Pendergrast, p. 319.

Coffee Break

Diluted Coffee: Trademark Law Basics

As the coffee industry became more competitive and commercialized in the United States in the twentieth century, disputes over trademark rights were a natural consequence. A coffee business is much like any other in this respect: one of its most valuable assets is the name under which it markets and sells its product, whether that is Hills Bros., Illy, or Starbucks. Trademarks in the United States are protected by the Lanham Act (the Trademark Act of 1946, as amended).[1] Under the Lanham Act, a "trademark" is a word, symbol, or device used to identify a producer's goods or services sold. "Trade dress" is the entire selling image of a product, including its packaging. The purposes of trademark law are to prevent consumer confusion as to the source of the product, and also to prevent unfair business competition.

In the United States, the first user of any trademark is protected from any subsequent use of a mark that looks like or is confusingly similar to the protected mark in connection with similar goods or services, or any likely area of expansion. Trademarks have received common law protection (through precedents in court decisions) and also through the laws of various states governing unfair competition. Additionally, a trademark that is registered with the U.S. Patent and Trademark Office and bears the symbol "®" has federal protection under the Lanham Act.

Trademark rights are exclusive to the holder of the mark and the mark cannot be used without the consent of the holder under a license—an agreement under which the trademark owner allows another to use the trademark with respect to specific delineated products. When parties claiming the same trademark for different products resolve their dispute, they at times will enter into a settlement agreement and agree to the entry of a consent decree with the court which provides for a division of the

86

rights, with one party, for example, having rights to use the brand with respect to coffee as a beverage, and the other having rights to the mark for another, different use, such as with cheese or another food product.

Trademark infringement occurs when another violates the exclusive rights of the trademark holder to the use of that trademark for similar goods and services. When the use is in connection with a product that is not identical, then the use has to create a *likelihood* of confusion for the actual or potential consumers of the trademark owner's product, regardless of whether the owners of the competing trademarks are competitors.

One problem that trademark owners continually face from potential infringers is that of trademark "dilution." Dilution can occur when the trademark ceases to signify a single source for the product; in other words, where the link between the mark and its owner becomes blurred. This is not a light matter: trademark owners have to be vigilant in protecting their marks, even when it appears that they are "beating up" a small company that is not really a threat from a competitive perspective, or they risk losing the mark entirely. Classic examples where this has happened are aspirin, escalator, linoleum, and zipper, which once were all trademarks. "Zipper" was originally a unique word registered as a trademark for overshoes with fasteners. But the word quickly gained popularity for any type of fastener. The trademark owner sued to protect its trademark but this effort was in vain because at the time, federal trademark law did not protect owners against uses that were not directly competitive, even if they diluted the mark. The law has now changed.

Under amendments to the Lanham Act in 1996, the owner of a famous mark is allowed to prevent another's commercial use of the mark if the use begins after the mark has become famous and causes dilution of the distinctiveness of the mark. The statute spells out factors to be considered to determine whether a mark is "famous": how distinctive the mark is or has become, how long it has been used in connection with the goods or services

Coffee Break (continued)

with which it is used, how much advertising and publicity surrounds the mark, how widely the mark is used, to what degree the mark is recognized, and how similar it is to other marks.[2]

The difficulty that companies still faced despite the 1996 law was evidenced in a U.S. Supreme Court ruling in 2003[3], in which the law was interpreted to require proof of actual dilution of the mark, something that was not always easy to do. In 2006, Congress amended the law to permit owners of famous trademarks to prove the *likelihood* of dilution rather than actual harm to their trademark, in the form of either blurring or tarnishment.[4]

"Blurring" occurs when the public associates a trademark with someone else's goods or services and such association "impairs the distinctiveness of the famous mark." There are a number of factors under federal law that courts can consider to determine whether there is dilution or blurring: (1) the degree of similarity between the mark and the famous mark, (2) the degree of distinctiveness of the famous mark, (3) the extent to which the owner of the famous mark is engaging in substantially exclusive use of the mark, (4) the degree of recognition of the famous mark, (5) whether the user of the mark intended to create an association with the famous mark, and (6) any actual association between the mark and the famous mark.[5]

Dilution by tarnishment is "an association arising from the similarity between a mark . . . and a famous mark that harms the reputation of the famous mark.[6] A mark is tarnished, for example, when it is linked to products of shoddy quality, or is portrayed in an unseemly context, with the result that the public associates the lack of quality in the imitator's goods with the products of the owner of the famous mark.

Some courts also look for blurring using a multipronged test established in the early 1960s, the so-called "*Polaroid* Factors"[7]: (1) strength of the trademark, (2) similarity of the marks, (3) proximity of the products and their competitiveness with one another, (4) evidence that the senior user may "bridge the gap" by developing a product for sale in the market of the alleged infringing product, (5) evidence of actual consumer confusion, (6) evidence that the imitative mark was adopted in bad faith, (7) respective quality of the products, and (8) sophistication of consumers in the relevant market.

A further difficulty arises where two parties have legally registered marks that are noncompeting. Courts are then faced with making Solomon-like decisions to determine whether there is any *likelihood* of confusion and what to do if there is. Where more than one party has legally registered marks that are noncompeting, the courts use a multifactor inquiry to determine whether there is any likelihood of confusion (so-called "*Lapp* Factors," named after the Third Circuit's decision in *Interpace Corp. v. Lapp Inc.*[8]: 1) the degree of similarity in the marks, 2) the strength of the mark of the person claiming infringement, 3) the price of the goods or other factors indicative of the purchaser's level of attention when making a purchase, 4) the length of time the defendant has used the mark without evidence of confusion, 5) the intent of the defendant in adopting the mark, 6) evidence of actual confusion, 7) whether the goods are marketed through the same channels of commerce and advertised in the same media, 8) the extent to which the parties' sales efforts are the same, 9) the relationship of the goods in the minds of consumers because of similarity of function, and 10) other facts suggesting that the consuming public might expect the owner to manufacture a product in the defendant's market.

1. 5 U.S.C. §§1125 *et seq.*
2. 15 U.S.C. §1125(c).
3. *Moseley v. Secret Catalogue*, 537 U.S. 418, 433 (2003).
4. 15 U.S.C. §1125(c)(1).
5. 15 U.S.C. §1125(c)(2)(B)(i)-(vi).
6. 15 U.S.C. §§1125(c)(2)(C).
7. *Polaroid Corp. v. Polarad Elecs. Corp.*, 287 F. 2d 492 (2d Cir. 1961).
8. 721 F.2d 460, 462-63 (3d Cir. 1983).

Chapter Nine

Fishy Coffee:
The Importance of the Brand, Part II

Louis Ender, Inc. v. General Foods Corporation,
476 F.2d 327 (2nd Cir. 1972)

T he trademark issues in the prior chapter were fairly clear cut: as between two coffee sellers, both of which operate under the same or comparable name, the one with the right to use its company name on the coffee it sells will be determined by straightforward legal principles, such as prior use rights and trademark registrations. The question becomes less simple when the brand is a made-up name that both have been using for very different products for a long time and one or both desire to expand into adjacencies where there is a possibility of consumer confusion. Which one should have the right to do so and which one needs to stand aside?

This is the story of a company that sold fish, namely sardines, under the brand "Maxim," and another that sold coffee under the same name. It would appear that fish is about as far removed from coffee as one can get. But of course, things are never so simple. And coffee historians know that fish actually has a close relationship to coffee: nineteenth century pioneers who needed to clarify the grounds in their cowboy coffee were advised to use eggs and, if eggs weren't available, to substitute salt cod.[1] But Louis Ender, Inc. and General Foods Corporation weren't thinking about cod when they entered into this litigation.

Louis Ender was a wholesale grocery business based in New York. It had acquired the trademark, "Maxim," which was first registered with the U.S. Patent Office in 1908, specifically for use in the sale of sardines. Before 1965, this trademark had continuously been used in connection with sardines.

General Foods Corporation was formed in 1929, as the successor to Postum, by Marjorie Merriweather Post and her husband, E. F. Hutton. The company owned a wide variety of brands for food products and was the largest processor and marketer of coffee in the United States at the time of the litigation. Its products included regular vacuum-packed and instant coffees sold under the "Maxwell House" brand, as well as other coffee brands. It controlled about 45 percent of the retail coffee market in the 1960s. In 1964, the company introduced a new instant coffee, the first freeze-dried instant coffee. Because the freeze-dry process was a new technology for instant coffee, General Foods wanted a mark that would differentiate this type of instant coffee from regular Maxwell House soluble coffee, but that was nevertheless suggestive of the "Maxwell House" brand. It settled on the name "Maxim."

In its trademark search, General Foods discovered that the mark had been registered for sardines, but not for any coffee product. To avoid any possibility of later disputes, however, the company obtained a consent agreement from Louis Ender on July 31, 1963, through its agent, Alexander A. Forgaco. Forgaco later assigned the agreement to General Foods. It is likely that Louis Ender company executives did not realize that Maxwell House was to be the beneficiary of the agreement.

---

1. Pendergrast, p. 47.

Under the agreement, Louis Ender granted its consent to the registration and/or use of the name "Maxim" limited to coffee in any form and tea in any form and acknowledged that such use of the name "Maxim" was not likely to cause confusion or deceive purchasers. Louis Ender also agreed not to use the name "Maxim" on any coffee, coffee product, beverage, beverage product, or any preparation for use in making any beverage or beverage product.

On January 21, 1964, General Foods filed an application with the U.S. Patent Office for registration of the trademark "Maxim" for coffee. In this application, General Foods made several declarations that Louis Ender later contended were false: (1) that the trademark was first used by General Foods in interstate commerce on November 29, 1962, (2) that to the best of General Foods' knowledge and belief no other person had the right to use the mark in commerce, and (3) that General Foods believed that it was the owner of the mark it sought to register. The trademark registration was granted on September 21, 1964.

In the fall of 1965, Louis Ender for the first time began marketing canned fruit juices under the name "Maxim." General Foods notified Louis Ender that the sale of the juices under the name "Maxim" was a violation of the consent agreement, but Louis Ender maintained that fruit juices were not "beverages" or "beverage products" within the meaning of that agreement. The parties were unable to settle their dispute and in May 1967, General Foods sued Louis Ender in the Supreme Court of New York, seeking an injunction to prevent Louis Ender's continued use of the name "Maxim" in connection with the sale of juices.

General Foods alleged that Louis Ender had breached its contractual obligations under the consent agreement. It also claimed that Louis Ender's "continued and deliberate" use of the name "Maxim" for orange juice and other fruit juices was intended to create confusion and infringed on General Foods' right to use the name. This was, according to General Foods, an unlawful and unfair business practice in violation of New York general business law.

On July 16, 1970, before any decision had been handed down in the state court suit, Louis Ender began an action in the U.S. district court against General Foods, seeking damages and the cancellation of General Foods' trademark registration for "Maxim" on the grounds that its original application for the trademark contained false statements. The damages that Louis Ender claimed were the expenses it had incurred in defending General Foods' state court lawsuit. General Foods moved to dismiss Louis Ender's federal court suit, arguing that the company had failed to state a claim on which relief could be granted. The district court denied General Foods' motion but stayed (postponed) all proceedings in the federal action until the state court rendered a decision.

In May 1971, the state court granted a permanent injunction against Louis Ender's use of the "Maxim" trademark in connection with the sale of fruit juices. Louis Ender unsuccessfully appealed.

Then General Foods filed another motion in the federal district court action to dismiss Louis Ender's complaint, and also moved for summary judgment in the case against Louis Ender on the grounds of "collateral estoppel." This is a legal doctrine under which an earlier decision rendered by a court in a lawsuit between parties is conclusive as to the issues so that they cannot be relitigated in subsequent proceedings involving the same parties, whether or not in the same court. Louis Ender then amended its complaint in federal court to allege constitutional claims, arguing that the state court action had denied it due process of law.

The district court granted General Foods' motion for summary judgment, holding that the issues on which Louis Ender had based its claim had been finally and conclusively determined adversely to Louis Ender in the New York State courts and therefore could not be retried in the district court. In addition, the district court could see no "discernable constitutional questions."

Louis Ender appealed.

General Foods contended in its appellate court briefs that the state court's determination that it had not fraudulently obtained its "Maxim" trademark registration and that General Foods' trademark was valid and General Foods had "estopped," that is, prevented, Louis Ender from making the same claims in its federal lawsuit. However, the appellate court did not agree that the factual issues litigated in the state court action were conclusive as to the issues that Louis Ender sought to litigate in the federal courts. General Foods' suit in state court was based on New York business law governing unfair competition. That law provided: "likelihood of injury to business reputation or of dilution of the distinctive quality of the mark or trade name shall be a ground for injunctive relief in cases of infringement of a mark registered or not registered or in cases of unfair competition. . ."

The decision in the state court in favor of General Foods was based on the theory that Louis Ender's conduct in labeling the canned juices with the name "Maxim" was unfair competition. Louis Ender had raised the issue of General Foods' allegedly false declarations in its trademark application as a defense against General Foods' unfair competition claim. It had wanted the New York state court to consider that General Foods, which was seeking "equitable" relief in the form of an injunction against Louis Ender, should not be entitled to that form of relief because the company had "unclean hands," having lied on its trademark application.

For the New York court, whether or not General Foods had acted fraudulently in filing its trademark application was irrelevant to its decision because General Foods had an action for unfair competition against Louis Ender that was independent of General Foods' registered trademark. Accordingly, the state court was not required to judge on the validity of General Foods' registered trademark or to determine the truth or falsity of its declarations in support of its application for registration. The New York business law explicitly provided that the law applied to protect a trademark whether it was "registered or not registered."

Therefore, the two cases were different. However, for Louis Ender, this was a distinction that made no difference. The company was out of luck in federal court, but for a very simple reason: it had no damages. When filing its federal court action, the only "damages" that it had claimed to have suffered due to General Foods' allegedly false statements in its trademark application were its expenses in defending the state court action. And this was a case where the allegedly false statements were "totally irrelevant." And because these statements were irrelevant, Louis Ender's claimed "damages" did not result at all from General Foods' allegedly invalid trademark registration. General Foods had prevailed against Louis Ender in state court on the theory of unfair competition, which did not require a trademark registration at all.

Because Louis Ender had claimed no damages in its federal action other than those litigation expenses, it had no right at all to be in federal court. A prerequisite for filing a federal court action is a valid claim for damages.

Louis Ender had also claimed in its amended complaint that it had suffered from the lack of due process in the state court action because the trial judge was killed in an automobile accident and the replacement judge had refused to grant a new trial. But the federal appeals court could not see how any of this involved General Foods. General Foods had done nothing to deprive Louis Ender of its constitutional rights. The company's proper course of action for this alleged deprivation would have been to raise this claim in its appeal to the state appellate courts. Louis Ender had not raised this issue in its unsuccessful appeals in that forum.

It seems that this is simply a case of sour grapes, or sour grape juice perhaps. It is obvious that Louis Ender felt it had been "cheated" by General Foods when General Foods initially obtained the consent agreement and then later went around Louis Ender's back to file its application for a trademark registration. Whatever may have been the source of its annoyance, however, the company learned that trying to avoid one court's jurisdiction by filing dubious claims in another does not get one very far. It's like a sardine trying to swim upstream.

Instant Coffee

Coffee has always depended on technology to gain popular acceptance. Long ago, when coffee was consumed solely as part of a religious ritual, the extensive labor required to prepare it was not a problem because the preparations— removing the pulp, roasting, grinding, boiling— were all part of the ritual itself. But once coffee entered the mainstream to become an internationally popular beverage, people began seeking easier ways to grow it, harvest it, roast it, and prepare it to drink. By the mid-1840s, patents were issued in the United States and Europe for industrial-scale coffee-roasting equipment.[1] By the turn of the twentieth century, a number of inventors held patents for espresso machines and other coffee brewers.

One of the biggest goals was the quest for an instant coffee: a coffee that could be prepared quickly, with minimal effort. In 1910, a soluble coffee was introduced in the United States, called "G. Washington Refined Coffee."[2] This instant coffee was composed of crystals formed from boiling coffee until the liquid evaporated. When the United States entered World War I, the army requisitioned all of the coffee produced under this brand for soldiers serving on the Western Front.[3] However, because these early soluble coffees lacked the flavor of fresh- brewed coffee, they did not attract a large number of consumers until the Depression years.

In 1938, Nescafé was introduced into the coffee market.[4] This was an improved instant coffee in powder form that Nestlé developed, using technology from its baby formula business. Instead of boiling the coffee to form crystals, under Nestlé's process, the liquid coffee was sprayed onto heated towers. Coffee droplets turned to powder as they struck the sides of the tower.[5] To make the compound more palatable and to maintain flavor, carbohydrates were added.

Nescafé changed the attitude of consumers toward powdered coffees. It rapidly became an international phenomenon, and it remains the instant coffee of choice

in many European homes and in other parts of the world. Take your breakfast in a Turkish hotel and order coffee: you will likely be served a Nescafé (not the traditional Turkish coffee).

During World War II, instant coffee was included in soldiers' daily K-rations, and the major U.S. coffee companies, such as Maxwell House and Folgers, brought out their own versions.[6] After the war, as Americans sought greater convenience and desired to be liberated from the kitchen, instant coffee gained wider acceptance for its convenience and new brands were introduced. The quality of these coffees was generally poor, but the flavor was uniform and consumers seemed to accept instant coffee even if it was mediocre as long as it was "hot and wet and looked like coffee."[7] In the 1950s, instant coffee represented over 15 percent of all U.S. coffee sales.

For coffee lovers, these were the "dark ages" of coffee. Most of the instant coffees sold in the 1950s and 1960s were made up largely of bitter robusta beans, which were over-extracted to produce more coffee per pound of beans, thus increasing the manufacturer's profits.[8] To compensate for the inferior quality, flavor enhancers were added.

Because not everyone was happy with the deteriorating quality of coffee, and in particular the soluble coffees that were on the market, coffee companies were constantly seeking ways to improve on the technologies to produce a better instant coffee that would be competitive price-wise. Maxwell House led the efforts with its new patent applications for freeze-dried coffee.

Coffee Break (continued)

The coffee revolution that began in the last decades of the twentieth century when consumers began demanding fresher, more flavorful coffee somewhat dampened sales of instant coffee, which by then had acquired a reputation for tasting both weak and stale. While Nescafé managed to maintain a hold on the international market, sales of other instant coffees suffered. Manufacturers attempted to counter this trend by introducing lines of "gourmet" instant coffees, and by increased advertising of the convenience associated with them. But many consumers, enamored with the new convenience of a Starbucks on every corner, drive-through espresso bars, and hot coffee available at every gas station minimart, as well as with the new electric drip coffee-making machines that could be programmed to have a freshly brewed cup of coffee ready to drink when they awoke in the morning, preferred to wait a little longer for their coffee than drink something that failed to please their palates.

Nevertheless, the desire to have a "ready-to-go" beverage lives on. Nescafé still holds a strong position and Starbucks has introduced its own form of "instant coffee," with its Starbucks VIA™ Ready Brew. "A truly great cup of coffee that you can prepare by just adding water" claims its advertising campaign.[9] It remains to be seen whether Starbucks' new technology can succeed where others have tried and have only produced, as Starbucks notes, instant coffees that "taste flat and lifeless."

1. Pendergrast, p. 48.
2. George Washington Coffee Official Webpage: http://www.georgewashington coffee.com/Washington_Coffee.html.
3. Pendergrast, pp. 147-148.
4. Nescafé Official Webpage: http://www.nescafe.com/worldwide/en/nescafe/ Pages/history.aspx.
5. Pendergrast, p. 213.
6. Pendergrast notes that because coffee was so closely connected to the American soldier, it acquired a nickname, after GI Joe—"cuppa Joe." Pendergrast, p. 224.
7. Pendergrast, p. 240, quoting a 1950 Consumers Research Bulletin.
8. Pendergrast, p. 262.
9. http://www.starbucks.com/via.

Chapter Ten

Freeze-Dried Coffee:
Patent Rights

Application of William P. Clinton,
527 F.2d 1226 (Fed. Cir. 1976)

U nlike many food products that can be consumed in their
"natural" state, coffee has always demanded technological innovation in order to be consumed and enjoyed. The
coffee bean grows inside a red berry on a tree. Who would have
thought that inside was hidden a little green bean which, when
roasted and ground, could produce a satisfying and stimulating
beverage? Some experimentation was required to gain that
insight. The green coffee bean requires extensive processing:
removal from the cherry, curing, and roasting, stated simply.[1] But
because the cost of coffee cultivation, transportation, and processing is high, and the demand for inexpensive coffee is also
great, over the centuries, and particularly since the mid-nineteenth century, coffee producers have sought strategies for
reducing this cost. At the same time, they've sought to mecha-
nize some of the hand labor that is required for coffee preparation. Hence, methodologies were invented to sort the coffee
beans more efficiently, to roast large volumes of coffee at once,
and to package it (such as the vacuum seal first utilized by Hills

---

1. *See* Coffee Break, "Coffee Basics: The Bean and Beyond."

Bros. in the early twentieth century). Many patents have been taken out by inventive coffee enthusiasts for coffee technologies, such as roasters.[2] Instant coffee alone has been an inventive field for over a century.[3]

An easily transportable and convenient coffee product has been long desired. In the nineteenth century, pioneers who carried packets of green coffee beans across the plains and who then were obliged to roast them, grind them, and boil the grounds over a campfire every night and morning would have been delighted to have a product that they could just mix in a cup of hot water. During the Civil War, because ground coffee quickly grew stale, Union soldiers carried portable coffee grinders and some of the more inventive among them carried rifles that came equipped with coffee mills in the rifle butts.[4]

As soon as it was introduced, cheap instant coffee gained significant market share, particularly in a post-World War II United States where convenience was king.[5] Consumers seemed more than willing to sacrifice any semblance of taste for convenience. By the 1960s, instant coffee represented almost 20 percent of U.S. coffee sales.[6]

Nevertheless, the taste of instant coffee left much to be desired and coffee producers engaged in extensive research to develop a method of production that would yield a better coffee. In 1960, General Foods introduced instant Yuban, which used all arabica beans and was therefore superior to most other instant coffees then being sold, which were made from a blend of main-

2. Pendergrast, p. 48.

3. "Coffee technology history highlights," *Tea & Coffee Trade Journal*, February 20, 2004, http://goliath.ecnext.com/coms2/gi_0199-157321/Coffee-technology-history-highlights.html.

4. Pendergrast, p. 49. *See also*, Davis, William C., *A Taste for War: The Culinary History of the Blue and the Gray*, Stackpole Books: Mechanicsburg PA, 2003, p. 27.

5. Pendergrast, p. 240.

6. Pendergrast, p. 240.

ly robusta beans. And then, in 1964, the company introduced its new Maxim, which represented a technological breakthrough: the first freeze-dried coffee, which offered a better flavor. Recognizing that this was a major technological development in the field, the scientists at General Foods filed multiple patent applications to fully cover this new technology, even at the risk of duplicating their own prior patent applications. One of these scientists was William P. Clinton.

In May 1969, Clinton applied for a patent for improvements to freeze-dried coffee. The prior applications that Clinton and his fellow scientists had filed had been approved so it was a surprise when all of Clinton's patent claims were rejected by the patent examiner on the grounds that the processes disclosed in this most recent application were covered by "prior art" and/or were too "obvious." "Prior art," in the patent law context, constitutes all information that has been made available to the public in any form before a given date that might be relevant to a patent's claims of originality. If an invention has been described in prior art, a patent on that invention is not valid. Even if the subject matter sought to be patented is not exactly shown by the prior art, and involves one or more differences over the most nearly similar thing already known, a patent may still be refused if the differences would be obvious. The subject matter sought to be patented must be sufficiently different from what has been used or described before that it may be said to be "nonobvious" to a person having ordinary skill in the area of technology related to the invention.[7] For example, the substitution of one color for another, or changes in size, are ordinarily not patentable.

Clinton appealed but the decision of the patent examiner was affirmed by the Patent and Trademark Office Board of

---

7. Section 103 Patent laws, 35 U.S.C. §103(a).

Patent Appeals. The process improvements claimed by Clinton were straightforward: roasted and ground coffee was percolated until a coffee extract containing 20 percent to 35 percent soluble coffee solids was obtained. This initial coffee extract was then concentrated by partially freezing it to form ice crystals and concentrated coffee extract. This extract, which contained 35 percent to 55 percent soluble coffee solids, was separated from the ice crystals and frozen, then dried. The remaining concentrated coffee extract was first cooled and the frozen extract (the crystals) was ground to a granular particle size.

Because at least five prior patents addressed the process of freeze drying coffee, including a patent that Clinton himself had obtained, the examiner could not see anything unique about Clinton's new discovery and determined that this process would have been obvious to anyone with coffee processing skills.

In his appeal, Clinton admitted that the individual steps of freeze concentrating and freeze drying a coffee extract were disclosed in the prior art, but he contended that there was no suggestion in the prior art to *combine* these individual steps. He contended that it would not have been obvious to apply these procedures. He also contended that, when all the prior art was considered as a whole, a person of ordinary skill in the process of producing soluble coffee would not have a sufficient basis for predictably recreating the steps that Clinton set forth in his application.

The court disagreed. In their view, a person of ordinary skill would have had sufficient motivation to combine the individual steps that made up the process Clinton claimed to have invented. For example, the court noted, a process invented by a certain Flosdorf in 1950 for freeze drying fruit juices and extracts suggests subjecting coffee extract to a combination of freeze concentration and freeze drying. A prior patent obtained by a certain Cottle in 1956, which disclosed a process for preserving beverages by freezing them, granulating the frozen material, and freeze drying the frozen granules, also disclosed that this process may result in the formation of sediment that could be removed by cooling and clarification. Even though Cottle's process did not disclose sediment formation in coffee extract in particular, the court thought it would have been within the ability of a coffee researcher of ordinary skill who was aware of Cottle's process to subject a coffee extract to gradual cooling and to remove any resultant sediment prior to freeze concentration.

Obviousness, the court noted, does not require absolute predictability but rather a reasonable expectation of success.

Clinton also maintained that what was lacking in the prior art was a discovery of an optimal moisture level in the end product of between 1 percent and 2.5 percent. Above this moisture range, the soluble coffee product caked and developed off-flavors from storage. However, if the extract was dried to a level below 1 percent moisture, this overdrying could cause an excess removal of aromatic substances essential to produce a good coffee flavor.

The court admitted that the claimed final moisture content was critical, but again believed that a person with ordinary skill in the art would have been motivated to produce a freeze-dried coffee with the optimal moisture content, because all the references to the freeze-drying process point out that freeze drying is an expensive method of removing water. In the court's view, the economics alone would have been a sufficient incentive.

In the end, the failure to obtain all the possible patents for the freeze-drying process did not limit the success of the Maxim product. Those who tried it believe that soluble coffee made from this process was superior to most other instant coffees then on the market. But instead of increasing the market share of all instant coffees, sales of Maxim actually eroded the sales of General Foods' own profitable Maxwell House coffee brands, including its soluble coffee, and so, after some trial period, the company removed the product from the market.

Coffee Break

Brazil's Black Frost

A Portuguese diplomat smuggled coffee tree saplings out of French Guiana and took them to Brazil. Brazil then soon became the foremost producer of coffee, so much so that by the beginning of the twentieth century, it had taken a three-quarters share of the world coffee production.

Brazil long maintained a goal of dominating global coffee markets, leading to an unsustainable growing practice: tropical rain forests were destroyed to clear areas for increased coffee production. These methods emphasized quantity over quality. Unfortunately, Brazil's climate is not optimal for coffee, even though it has managed to dominate production for over a century. The country has accomplished this by fighting its own climate. Coffee cannot tolerate a hard frost and it requires abundant rainfall. Brazil suffers from periodic cold snaps and drought, which have increased in intensity and frequency as its protective rain forests have been destroyed.

Brazil suffered a severe frost in July 1953 that significantly reduced the Brazilian coffee harvest for that year.[1] But this was nothing compared to the "Black Frost" of 1975.[2] That year, it snowed for the first time in Brazil's coffee-growing region, the Paraná. On the night of July 17, an enormous frost settled over the coffee trees, inflicting terrible destruction. Viewed from the air, the area looked as if it had been burned in a forest fire and the event was named the "Black Frost." Most frosts that hit Brazil are called "white frosts." These will kill leaves and flowers of young coffee trees, thus affecting the next year's harvest, but the tree generally will live. A black frost is different. This turns the sap of the tree black (hence the name) and kills the tree, turning it into something resembling a burnt-out stump.

Over half of Brazil's coffee trees were destroyed in the 1975 Black Frost. They would produce no crop for the 1976-1977 crop year. At the time of the frost, there were also wars in Ethiopia and Angola, and Uganda's production was suffering under the caprices of its ruler, Idi Amin. The coffee supply situation was

Coffee Break (continued)

very uncertain. Although the Brazilian government had some coffee reserves on hand, considering that Brazil then represented almost a third of coffee imports into the United States at the time, the situation was grave. In the wake of the frost, coffee futures soared and coffee traders began hoarding their short supplies.[3]

One consequence of the resulting high coffee prices was an effort to develop more efficient coffee-roasting techniques, essentially to "squeeze" more coffee from the limited supply of beans: so-called "high yield coffees." Ironically, this aided the growth of the specialty coffee industry in the 1980s and 1990s: as daily coffee became weaker, coffee lovers turned to gourmet coffee shops that could satisfy their craving for the real thing.[4]

1. "Brazil: The High Cost of Coffee," *Time*, Friday, Aug. 28, 1964, found at http://www.time.com/time/magazine/article/0,9171,876132,00.html.; *See also*, Pendergrast, p. 249.
2. Pendergrast, p. 317.
3. Talbot, John M., *Grounds for Agreement: The Political Economy of the Coffee Commodity Chain*, Bowman & Littlefield Publishers, Inc., 2004, p. 68.
4. Schoenholt, Donald, "Specialty Coffee Moves from Strength to Strength," *Tea and Coffee Trade Journal*, Oct. 1, 1991, found at http://www.allbusiness.com/manufacturing/food-manufacturing-food-coffee-tea/276455-1.html.

Chapter Eleven

What Goes Up Can Come Down:

The Wild World of Coffee Futures Trading

First Commodity Corp. v. Commodity Futures Trading Commission, 676 F.2d 1 (1st Cir. 1982)

n June 1975, John Ruddy was in a tight financial position. His daughter was getting married and he needed some extra money to pay the wedding expenses. He turned for advice to Richard Badoian, a sales representative at First Commodity Corporation of Boston. Badoian recommended that Ruddy buy several call options on coffee. These options cost Ruddy about $1,900 and gave him the right to buy 15 tons of coffee at a price of about $1,080 per ton at any time before December 31, 1975. Ruddy had no experience in the world of commodities trading but he trusted Badoian. He had no idea what he was getting into when he entered the chaotic world of coffee trading, particularly in 1975, when coffee supplies were fluctuating madly, causing the price to be extremely volatile.

Later that month, Ruddy and Badoian talked about the status of Ruddy's call options. The price of coffee had begun to fall and Ruddy was concerned. As he testified later, he asked Badoian to "take any action necessary to protect me the same as you would if it was your money." Badoian told Ruddy that First Commodity expected a "temporary downtrend" in the coffee market. Being a coffee specialist, Badoian was an optimist. He suggested that Ruddy "take advantage of this additional chance to make money by placing a hedge."

Ruddy had no idea was a "hedge" was. He testified at trial that he was thinking in terms of a hedge fence.

He had the impression, from what Badoian told him, that the "hedge" would make money for him if the price of coffee fell, and that he could lose the price of the call options, commission costs, and the deposit or margin on his short sale futures contract *only if* "coffee stayed within a very limited price range." Ruddy specifically asked Badoian if the hedge would hurt his "up" position (if coffee prices rose) from his call options, and Badoian responded, according to Ruddy's testimony, "Definitely not. You can pick up extra money and when coffee goes up, we [First Commodity] just automatically pick up the hedge for a small fee."

Ruddy added that he told Badoian to "do nothing to hurt my up position." And Badoian told him that he would make enough to pay for a fine wedding for his daughter. Badoian sold several short futures contracts for Ruddy's account on the London futures market, offsetting Ruddy's call options.

Then the price of coffee stopped its fall.

A "killer" frost in Brazil on July 17, 1975,[1] in fact led to fears of shortages of coffee and this led to shortages on the coffee futures markets, which in turn caused the price of coffee to sharply increase. Ruddy thought he was a rich man. Ecstatic, he called First Commodity on July 21 but was unable to reach Badoian. He spoke with another manager in the office and was told that First Commodity had decided not to remove Ruddy's

---

1. *See* Coffee Break, "Brazil's Black Frost."

short hedges when the price of coffee began to go up because doing so would have been too expensive. Gradually, through subsequent conversations with a lawyer at the Commodity Futures Trading Commission (CFTC), it began to dawn on Ruddy that he was not going to be rich. In fact, because of the "hedge," he had realized no profit at all from his call options when the price of coffee began to go up.

Ruddy then filed a reparation complaint with the Commission, seeking to recover from Badoian and First Commodity the lost profits on his call options. The gist of his complaint was that Badoian had lied to him, first by letting him believe that the hedge purchases were safe, and then by telling him that First Commodity would pick up the hedge if coffee prices rose.

The CFTC agreed with Ruddy, finding that Badoian had violated its Rule 30.02, which makes it unlawful to "deceive or attempt to deceive" or to "make . . . any false report or statement" to a customer in connection with the sale of commodity futures contracts on foreign exchanges. (Badoian had used the London futures market to place Ruddy's hedge.) It ruled that Badoian had made material misrepresentations to Ruddy about the effect of the short futures contracts on Ruddy's "up" position and that Ruddy had reasonably relied on Badoian's assurances to his detriment. The Commission also found that Badoian had "willfully" made the representations at issue. Badoian and First Commodity were ordered to pay Ruddy approximately $10,000 in damages.

They sought court review.

Badoian and First Commodity argued that the CFTC lacked the power to hold them liable under Rule 30.02 because the rule was inconsistent with the Commission's authorizing statute. This was so, they maintained, because Rule 30.02 lacked a "scienter" requirement that all antifraud regulations must have. In fraud cases, "scienter" means that a person knew that he was making false representations, *with intent* to deceive. In other words, they argued, even though Badoian and First Commodity may have deceived Ruddy, even though they may have led him into unwise investments without explaining the risks, even though they might have taken advantage of him, even though they had behaved carelessly, they did not do so *intentionally*, so they should not be responsible to him for his lost profits. It was his own fault for believing them that he was in his financial predicament.

The Commission disagreed, maintaining that it had the required authority to issue an antifraud rule without any scienter requirement.

The appellate court could see the logic in First Commodity's argument. The statute governing fraud in commodity futures trading[2] requires proof of scienter in connection with fraud in domestic futures transactions. Therefore, it would seem logical to argue that, just as the antifraud provision in Section 10(b) of the Securities Exchange Act requires proof of scienter in enforcement actions under Rule 10b-5,[3] and the antifraud statute for commodity futures compels the Commission to prove scienter when enforcing its rules under the statute against fraud in domestic transactions, the same rules should apply to transactions in foreign contracts. However, the court noted, these statutory provisions are not applicable.

The court acknowledged that it would be reasonable to conclude that Congress did not intend to give the CFTC significantly broader authority to regulate fraud on foreign exchanges than

---

2. 7 U.S.C. §6b.

3. 15 U.S.C. §78(b), 17 C.F.R. §240.10b-5.

4. The Commission only received the authority over foreign futures transactions in 1974 amendments to the Commodity Exchange Act. These amendments gave the Commission "exclusive jurisdiction" with respect to transactions involving futures contracts "traded . . . on a contract market . . . or [on] any other board of trade, exchange, or market." 7 U.S.C. §2.

it had on the domestic front.[4] However, the court also found countervailing arguments to support the Commission's position that it did not have to prove scienter. First, the language in the statute did not contain any scienter limitation. Second, because the Commission did not have the power to regulate foreign futures exchanges directly, there were special, additional risks involved in foreign futures transactions that would not be present in domestic transactions. Third, in another section of the law governing "trading advisors," a provision outlawing conduct that "operates" as a fraud does not have any scienter requirement. Finally, the antifraud rules that the Commission had promulgated to govern options contracts (as opposed to futures contracts) did not limit liability for fraud to situations where scienter was present.

Having gone through this very comprehensive analysis, however, the court decided that it did not actually have to rule on the issue because the CFTC did not need to find an *actual* intent to misrepresent a fact or deceive in order to find First Commodity liable to Ruddy in this particular case. It was able to base liability on their recklessness. A "reckless" misrepresentation is one that strays so far from standards of ordinary care that it becomes very difficult to believe that the speaker was not aware of what he was doing. Under comparable securities fraud case law dealing with scienter, "willful" behavior has been liberally defined to include "reckless" conduct. In *Ernst and Ernst v. Hochfelder*,[5] for example, the U.S. Supreme Court incorporated recklessness into scienter as "a mental state embracing intent to deceive, manipulate, or defraud" under SEC Rule 10b-5 and Section 10(b) of the Securities Exchange Act of 1934.

The court was convinced that, even if the securities cases

---

5. 425 U.S. 185, 96 S. Ct. 1375, 47 L. Ed. 2d 668 (1976).

based on recklessness were not sufficiently on point, the Commodity Futures Trading Act authorized the Commission to predicate liability for fraud in foreign futures transactions on a reckless state of mind. Accordingly, if Ruddy's testimony as to his conversations with Badoian was to be believed (and the court could not find a reason to disbelieve it), a finding of reckless behavior by Badoian and First Commodity became inevitable.

Ruddy wanted to know if the "hedge" would hurt his "up" position and Badoian knew that this was important to him. Badoian assured Ruddy that the hedge would not hurt his "up" position, as the court noted, but this assurance was totally false. The hedge did not merely hurt Ruddy's "up" position, as the court noted, it completely "destroyed it, eradicated it, wiped it out." While Ruddy held the hedge, he simply had no "up" position. And Badoian had to have known this, given his experience as a trader in the commodity futures markets. Given the nature of the call options and short futures contracts and the way in which they work together, the court found it "nearly inconceivable" that a commodities broker would not know that he was leaving Ruddy with a false impression of the risks.

According to the court, the best that could be said for Badoian was that he may have believed that Ruddy would not be hurt because he (Badoian) intended to sell or dispose of the hedge if the price of coffee began to rise. Perhaps he did intend to do this at the time he gave his assurances to Ruddy, but in fact he did not do so. But that is still not the answer he should have given Ruddy in the first place. He should have explained to Ruddy what the effects of the hedge would be while Ruddy held the hedge, not after it was gone. The potential impact of the hedge on Ruddy's "up" position may have been obvious to Badoian, the court acknowledged, but it was not necessarily obvious to Ruddy, who was, after all, an unsophisticated investor.

According to the court, Badoian behaved recklessly at best.

The CFTC had found that Badoian's conduct was "willful," in "careless disregard" of the truth. The court thought that this word usage was unfortunate because the word "careless" normally suggests mere negligence. The court did not believe, however, that the Commission, by using this phrase, really thought that Badoian was simply negligent. The court therefore affirmed the Commission's decision because the justices believed that the defendants were more than just negligent—they had behaved willfully; they were reckless. The court ruled that the Commission had adequate power to predicate liability upon that state of mind.

Revenge may be a dish that is best served cold, but justice is better, like coffee, when served hot. Poor Ruddy finally got reparation for his losses from 1975, but he had to wait until 1982—too late, one assumes, to provide the needed cash for his daughter's wedding.

Coffee Break

Coffee Commodity Futures Trading: A Primer

"I acquired enough information about speculation in coffee to cause me to make a resolution never to touch it except as a beverage."[1]

Coffee is a food product but it is also a commodity, which is bought and sold in secondary commodities markets on a global scale. Anyone investing in the financial products bought and sold on a commodity exchange needs to understand the inherent risks in the enterprise. For some, it is a hard-learned lesson.

Trading in coffee as a commodity is not new. The Dutch were the first in Western Europe to grow coffee and they were also the first to create a secondary market for its purchase and sale. The Amsterdam Stock Exchange was established in the late fifteenth century. As early as 1639, at least 360 types of commodities were traded there. Some were mundane, such as grain, salt, and herring, while others were considered luxury items, such as textiles, sugar, coffee and spices.[2] Commodities were purchased ahead of delivery, sometimes even years ahead, which was an enormous stimulus to trade. These were called "futures contracts." Like any other financial market, manipulation by unscrupulous buyers and sellers was always a risk.

In order to invest in the coffee commodity exchange, the investor needs to understand a common vocabulary.

A futures contract is a standardized contract to buy or sell a specified commodity (coffee) of standardized quality (such as all arabica) at a certain date in the future and at a market-determined price (the futures price). A futures contract gives the holder the obligation to make or take delivery under the terms of the contract. Instead of entering into a futures contract, where one has to fulfill the contract (either to buy or sell the commodity) on the settlement date, an investor may also purchase an option, either a call option or a put option, which grants the buyer the right, but not the obligation, to buy or sell the commodity in

120

question. If the investor has a put option, that investor has the right (but not the obligation) to sell the underlying asset (such as coffee) at a fixed price. In the event of a market decline, the option holder may exercise these put options, obliging the counterparty to buy the underlying asset at the agreed upon (or "strike") price, which would then be higher than the current quoted spot price of the asset.

On the other hand, if an investor has purchased a call option for coffee, then he has a right to buy a specified quantity of coffee at a particular strike price at any time until the call option expires. For example, if you purchase a coffee call option on January 1, 2011, with an expiration date of December 31, 2011, and a strike price of $1,000/ton, you would have the right to buy the specified tons of coffee at $1,000/ton at any time during 2011. If the market price of coffee goes above $1,000/ton at any time during 2011, you can sell the call option at a profit as long as the market price exceeds the strike price of $1,000 plus the cost of the option, including commissions on the transaction.

A futures contract, on the other hand, is a firm commitment to deliver or receive a specified amount of a given commodity at a particular price and time in the future. It is more than an option: it is an actual purchase or sale. When trading futures contracts, being "short" means having the legal obligation to deliver something at the expiration of the contract, although the holder of the short position may alternately buy back the contract prior to expiration instead of making delivery. Short futures transactions are often used by producers of a commodity to fix the future price of goods they have not yet produced. Shorting a futures contract is sometimes also used by those holding the underlying asset (i.e., those with a long position) as a temporary hedge against price declines. Shorting futures may also be used for speculative trades, in which case the investor is looking to profit from any decline in the price of the futures contract prior to expiration. A short position in a futures contract means the holder of the position has an obligation to sell the underlying asset later at a given price; if the price falls below the given price, the person

121

with the short position can buy the asset at the lower price and sell it under the future at the higher price. For example, a December "short" coffee future obligates the holder to deliver a specified quantity of coffee in December for the price specified in the contract, say $1,000/ton. The holder of the "short" futures contract hopes that the price of coffee will fall below $1,000 before he has to deliver the coffee. If that happens, then he can buy the coffee for the delivery time required by the contract at the lower price and keep the difference between the price paid and the $1,000 contract price received, less commissions. The lower the price of coffee falls, the greater the "short" party's profit.

A short futures contract can act as an offset, or hedge, against a call option. If an investor holds a call option, for every dollar that the price of coffee rises, the option increases in value by a dollar. At the same time, if the investor holds a short futures contract on coffee, every dollar that the price of coffee rises makes the contract worth about a dollar less. When an investor holds both a call option and a short futures contract, the gains and losses cancel one another out.   As a result, even if the price of coffee rises to, say, $5,000 per ton, an investor holding both (covering one ton of coffee at $1,000/ton) will not make money. The call option gives him the right to buy the $5,000 coffee for $1,000. However, the futures contract requires the investor to deliver that same coffee to a buyer who is only obligated to pay $1,000. This type of investment would not be wise in a rising market because when the call option and the futures contract offset each other, as the price of coffee rises, no matter how high the price goes, the investor will not be able to recover the cost of the option and the trading commissions.

If the investor is betting on a falling market, however, the dynamic changes. The value of the call option and the futures contract do not precisely offset each other as the price of coffee falls. The person holding a call option cannot lose more on that investment that the cost of the option itself, because he holds only a *right* to buy, not an obligation to buy. If the price of coffee falls, his right becomes worthless and he is out what he paid for the option, but he simply won't exercise it. If the price of coffee falls to $400, on a $1,000 call option, the investor would make $600 on the futures contract because the holder of that contract has the obligation to buy the coffee for $1,000 a ton, even though the value of the coffee is now far less.

The investor holding both a call option and a short futures contract has hedged in the following sense: if the price of coffee rises, the investor cannot make money; he will lose the cost of the option and the trading commissions, but he will not lose more than that. If the price of coffee falls a little, he may lose part of the cost of the option and commissions. If the price falls a bit more, he may break even; and if the price falls far enough, he could make a profit.

1. Cyrus Townsend Brady, *The Corner on Coffee* (Preface), cited by Pendergrast, p. 68.
2. Hart, Marjolein 't, Jonker, Joost, van Zandin, Jan Luiten, eds., *A Financial History of the Netherlands*, Cambridge University Press, 1997, p.53.

Chapter Twelve

He Was Dunked by Dunkin' Donuts:
Coffee House Franchise Agreements

Intercontinental Investors v. Georgia Donuts, Inc.,
162 Ga. App. 685, 292 S.E. 2d 107 (1982)

The American dream, some say, is to be an entrepreneur—
to run one's own business. Many people lack the know-
how or capital to put together a successful enterprise but
they have good management skills. For these people, a franchise
may be the best solution. This business relationship in the best
of scenarios marries two sorts of business persons: the first, the
good manager without capital or a great idea, and the second, an
innovator with a great idea and a financing source who wants to
quickly expand her concept but does not want to directly operate and manage additional stores. The franchisor lends her trademark and/or trade name and a business system to a franchisee
who pays an initial fee and an ongoing royalty for the right to do
business under the franchisor's name, using the franchisor's system. There are many examples of successful franchises, including Burger King and McDonald's. One of the first franchises was
the Singer Sewing Machine dealer.

Franchises are not for everyone. In order to obtain a franchise, a person has to invest some upfront capital and then agree to a set of nonnegotiable contract terms and conditions. In some cases, the franchisor also either leases the location to the franchisee or approves the selected store location. Often nothing prevents the franchisor from franchising another store in the vicinity. Because the goal of the franchisor is to control a chain of independently owned but indistinguishable establishments using the franchisor's brand and its system, it requires commonality in the requirements and obligations of all franchisees. Having each franchisee operate under different terms would not be efficient, could create potential quality control issues, could cause potential difficulties for the franchisor in managing its brand, and might hinder the consistency in products and services that franchisors want in all their locations.

Some franchisees are very capable of adhering to the strict requirements of the franchise agreement; others chafe at the loss of their independence. This is particularly true when the franchisee discovers that his business is earning less than the anticipated profits and the franchisor refuses to agree to modifications to product offerings, for example, or requires that the franchisee buy ingredients from a national supplier rather than procuring less expensive products locally. When a franchisee acts against the requirements of the franchisor, he is in breach of the agreement and risks forfeiture, which means not only the loss of the franchise but also the capital that the franchisee has invested to acquire the franchise rights and to establish his business. This often represents the loss of thousands of dollars in investment. This was the fate of a small Georgia company that had acquired a Dunkin' Donuts franchise in that state.

Dunkin' Donuts has been referred to as a "stealth" coffee house.[1] By the 1990s, the company had over 3,000 franchise out-

1. Pendergrast, p. 387.

lets throughout the United States, making most of its profits from coffee sales, but "disguised as a donut company."[2] Its beginnings were humble. In 1946, Bill Rosenberg started a small business, that he called Industrial Luncheon Services, delivering meals and snacks to workers in the Boston area. In 1948, he opened his first donut shop, called the Open Kettle in Quincy, Massachusetts. Two years later, in 1950, he changed the name of his shop to Dunkin' Donuts, selling coffee, donuts, and baked goods. In 1955, he entered into his first franchise agreement for a Dunkin' Donuts store. Today, Dunkin' Donuts claims to be America's largest retailer of coffee-by-the-cup, serving nearly 1 billion cups of brewed coffee every year.[3]

In 1980, a small business called Intercontinental Investors obtained a franchise to operate a Dunkin' Donuts retail store in Georgia. It also entered into a lease with Georgia Donuts, which was a wholly owned subsidiary of Dunkin' Donuts of America, for the premises where Intercontinental would operate its store. The lease required the franchisee to pay base rent as well as percentage rent equal to 7 percent of its gross sales above a certain amount. "Gross sales" was defined as "all sales made by the lessee on the premises." This term was used in the franchise agreement in the same way. The lease also provided that it was contingent on the franchise agreement remaining in effect, and it permitted the landlord to terminate the lease if the franchise agreement was terminated "for any reason."

Under the franchise agreement, the franchisee agreed to pay Dunkin' Donuts, the franchisor, 4 percent of gross sales as an advertising fee and 4.9 percent of gross sales as a franchise fee. The agreement also provided that if there was a default under the

---

2. Pendergrast, p. 387.

3. Dunkin' Donuts Official Web site: https://www.dunkindonuts.com/aboutus/credentials/History.aspx.

franchise agreement, then the franchisor could revoke the agreement unless the franchisee cured the default. However, under that agreement, the franchisee would have no opportunity to cure if the franchisee underreported its gross sales.

Intercontinental moved into the premises in February 1980 and began operating its store. Within a year, it was in trouble. Between February 1981 and September 1981, it had received five notices for nonpayment of rent. On September 24, 1981, Georgia Donuts sent a final letter to Intercontinental demanding that it surrender the premises because it had failed to pay $1,469 in percentage rent on May 15 and on September 15. Georgia Donuts then sued Intercontinental to recover possession of the leased premises. And Dunkin' Donuts terminated the franchise.

Intercontinental claimed that there was an ambiguity in the definition of "gross sales" in the lease and in the franchise agreement. It argued that the percentage rent requirement only applied to *retail* sales and that it should not have been required to report and pay percentage rent on *wholesale* sales because these were not made *on* the premises. These were sales outside the premises: sales personnel delivered coffee and donuts to offices and other workplaces at a lower, nonretail price. There was no way that Intercontinental could operate profitably without these sales and there was no way it could make a profit if it was obliged to pay 7 percent, 4 percent, and 4.9 percent respectively of these sales to Dunkin' Donuts. If the wholesale sales were not included, then sales on the premises were not sufficient to trigger the percentage rent requirement.

Intercontinental also argued that even if there was an underreporting of gross sales under the lease, this should not have entitled Dunkin' Donuts to terminate the franchise, especially where it stood to lose its significant capital paid to acquire the franchise because of a dispute over less than $1,500. In other words, Intercontinental claimed that the franchise agreement—and particularly its onerous default and forfeiture provisions—was an adhesion contract. Many legal experts would agree that a franchise agreement is an adhesion contract, but that does not mean that it is not legally enforceable. It only means that one party to the agreement, the franchisee, has little or no ability to negotiate revisions to the contract. However, sometimes courts have ruled that an adhesion contract is so one-sided, favoring one party to the significant detriment of the other, and is therefore so harsh in its impact on the weaker party, as to be unenforceable.

Unfortunately for Intercontinental, the Georgia court did not accept this argument. The court agreed that allowing Dunkin' Donuts to terminate the franchise agreement over such a small amount in dispute was a "harsh result." However, it noted that "where the essentials of a contract are present and no rule of law appears to have been transgressed, the courts are powerless to interfere." There was, in other words, nothing the court could do to prevent the loss of the franchise. That was just the way the donut crumbled.

Coffee Break

Coffee and Health:
Turkish Delight, C.W. Post,
and Dunkin' Donuts

"We pray that drinking COFFEE be forbidden . . . How
else is it possible they should run a whoring to spend
money and time on a little base, black, thick, nasty, Bitter,
Stinking, Nauseous, Puddle-water. . .Wherefore we pray that
drinking COFFEE be forbidden to all Persons under the Age
of Threescore and that Lusty Nappy Beer . . be Recommended
to General Use."[1]

Coffee has frequently been criticized for having a detrimental
effect on health. It has also been lauded as the world's most
popular stimulant. Coffee produces needed boosts of energy, due
to its caffeine content. Health claims for and against coffee have
always been controversial. Caffeine is an organic compound that
affects the brain by blocking the neurotransmitter that makes a
person drowsy. It also causes the heart to beat more rapidly and
constricts the blood vessels. Those who consume large amounts
of coffee may suffer from high blood pressure as well as excess
stomach acidity. (But oddly enough, it may also help some people
digest food.) It has been blamed for bone loss in older coffee
consumers.[2] Coffee can trigger or worsen anxiety and insomnia.
It can interfere with iron absorption. One can readily become
dependent on coffee to get through the day. It is addictive.

For every negative statement, there have been positive
findings. Most recently, for example, coffee is claimed to lessen
the risk of type-2 diabetes and gallstones, as well as to help
prevent cirrhosis of the liver. According to recent Finnish
studies, regular intake of coffee may also prevent dementia and
Alzheimer's disease. There may be a correlation between regular
consumption of the beverage and reduced risk of death from
heart disease, cancer, and other inflammatory conditions.[3]

Concerns about coffee's effects are not new. Seventeenth
century housewives protested against London coffee shops,

out of fear that coffee was having a negative impact on their husbands' health and virility. These arguments were particularly vociferous in the nineteenth century when marketers of coffee substitutes gained inroads against coffee sales.

One of the loudest was C.W. Post, the inventor of Grape-Nuts cereal. During the Civil War, when coffee was at times in short supply, Americans had acquired a taste for toasted grain-based coffee substitutes. Manufacturers of these products found a way to maintain consumption in the post-war years by touting the health benefits of their products while attacking coffee as a dangerous beverage. Battle Creek, Michigan, was the location of several health spas, including the famous sanitarium run by John Hartley Kellogg, known as the father of the modern breakfast cereal, and another operated by his rival, C.W. Post. Kellogg produced a "Caramel Coffee," a substitute for coffee and tea, both of which Kellogg disparaged as harmful drugs.[4] C.W. Post produced Postum, a grain-based product, mixed with molasses.

Coffee Break (continued)

Due to Post's canny marketing techniques, Postum soon became profitable and made Post a very wealthy man. He attacked coffee directly and relentlessly, playing up caffeine's addictive nature and warning of coffee's health hazards, including some invented by Post. For example, he claimed that drinking coffee would cause loss of eyesight. His ads put coffee in the same class as other dangerous drugs, such as cocaine, morphine, nicotine, and strychnine.[5] Coffee producers seemed unable to counter Post's assaults.

But Post was not alone. By the turn of the century, many doctors advised against daily consumption of coffee, concerned particularly about coffee's potential cause of common ailments of the time: heart palpitations, nervousness, indigestion, and insomnia. [6] Over the next decades, health concerns repeatedly surfaced. In the 1960s, the worries centered on heart disease and potential links to coffee. In the 1970s, it was cited as a potential cause of stomach ulcers and various cancers, as well as birth defects if consumed by pregnant women.[7] In the 1980s, new concerns were raised, with pressure on the U.S. Food and Drug Administration to require warning labels on coffee and tea packaging.[8]

Through it all, Americans have continued to drink coffee. However, concerns have been sufficient enough to inspire coffee producers to put greater technological expertise against caffeine to create a viable decaffeinated coffee. By the end of the twentieth century, "decaf" was as commonly served in most offices, restaurants, and coffee houses as the caffeinated product. This has, however, not decreased the consumption of caffeinated coffee.

Although whether coffee is harmful to health may be controversial to this day, there is no doubt that many of the products frequently consumed with coffee can be detrimental. Although many coffee drinkers will take their beverage black, others add large helpings of both milk or cream and sugar. In Turkey, coffee is served not just with sugar, but with Turkish

Delight, very sweet delicacies, on the side. In Austria, whipped cream is liberally heaped on cups of coffee served in Konditerai.

And who is not fond of a cup of coffee with a sweet pastry? At their "elevenses," many British people will have their ritual biscuit, which is called a cookie in America. And it is just as traditional for Americans to have a doughnut with their coffee. Dunkin' Donuts, one of America's largest coffee retailers, also serves many varieties of its donuts with the billion cups of brewed coffee that are served in its shops every year.[9] The donut—probably derived from the Dutch *olykoeks* (sweet fried cakes)—had achieved iconic status, with an accompanying cup of coffee, before World War I. During the Great Depression, free soup, coffee, and doughnuts were handed out to the unemployed.[10]

In terms of risk, where obesity is cited as a true health issue for Americans, it may be less likely that the cups of coffee we drink will harm us than those sweet nothings we all enjoy consuming with them.

---

1. Petition of English Women seeking to close coffee houses, London, 1674, cited in Allen, p. 108.
2. Pendergrast, p. 413.
3. "Your Health: Coffee Cures?" *Body and Soul*, Sept. 2009, p. 127.
4. Pendergrast, pp. 96-97.
5. Pendergrast, p. 99.
6. Pendergrast, p. 103.
7. Pendergrast, p. 301.
8. Pendergrast, p. 339.
9. Dunkin' Donuts Official Website: https://dunkindonuts.com/aboutus/Credentials/History.aspx.
10. *See* http://www.picturehistory.com/product/id/939.

Chapter Thirteen

A Smuggler's Tale:
The International Coffee Agreement

U.S. v. Patel, 762 F.2d 784 (9th Cir. 1985)

O n November 9, 1983, Hemant Patel, his brother Raoji Patel, and their companies, Bridgewater Development Company and Pacific Food and Beverages, were indicted by the Federal Grand Jury in San Francisco for coffee smuggling, conspiracy to defraud the U.S. government, and for making false statements to the government. They pleaded not guilty to all counts.

Coffee smuggling? What would be the benefit of smuggling such a ubiquitous product as coffee?

Over the past decades, millions of illegal profits have been made by people willing to risk criminal prosecution for bringing illegal substances—such as cocaine or heroin—into the United States. Despite its stimulating properties, coffee has never been viewed as a controlled substance. However, during a short period between the 1960s and the 1990s, new laws and quotas were put into place intended to regulate and limit the supply of coffee imported into the United States. Despite these laws, and in fact in some cases because of the way that these laws were structured, many pounds of coffee arrived illegally, with false bills of lading and customs declarations. The Patel case involved one such shipment that did not successfully slip through.

During the post-World War II years, in the face of low coffee prices, coffee producing countries, particularly in Latin and South America, campaigned for an international treaty that would establish quotas for coffee imports and stabilize global coffee prices. Even before the war, Brazil in particular had used various means to try to establish higher coffee prices. Largely, these requests were rebuffed by coffee-consuming countries—and particularly the United States—that were opposed to setting an artificial quota system and were anxious about the domestic political repercussions that could result from artificially high coffee prices. After 1959, however, when Fidel Castro overthrew the Batista dictatorship in Cuba, the U.S. view of Latin America changed.[1] In 1960, Castro entered into trade agreements with the Soviets and began nationalizing American businesses in Cuba. Fearing growing Communist influence in Latin America, the United States lent its support to a coffee quota agreement.

In 1962, the United Nations convened a coffee conference and the long-sought-after coffee agreement was negotiated—the International Coffee Agreement of 1962. This agreement (ICA) set basic quotas, with Brazil allowed the most. The ICA required that every coffee shipment be accompanied by a "certificate of origin," a re-export certificate. Countries with low coffee consumption, such as China, Japan, and the Soviet Union, were exempt from the quota system. The U.S. Senate ratified the ICA in May 1963, but the implementing legislation was not enacted until almost two years later, in February 1965, due to the unpopularity of the treaty.[2] At that time, the United States began monitoring certificates of origin.

---

1. Pendergrast, p. 274.
2. 19 U.S.C. §§1356a-1356e.

As noted, certain countries such as the Soviet Union, China, and Japan (so-called "Annex B nations," which meant that they were considered to be new coffee markets) were exempted from the quota system to encourage coffee consumption in those countries.[3] In addition, the ICA did not restrict sales to nonmember countries that had not signed on to the ICA, such as Hong Kong and Guam. The result of those exemptions was to create two pricing systems for coffee: coffee beans that claimed a high price in ICA member countries could be sold for less money to Annex B and nonmember countries because there were no quotas in place with respect to them. This presented opportunities for dealers to easily evade the law by buying coffee to be shipped into a nonmember country, for example, and then reselling the cheaper beans into the United States at a profit. This was called "tourist coffee." It is estimated that millions of dollars worth of illegal coffee was smuggled out of Latin American countries using this strategy.[4]

The ICA lapsed in 1972, when the member countries could not agree to new quotas. However, after Brazil's terrible frost in July 1975,[5] and a devastating earthquake in Guatemala in 1976, coffee prices became extremely volatile and concerns over political unrest grew. The United States agreed to join another International Coffee Agreement in 1976. However, even with the new quotas in place under the 1976 ICA, substantial price volatility continued. In 1981, the first enforcement year, coffee prices fell so low that the quotas were temporarily cut. They then rose again so that, by 1983, despite strong reservations, the free-trade Reagan administration ratified the ICA. If anything, this only encouraged the free flow of "tourist coffee," which by some

---

3. Pendergrast, pp. 294-295.
4. Pendergrast, p.295.
5. *See* Coffee Break, "Brazil's Black Frost."

accounts sold to nonmember countries at discounts of 50 percent or more, much to the consternation of ICA member countries. Smuggling was rampant and counterfeit certificates of origin were freely available. In 1983, U.S. Customs confiscated $26 million in illegal beans.[6] One of these confiscated shipments belonged to the Patels.

On March 31, 1984, a jury found the Patels guilty of smuggling and conspiracy. Hemant Patel was sentenced to one year in prison and ordered to pay a $10,000 fine on the conspiracy count and five years' probation and a $10,000 fine on the smuggling count. Raoji Patel was placed on five years' probation and fined $20,000, and each corporate defendant was fined $20,000. They appealed.

In July 1982, Hemant Patel approached Joseph McDonald, the director of the Department of Commerce for the Territory of Guam, with a proposal to ship raw coffee beans to Guam for transshipment to the United States. Patel represented to the Guam government that he intended to establish a coffee-processing business on Guam. McDonald advised Patel that under the U.S. Tariff Schedules, the coffee could enter the United States exempt from tariffs, duties, and the coffee quotas, as a product of Guam, if the raw coffee beans were processed on Guam, because Guam was a territory of the United States.

In December 1982, Hemant Patel purchased 3,000 tons of processed coffee beans from Honduras. Patel represented to the Honduran coffee dealer that the coffee was destined for Hong Kong which, like Guam, was a nonmember country not subject to the ICA. He was, therefore, able to buy the coffee at $54 per bag instead of $120 per bag, which would have been the price if the coffee had been destined for shipment to the United States,

---

6. Pendergrast, p. 347.

a member of the ICA. A Certificate of Origin for the coffee was forwarded to the International Coffee Organization in London, which kept track of global coffee shipments, indicating that the coffee shipment was destined for Hong Kong. Instead, Patel arranged for shipment of the coffee to Guam.

When the Honduran coffee arrived in Guam, Anil Patel, Hemant's relative, explained to Guam customs authorities that the discrepancy between the country of destination shown on the ship's manifest and the country shown on the port clearance documents arose because a third buyer at sea had diverted the ship to Guam. Anil Patel also told the customs officials that the beans were being graded and processed on Guam, which was not the case (the coffee had already been graded and processed in Honduras).

Once in Guam, the coffee was off-loaded, tagged with a card reading "Processed in Guam, USA" and loaded onto a ship headed to the United States. By this time, Joseph McDonald was no longer employed by the Guam government, but had been retained by the Patels as a "consultant." In February 1983, McDonald obtained a Certificate of Origin from the Guam Customs Department for the Honduran coffee, which already was in transit to the United States. The Certificate of Origin identified the shipment as "processed agricultural beans," not coffee.

When the coffee reached the United States, the Food and Drug Administration insisted that the Patels identify the beans more specifically. Raoji Patel informed his import broker that the Latin name for the beans was "caffea." When the broker provided this information to the U.S. Customs officials, the coffee was seized. Proceedings were then instituted to forfeit the illegally smuggled coffee and the Patels were tried.

On appeal, the Patels argued that there was inadequate evidence to find them guilty and that the instructions describing the

ICA quota exemptions and customs laws that were given to the jury at trial were wrong. The Patels claimed that the government had not proved that the ICA quotas were in effect at the time the coffee was imported into the United States. Proof of the existence of the quotas was required for them to be found guilty of importing coffee contrary to the law. Because the jury instructions had stated that the government had to have proved this fact for the Patels to be found guilty, the court believed that the jury, in rendering its verdict, must have necessarily found that the quotas had come into effect by the time the coffee reached the United States in early 1983 (the coffee had been shipped in late 1982).

The instructions gave the jury two choices. If the jury found that the coffee was a product of Honduras, then the coffee shipment must have been accompanied by a Certificate of Origin form and export stamps certifying that the coffee was exported under Honduras' export quota. On the other hand, if the jury found that the coffee was a product of Guam, then the coffee must have entered the United States from an ICA nonmember country, and subject to the United States' import quota. To prove that the Patel's importation of coffee into the United States was contrary to law, the government had to establish that the Patels knowingly and fraudulently imported the coffee into the United States.

The Patels also argued that the trial court abused its discretion by instructing the jury that a headnote in the tariff schedules under the ICA did not apply to the Patels' importation of coffee. This headnote was the one McDonald had referred to when he advised the Patels that the coffee could enter the United States as a product of Guam, exempt from tariffs, duties, and import quotas, because Guam was a U.S. territory. This headnote (Headnote 3(a)) provided an exemption for "articles grown or produced if they do not contain foreign materials of more than 50% of their total value."

The Patels argued that the coffee they imported should be characterized as a product of Guam and exempt from duty under Headnote 3(a) processing standards. They also argued that Headnote 3(a) not only exempted the coffee from tariffs and duties but also from the quota restrictions imposed by U.S. law on non-ICA member countries because the ICA made clear that only "conflicting bilateral obligations" would take precedence over the ICA. The trial court had ruled that Headnote 3(a) was not relevant in determining whether the importation of coffee by the Patels into the United States was lawful because Headnote 3(a) only applied to tariffs and duties, not quotas. It therefore declined to treat Headnote 3(a) as a "conflicting bilateral obligation" that would preempt the ICA import quotas. Under this reasoning, even if the coffee imported by the Patels could have been characterized as a product of Guam, rather than Honduras, the quota provisions of U.S. law governing imports from nonmember countries still applied and the Patels were required to comply with those quotas under the ICA.

The appellate court agreed that Headnote 3(a) only applied to tariffs and duties and not quotas.

The Patels also argued that the trial court abused its discretion by failing to instruct the jury, as requested by the Patels' counsel, that under Headnote 3(a), the Honduran coffee could have been Guam coffee, with sufficient processing in Guam. Instead, the jury was instructed that, to qualify in Guam for a valid certificate of origin stating that the coffee was a product of Guam, the coffee had to have been manufactured in Guam from materials grown, produced, or manufactured in Guam. The trial court thus rejected the "value added" formula in Headnote 3(a) which defined a product of Guam as one that did not contain foreign materials with over 50 percent of the value of the product. In effect, the court's instruction to the jury precluded its members from finding that the Patels' coffee was a product of Guam because it was processed from foreign (Honduran) raw materials.

The Patels urged the appellate court to consider the "value added" definition even if the trial court had already determined that Headnote 3(a) was not applicable to the quota restrictions at issue. They argued that the failure of the trial court to instruct the jury about this definition denied the Patels the right to present their theory of the case.

But the appellate court felt that the Patels' arguments were just too much of a stretch. It found that, because the district court correctly ruled that Headnote 3(a) did not apply, an instruction concerning the definition of a "product of Guam" was not required and could have confused the jury. Furthermore, the appellate court held the viewpoint that in order for a raw material from one country to become a "product" of another, some transformation of the product must take place so that a new, distinctly different article emerges. The trial court could have instructed the jury to determine whether the Honduran coffee had undergone a sufficient degree of change in Guam to have become a product of Guam, but this would have been irrelevant because the issue was not whether the Patels were exempt from duties but rather whether they had violated a law establishing quotas.

Therefore, the court determined, whether or not the coffee was from Honduras or Guam as a place of origin, the law required that the coffee be accompanied by the appropriate documents. Instead, the coffee entered the United States falsely identified as processed agricultural beans and without complying with the applicable quota.

Finally, the Patels argued that they were denied the right to a unanimous jury verdict as required by the Sixth Amendment, because some jurors may have convicted them because the import requirements for Honduran coffee were not satisfied and others could have found illegal conduct because of noncompliance with the requirements of Guam. The appellate court disagreed. In its view, "no reasonable juror" could have concluded that the coffee came from Guam. This was so because the Patels did not satisfy the requirements of either country. Rather, the coffee was imported as "processed agricultural beans."

For the appellate court, as for the jury in the case, the bottom line was that the Patels had lied about the origin of the coffee and about the contents of the shipment into the United States. As the prosecutor in the case had noted in his closing argument: "had the defendants processed the coffee [in Guam], as they said they would do, they wouldn't be in any of this mess."

As a final rebuff to the Patels, the trial court assessed $8,920 against Hemant Patel for the cost of transferring the case at his request from San Francisco to Guam because the court viewed his request for the change of venue as a "strategic attempt to obtain a more favorable jury" rather than an effort to avoid inconveniencing witnesses. The defendants only called one Guam resident as a witness at trial.

Smuggling was an illegal and risky venture, but the Patels compounded their crime by lying to the government, which is always a bad idea, especially when the lie insults one's intelligence. "Processed agricultural beans"? What were they thinking?

Coffee Break

The Regulation of Coffee: From Turkey to the ICA

According to legend, Pope Clement VIII, faced with the rising power of the Ottoman Empire in the seventeenth century, was asked by Catholic prelates in Italy to ban coffee, the favorite brew of the Islamic lands now beginning to make inroads into Western Europe, as an "infidel brew." It was feared that Christians who drank it might lose their souls to the devil. But before taking action, the Pope insisted on tasting it. One sip and he was hooked. Rather than ban it, he decided instead to baptize coffee, making it a Christian beverage.[1]

Coffee: a drink that has been both banned and baptized. Since its discovery, coffee has provoked passion and fear. From its early days in the Islamic world, the popularity of coffee was controversial. Many were suspicious of both the effects that caffeine had on those who consumed coffee and the gatherings in which it was consumed. These seemed debauched to some and subversive to others. Coffee houses were thought to be spawning grounds for sedition. Efforts were launched and persisted from time to time but without success to declare coffee to be an intoxicant forbidden by Islamic law. Fatwas—legal injunctions against coffee houses—were occasionally issued. For example, in 1511, the coffee houses of Mecca were closed by the edict of Khali-Beg, the local governor, who saw coffee as a source of troublemaking. But the Sultan of Cairo, who was a habitual coffee drinker, reversed the edict.[2] However, not much later, in 1539, the tables were turned and Cairo's coffee houses were raided and closed during Ramadan.[3] This only endured a short time and since, coffee houses in Cairo have thrived.

Coffee houses achieved such popularity in Constantinople (now Istanbul) in the sixteenth century that Sultan Murat IV closed them all, fearing sedition; they were to remain dark until the last part of that century. Persons caught drinking coffee were beaten and repeat offenders were sewn into leather bags and thrown into the Bosporus.[4] However, almost as soon as the Sultan's edict went into effect, the coffee house patrons, unwilling to give up their favorite passion, took their money and their social life elsewhere, out of Istanbul, to nearby towns. In Bursa, across the Marmara Sea, there were 75 coffee houses during this time.[5] The moralists and the anti-seditionists were fighting a losing battle. Coffee's power was too strong. The coffee house was by then too entrenched into Turkish society. The "tavern without wine" provided a respectable gathering place for men to socialize and entertain away from home.

Other similar efforts elsewhere also failed. In the 1700s, Frederick the Great, wanting to promote German beer as the country's national beverage, tried a different tack: he prohibited coffee roasting, except in official government establishments. This, of course, raised the price of coffee beyond the reach of the poor, who then turned not to beer but to coffee substitutes, such as toasted chicory or barley. Those with the means to do so bought coffee on the black market, roasting it surreptitiously. Government spies, named "coffee smellers," were sent into the streets to locate clandestine roasters. But the Germans were too fond of their "kaffee" to give it up and this effort to limit its consumption failed.[6]

More recent efforts to regulate coffee have turned more to the production side rather than consumption. As a larger and larger number of coffee plantations were developed in the nineteenth century, efforts to regulate and limit coffee production were attempted, all without lasting success. Brazil achieved some success initially when it attempted its valorization scheme at the turn of the twentieth century. However, local and national edicts prohibiting additional production ultimately failed. Whenever coffee prices rose in response to shortages of coffee on the world market—whether created by natural events, such as frost or pests, or market manipulation—growers would increase plantings to take advantage of the higher prices and to meet the increased demand. This in turn led to an oversupply of

Coffee Break (continued)

coffee within a few years when those plantings matured, which in turn caused coffee prices to plummet, sometimes dramatically, particularly on the futures markets.

Coffee-growing countries clamored for international regulation that would establish coffee quotas on a worldwide basis and thereby control supply and demand, in order to keep coffee prices from falling precipitously. The negotiations for such a treaty began following the end of World War II and continued into the 1990s. During this time, several agreements (each known as an International Coffee Agreement or ICA) establishing the desired quotas were instituted. The first of these came into effect in 1965.

This first agreement set up the International Coffee Organization, ICO, in London under the auspices of the United Nations to manage the agreements under the ICA.[7] This agreement was followed by a second five-year agreement in 1968. These two agreements contained provisions for the application of a quota system under which supplies of coffee in excess of consumer requirements were to be withheld from the market.[8] The basic quotas under the ICA were established based on the volume of world coffee exports at the time.[9] Brazil, then the world's largest coffee-exporting country, was allowed the largest quota, 18 million bags. Colombia was next, then certain African countries. However, countries with low coffee consumption, such as Japan, China, and the Soviet Union (so-called "Annex B countries"), were exempted from the quota system in order to encourage consumption there. This provided an incentive to exporters to ship as much coffee as they could to those exempt countries. This two-tier structure of the ICA opened up opportunities for fraud and smuggling—so-called "tourist coffee." Under other provisions of the ICA, production and diversification policies were initiated to limit supplies of coffee and promotion activities instituted to increase consumption.[10] However, these were voluntary and largely ineffective.[11]

That ICA expired in 1973, but it was renewed again in 1976. However, because coffee prices at the time were high,

there was no real quota system in place. High coffee prices continued into the 1980s. Finally, amid continued coffee market volatility, the agreement collapsed and its quota system was suspended automatically in 1986 when the average price stayed above the threshold price of $1.50 per pound.[12] With the suspension of the quota system, coffee prices began to fall. Latin American countries formed a coalition to limit exports, with little success. These efforts, however, caused the negotiations for a new agreement to stall as U.S. legislators railed against the South American cartels.

Finally, in late 1987, a new ICA was put in place, but retaining the provisions that had engendered earlier concerns. The two-tier market created by the ICA encouraged the smuggling activities that had been problematic in the 1970s. Because of these problems, this ICA was short-lived. By early 1989, negotiations over the renewal of the quotas deadlocked. On July 4, 1989, the International Coffee Organization, established under the first ICA, suspended all export limits.[13]

Coffee Break (continued)

The fall of prices to record lows during coffee years 1990-91 and 1991-92 created an impetus to negotiate a new agreement. This finally came into effect in 1994. The provisions of the 1994 agreement largely encouraged activities by the ICO that would advance coffee consumption, as well as promote actions and exchanges to enable the sustainable management of coffee resources and processing. Neither a later agreement in 2001, nor one that became effective in 2005, had any quota or mandates to limit coffee production, but both agreements contained provisions that encouraged member countries to develop a sustainable coffee economy. In September 2007, the terms of a new International Coffee Agreement, the seventh agreement since the 1960s, were agreed upon in a meeting in London. The goal was to strengthen the ICO's role as a forum for intergovernmental consultations, to facilitate the international coffee trade, and to promote a sustainable coffee economy for the benefit of the coffee industry, but especially of small-scale farmers in coffee-producing countries.[14]

---

1. Sonnenfeld, p. 387.

2. Kolpas, p. 17. Khair Beg was a corrupt official. Only a year after his ban was lifted, he was executed for his transgressions.

3. Allen, p. 62.

4. Allen, pp. 112-113.

5. Schiffer, Reinhold, *Oriental Panorama: British Travelers in 19th Century Turkey*, Amsterdam and Atlanta, GA, Rodopi, 1999, p. 216.

6. Pendergrast, p. 11-12.

7. International Coffee Organization Official Webpage: http://www.ico.org/mission.asp.

8. Discussed at http://www.ico.org/history.asp.

9. Pendergrast, p. 277.

10. International Coffee Organization Official Webpage: http://www.ico.org/history.asp.

11. Pendergrast, p. 277.

12. Pendergrast, p. 362.

13. Pendergrast, p.363.

14. International Coffee Organization Official Webpage: http://www.ico.org/history.asp.

Chapter Fourteen

Hot Coffee

McMahon v. Bunn-O-Matic Corp.,
150 F.3d 651 (7th Cir. 1998)

"You don't buy cold coffee." —Jack McMahon

Jack and Angelina McMahon were on a long-distance road trip when they stopped to refill their car at a Mobil gas station. During the break, Jack went inside the minimart to buy a cup of coffee. He took a medium-sized Styrofoam cup and filled it with hot, black coffee to within 3/4 inch from the top, leaving some space because, as he later testified, the coffee would "seep down" the side if the cup were filled to the brim. "If you take the lid off," he said, "I don't want it running on my hands because it's too hot. It's scalding."

He returned to the car and put the filled coffee cup into the car's cup holder—the one closest to the passenger seat, occupied by his wife, Angelina. They drove to the toll road. Once they were clear of the gate, Jack asked his wife to open the coffee for him. This had been their customary procedure: she would pour the hot coffee from the full cup into an extra empty cup that they kept in the car, until it was half full, while Jack drove. She would then hand him the half-filled cup to drink while he was driving.

On this day, however, things went terribly wrong. As Angelina was pouring the hot coffee into the second cup, the Styrofoam cup collapsed and the hot coffee spilled into her lap. She suffered second and third degree burns on her thighs and abdomen.

This is a case of "seek the deepest pocket." The McMahons did not sue the person who sold them the coffee; they sued the cup manufacturer and the lid maker, who both settled. They also sued Bunn-O-Matic Corporation, the manufacturer of the coffee maker, in federal district court for product liability. They argued that the temperatures at which the Bunn coffee maker brewed and served coffee—195°F during the brewing cycle, and 179°F as the holding temperature—were excessive and that its design was therefore defective.

Bunn moved for summary judgment, which the trial court granted. The district court judge noted that both McMahons had conceded in their depositions that "hotness" was one of the elements that they valued in coffee, and they sought out hot coffee even though they knew it could burn. In fact, they took precautions to prevent the coffee from burning them, including Angelina's practice of using two cups to avoid spills. The judge believed that these concessions foreclosed any possibility of recovery at trial.

The McMahons appealed.

"Why are we here?" the appellate court essentially asked in its opinion, affirming the dismissal of the case.

The McMahons had filed their case against Bunn-O-Matic on the theory that it made and sold *coffee* as opposed to selling a *tool* that retailers used to make coffee. It was a mystery to all why the McMahons chose to sue the coffee maker manufacturer instead of the retailer who sold McMahon his hot coffee. The court could not understand why Bunn had not challenged this odd theory of the case. Why should a tool manufacturer be liable in tort for injuries caused by a product made from that tool? If a restaurant fails to cook food properly and the guest comes down with food poisoning, the court wondered, is the oven's manufacturer liable?

In the same light, the court could not understand the McMahons' assertion that they should have received warnings about the coffee. How, the court asked, is a manufacturer of coffee-making machines supposed to deliver such a warning? Most consumers who buy a cup of coffee at a retail establishment never see the machine that makes the coffee. The cup of coffee is brought to the consumer at the counter or is delivered through a take-out window. The consumer would not be in a position to read whatever warnings may be on the coffee maker. Warnings, if required, should go on the restaurant menu or on the cup containing the take-out coffee. Again, why should Bunn have that responsibility?

The court was also disconcerted by the McMahons' assertion that hot coffee is especially dangerous to take-out customers because they are more likely to spill it. What has this to do with the claim that a machine is defective, as opposed to a claim that the coffee vendor used the wrong machine for the job? Coffee can be sold in china cups without the risk of destabilizing them (as opposed to Styrofoam cups). Coffee served in-house (as opposed to take-out) posed no risk of jostling in a moving car. The court continued, "it cannot be that producing hot liquids makes a machine defective any more than a knife is defective because the blade is sharp." Perhaps it should be the case that vendors who sell take-out coffee in Styrofoam cups must keep the coffee at cooler temperatures or use stronger cups better able to withstand the heat of very hot coffee. But, the court noted, both the McMahons and Bunn treated the McMahons' complaint as if the coffee machine maker and the coffee retailer were the same. The court found this to be very odd. However, because this was the case they received rather than the case they should have had (versus the retailer), the justices were obliged to consider it as the parties presented it, not as it should have been presented.

The court first considered whether Bunn should have provided a warning about the dangers of hot coffee. The McMahons had both admitted in their depositions that they knew that coffee was hot and that it could cause burns. For this reason, in fact, they took elaborate steps—pouring half of the hot coffee from a full cup into an empty cup—to mitigate the risk of burns. The court conceded that if the coffee were unusually hot and capable of causing severe burns, it might be useful to provide some sort of warning, especially if this were a surprising feature that would otherwise be hard to observe. But, the court noted, from the record in the case, there was no evidence that a temperature of 179°F was unusually hot for coffee. The McMahons contended that this was an abnormally hot temperature but provided no evidence to back up that contention. The court also pointed out that the accepted industry standard serving temperature for coffee was between 175° and 185°F. If that were the case, then the coffee purchased by the McMahons was not unusually hot, and in fact, the court continued, coffee was generally hotter 20 years before when most home-brewed coffee was made in electric percolators where boiling water spurted over coffee grounds during the brewing cycle and took time to cool below 180°F.

The McMahons contended that home drip brewing machines in common use by the 1990s produced cooler coffee than the 179°F achieved by the Bunn machine, but the court reviewed some background engineering standards adopted for home coffee makers (ASTM standards) to discover that, on completion of the brewing cycle and for two minutes after, the coffee in the carafe would be between 170°F and 205°F. Therefore, some coffee makers are manufactured to a standard that assures that the coffee, once brewed at home, can be held at a temperature that does not fall below 170°F. In that case, the court concluded, coffee sold at 180°F by a highway minimart vendor, who would expect it to cool during the longer interval before it is actually consumed, would not have such an abnormal temperature as to require a "heads up" warning.

And the court also was dubious about holding Bunn responsible for providing a detailed warning about the severity of burns. Even assuming that ordinary coffee drinkers don't know that only three seconds of exposure at 179°F can cause a third-degree burn, the court wondered "how, precisely, is this information to be conveyed by a coffee maker manufacturer? Bunn can't deliver a medical education with each cup of coffee."

Moreover, the court observed that insistence on warning labels could be counter-productive. For one thing, the more information that must be squeezed onto a product label, the smaller the type and the less likely it is that the consumer will read or remember any of it. Long statements in all capital letters become illegible and, if in lowercase letters, they become boilerplate. And only a long, detailed analysis of the risks posed by hot coffee, accompanied by statistical detail of likelihoods and probabilities, would enable the consumer to appreciate whether or not the "superior taste of hot coffee justifies the incremental risk" of burns. Finally, the court stated, such a detailed warning about the risk of burns could obscure the principal message that the consumer should take away: that precautions should be taken to avoid spills. Under Indiana law, where the McMahons' accident happened, consumers are expected to educate themselves about "the hazards of everyday life—of matches, knives and kitchen ranges, of bones in fish, and of hot beverages."

The McMahons had argued that the Bunn-O-Matic was inherently defective—that its design was flawed. Under Indiana law, any person who sells "any product in a defective condition unreasonably dangerous to any user or consumer . . . is subject to liability." But, in order to prove a design defect, the plaintiff has to show not only that the design is defective, but also that the defective product is "unreasonably dangerous."

The McMahons argued that, even though they knew that hot coffee could cause burns, coffee made on Bunn's equipment exposed them to harm "to an extent beyond that contemplated by the ordinary consumer." The court doubted this, but decided that it did not need to judge whether a third-degree burn was such an unanticipated harm. Even if hot coffee were "unreasonably dangerous," the court stated, "the record did not permit a reasonable juror to conclude that the coffee maker was defectively designed."

The McMahons' theory was that Bunn's coffee maker was negligently designed because the temperatures at which it brewed coffee compromised the structural integrity of the Styrofoam cup, making it more flexible and more likely to collapse when its rigid lid was removed. But the court could not see how this was really Bunn's fault, rather than that of the cup manufacturer (who should have known that cups have to be sturdy enough to hold hot coffee), or the retailer (who should have chosen a cup designed to hold the hot coffee safely). However, the court added, even if there were only one type of coffee cup in the world, there was no empirical evidence that hot coffee made Styrofoam cups flexible.

The McMahons had provided an affidavit from an engineering professor who had opined that the ideal temperature at which coffee should be served was between 135° to 140°F. They theorized that it was more costly to serve coffee hotter than this "ideal" temperature, because of the higher cost of electricity required to increase the coffee's temperature. They asked how it could not be negligent to spend additional money for the purpose of making a product more likely to cause an injury. The court rapidly dismissed this argument also, noting that people spend money to increase their risks all the time. They take ski vacations; they attend hockey games; they engage in rock climbing.

To determine whether a coffee maker is defective because it held coffee at 179°F, the court decided that it needed to understand the benefits of hot coffee in relation to its cost. As for costs, the court noted that the record was silent. Were severe burns from hot coffee frequent or rare? On the other hand, the court saw benefits for all coffee drinkers who liked their coffee hot. The court failed to understand, without some way to compare the perceived benefits of a design change to keep coffee cooler (fewer and less severe burns) against the cost of doing so (less pleasure from drinking warm versus hot coffee), how designing a coffee maker to hold coffee at 179°F was a negligent inattention to risks.

It did not seem obvious that consumers derived no benefit from coffee served hotter than 140°F. In fact, to prove this point—and because the court seemed frustrated by the meager arguments made by both parties to the case—the justices (or more likely their law clerks) did some background investigation on their own by studying a treatise on coffee processing technology, while at the same time noting in a somewhat annoyed tone, "albeit unassisted by the parties." The court's independent research showed that there were good reasons for selecting a temperature over 170°F.

They learned, for example, that the smell and therefore the taste of coffee depend heavily on the oils containing aromatic compounds that are dissolved out of the coffee during the brewing process. Brewing temperatures ought to be close to 200°F in order to dissolve them effectively, but without causing the premature breakdown of these delicate molecules. Coffee smells and tastes best when these aromatic compounds evaporate from the surface of the coffee just as it is being drunk. Compounds vital to good coffee flavor have boiling points in the range of 150° to 160°F, and the beverage tastes best when it is hot and the aromatics vaporize as the coffee is being consumed.

For coffee to beat 150°F when it is in the cup, it must be hotter in the pot. Pouring a liquid increases its surface area and causes it to cool; more heat is lost when the coffee makes contact with the cooler cup. Then, if the drinker adds cream and sugar, or uses a metal spoon to stir the coffee, the temperature falls even more. If the consumer carries the coffee out of the store for later consumption, it cools even further. All in all, the court was convinced that hot coffee was good and that the McMahons had not shown that the choice of a high temperature made coffee defective.

Even though the court felt sympathy for Angelina McMahon, who had been "severely injured by a common household beverage," without fault of her own, allowing the legal system to shift the costs of this injury to the coffee pot maker "would have had consequences for coffee fanciers who love their beverage hot."

Who would want a side effect of litigation to be a cup of lukewarm coffee, after all?

Coffee Break

The "Scalding" McDonald's Case

I had taken lunch with my friend, Margot, in a little Italian restaurant near her office, very near the Louvre in Paris. At the conclusion of our lunch, we ordered coffee. But Margot realized that she was running late and, when the waiter appeared with two demitasses of steaming espresso, she asked for an ice cube to cool the coffee so that she could drink it quickly. The waiter, an Italian, did as he was asked, soon returning with the single ice cube in a saucer. He watched, horrified, as Margot picked up the ice with her teaspoon and dropped into her coffee. "Ça," he told me, "c'est l'assassinat du café" (that is the assassination of coffee).

Coffee is meant to be consumed hot. And for Americans, it is also imperative that the coffee be convenient—ready to drink when we want it, without waiting, in the morning when we get up, and while we are on the road. My parents used to carry a big thermos with them whenever we took a trip, so that they could have their coffee while we traveled. Today, convenience stores at gas stations and fast food restaurants line our route, doing away with the need to carry it from home. A hot cup of coffee is no further away than the next freeway off-ramp and a McDonald's drive-through.

The most famous "hot coffee" case is a trial court verdict handed down by a jury in New Mexico in 1994, involving just such a drive-through restaurant. The $2.86 million award in *Liebeck v. McDonald's Restaurants* sent shock waves through the legal community and beyond. Even though the multimillion-dollar award did not hold—the trial judge reduced it to $640,000 and the parties settled for an undisclosed sum before an appeal was handed down—it nevertheless became a major news event and a *cause célèbre* for tort reform advocates. They saw it as representative of out-of-control juries and frivolous lawsuits. For many, it raised the question:

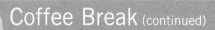

Coffee Break (continued)

haven't people who spill hot coffee on themselves while driving assumed the risk?

The facts of the case are more nuanced than the headlines would lead one to believe. Stella Liebeck was a 79-year old woman from Albuquerque who was a passenger in a car driven by her grandson. They stopped at a McDonald's restaurant to buy her a cup of coffee. While the car was still parked, she put the cup between her knees and opened the lid to add sugar and cream. In doing so, she spilled the hot coffee into her lap. Her sweat pants absorbed the hot liquid and she suffered third-degree burns. She was hospitalized for treatment and had to undergo two years of skin-graft surgeries.

Liebeck wrote to McDonald's asking that the company reimburse her medical costs and compensate her daughter's lost wages incurred while she was caring for her mother. The total demand was $20,000. The company offered $800. Liebeck then retained an attorney who filed a lawsuit against McDonald's alleging gross negligence and product liability, claiming that the coffee, at 170°F, was an inherently dangerous product likely to cause severe burns if spilled. McDonald's denied that its coffee was too hot. The company rejected a $300,000 settlement offer.

At the trial, Liebeck's lawyer introduced evidence that McDonald's had required its franchisees to serve coffee at 180°-190°F which, if spilled, could cause a third-degree burn in two to seven seconds. McDonald's attorneys explained that the coffee had to be hot when served at drive-through windows because, by the time the customer actually drank the coffee bought in this manner, it would have cooled and that consumers thought coffee served at temperatures lower than 170°F was too cool. Unfortunately for McDonald's, the plaintiff's attorneys also submitted documentation obtained through discovery showing that between 1982 and 1992 the company had received over 700 customer complaints of scalding from coffee and that McDonald's had previously settled claims for burn injuries in amounts in excess of Liebeck's claim.

160

The jury found that McDonald's hot coffee was responsible for Liebeck's injury and awarded her $200,000. Because Liebeck was also partially at fault—that is, she was careless in putting the coffee cup between her knees—this award was reduced by 20 percent to $160,000. But, in addition, they also awarded her $2.7 in punitive damages to penalize McDonald's for its corporate coffee policy, which they viewed as callous, putting its coffee consumers at unreasonable risk. One juror later explained this decision as a means of saying, "Hey, open your eyes. People are getting burned." [1]

Despite its notoriety, the *Liebeck* decision provoked few followers. As a McDonald's attorney noted in an interview after the trial, most people enjoy and accept hot coffee as a source of pleasure.[2] The risk of burns from spilled coffee has also been mitigated since the decision. In the years following the award, "to-go" coffee purveyors offered better cups and lids. The commuter cup—an insulated plastic or stainless steel coffee cup with a tight-fitting lid—became commonplace. And cup holders became a standard feature in every new car, so that no consumer has to risk spills by putting a coffee cup between her knees while driving.

1. Fleischer-Black, Matt, "One Lump or Two?" *law.com*, June 4, 2004, found at http://www.law.com/jsp/article.jsp?id=900005539201.
2. Fleischer-Black.

Chapter Fifteen

Frozen Coffee:
A Freeze-Out in the World of Coffee Distributors

Lichtenstein v. Consolidated Services Group, Inc.,
173 F.3d 17 (1st Cir. 1999)

Coffee has always been a brutal business. From its earliest days, when nations attempted to monopolize production and trade, to more modern times when coffee roasters have competed fiercely for a piece of this lucrative pie, the coffee business has not been for the faint of heart. And even within organizations, co-workers and co-owners constantly have needed to "watch their back" from the acts of supposed colleagues.

Arnold Lichtenstein learned this lesson about the coffee business the hard way, in 1990, after he was frozen out of the small coffee venture he had helped found, by his partner and colleague. He realized how vulnerable one can be when one is only a minority shareholder in a close corporation. He learned a basic law of the corporate jungle: don't put yourself in a minority position.

It all started in the early 1980s, when Lichtenstein worked as a salesman at a small company called Coffee Pause, in Massachusetts, which purchased and redistributed packaged coffee and related products. One of his co-workers with whom he became close was John Salterio. In 1986, Salterio left Coffee Pause to start a business in Philadelphia that he called Caribbean

Coffee Company. This company was engaged in the same field as Coffee Pause.

In about 1988, Lichtenstein left Coffee Pause and, with Salterio, started a business called Consolidated Services Group (CSG), which distributed coffee and bottled water. CSG was a partnership in which Lichtenstein had a 49 percent interest and Salterio had 51 percent. Their understanding was that Salterio would provide the start-up capital, handle the books, and run the company. Lichtenstein would make the sales and they would share the profits equally.

At some point, the two partners invited two other men, Peter Butera and Martin Keefe, to join them. Keefe had also worked at Coffee Pause with Salterio and Lichtenstein, and had been a minority owner of Coffee Pause. The four men agreed to form a corporation. However, Keefe expressed concerns about working for Salterio and in allowing Salterio to be in charge of the business—concerns that were more than justified, as we shall see. He only agreed to join CSG if there were a written agreement that protected him and Lichtenstein as minority owners. Keefe was asked to take care of getting this in place.

In 1989, Keefe asked an attorney he knew, Jonathon Fryer, to prepare the agreements and "do" an incorporation. Keefe told Fryer what terms were required and Fryer put together the agreement and the rest of the incorporation documents. Over a period of several days, the partners negotiated the terms of their deal, including remuneration and share distribution, as well as each party's duties to the corporation. Lichtenstein was put in charge of sales and business development, and was responsible for locating a coffee roaster and various suppliers. Salterio was to be the "internal specialist broker." Keefe was to be the salesperson and Butera was made the telemarketing expert.

Finally, on April 4, 1989, the four met over cups of coffee and signed an agreement to form either a Massachusetts or Delaware corporation to be called "Consolidated Services Group, Inc." An exhibit was to be attached to the agreement listing each person's capital contributions to the enterprise, but it was left blank. However, they had orally agreed that Salterio would contribute all the money necessary to capitalize the corporation, just as he had done with the previous partnership.

The four men also signed a Voting Trust Agreement, agreeing to deliver their shares in the company to the attorney, Fryer, who was to be the voting trustee. His sole obligation was to vote the shares of stock as directed in writing by each shareholder. They also signed an employment agreement, which contained a non-compete clause that prohibited any of them, for three years following termination of his employment, from participating in any business similar to that conducted by CSG within a 150-mile radius of the corporate headquarters. Salterio was elected president and clerk, Butera was treasurer, Lichtenstein was first vice president, and Keefe was second vice president. Salterio was issued 51 shares of stock, Lichtenstein 28, Keefe 15, and Butera 6. These were transferred to Fryer to hold as voting trustee.

Needless to say, things did not go as planned. It all looked good on paper but the relationships soon soured as the company tried to develop and grow the business.

Even though the corporation formation agreement had provided for a Massachusetts or a Delaware corporation, the company was incorporated in Maine, where Salterio lived. The corporation never formally voted to ratify the employment agreement. Even though Salterio told the others that "everything was taken care of," no assets of the CSG partnership were ever formally transferred to the corporation. The four men never held a shareholders' or board meeting. The corporation never filed a corporate tax return nor did it pay any corporate filing fees to the state of Maine. In fact, its authority to do business as a corporation was suspended by the state on September 13, 1991, as a result of the company's failure to file an annual report as required by Maine law.

The men referred to the business from time to time as Consolidated Services Group, Consolidated Services, Consolidated Services, Inc., and Consolidated Services Group, Inc. From November 1989 until August 1990, Salterio wrote checks from a bank account in the name of Consolidated Services Group, Inc.

In January 1990, Salterio executed a Master Agreement with New England Coffee Company, signing as the president of Consolidated Services Group, Inc. At the time, more than 80 percent of CSG's revenue was generated from coffee sales and most of those sales came from its brokerage contract with New England Coffee Company. Even though CSG never filed a corporate tax return for the tax years 1989 through 1993, Salterio included income and expenses from the Consolidated Services business on Schedule C (Profit and Loss from a Business or Profession) of his personal federal income tax return, effectively treating the income and expenses of CSG as his own (and benefiting from the company's net losses to reduce his own taxable income).

In the fall of 1990, Salterio terminated Keefe, claiming that he had failed to perform his duties. At the time, Salterio owed Keefe approximately $2,000. After discussions with the attorney, Jonathon Fryer, Salterio agreed to pay Keefe the $2,000, which was described as a payment for the purchase of Keefe's stock in the corporation. Salterio then told Lichtenstein that he had no money to pay him. Up to this point, Lichtenstein earned $500 in fixed salary under the employment agreement. Salterio told Lichtenstein that he could go into business for himself, working in the same field as CSG, provided he paid CSG 20 percent of what he earned. Otherwise, he would not be allowed to do any work that conflicted with Consolidated's business. However, Salterio told him that he would not object to Lichtenstein's doing consulting work. Lichtenstein told Salterio he would leave the business.

On October 31, 1990, Lichtenstein's attorney wrote to Salterio, offering an agreement under which Lichtenstein would resign as vice president of the company and sell back all of his shares in the corporation, but that Lichtenstein would be entitled to solicit the company's customers for his own account. On May 16, 1991, at the request of Salterio, attorney Fryer wrote to Lichtenstein informing him that, because the four incorporators had not completed the necessary documentation to establish the corporation, including ratifying the employment agreement, "the corporation never fully came into operation and was abandoned as a venture by the shareholders."

In November 1994, after allowing the situation to fester for some time, and seeing himself frozen out of his own company, Lichtenstein took action. His attorney wrote to Salterio to request inspection of the corporate books and records. Salterio refused, stating in response to the attorney's request that the corporation never had any assets, liabilities, or net worth. "Because the corporation never operated as such," he wrote, "there are no corporate records."

In January 1995, Lichtenstein sued CSG, John Salterio, and attorney Jonathon Fryer, claiming breach of contract, breach of fiduciary duty, and seeking to dissolve the corporation. Among other claims, he alleged that Salterio had misappropriated corporate assets and had failed to permit inspection of the corporate books and records in violation of Maine law. In response, Salterio's attorney stated that Salterio had not actually refused an inspection of the records but that he was still gathering them. However, he insisted that they were the records for the company from before the time the parties agreed to incorporate, when the company was operating as a "dba of Mr. Salterio," which he claimed "continued in that fashion after incorporation."

The trial court dismissed Lichtenstein's claims against attorney Fryer because there was no evidence that he had breached any fiduciary duties. As a voting trustee, he had fulfilled the only obligation he had, which was to vote the shares. Aside from this responsibility, Fryer had no other fiduciary or contractual relationship with Lichtenstein because he had not represented Lichtenstein once the incorporation papers were drawn up. The court did rule that CSG was a validly formed corporation under Maine law. The court found that, not only was a corporation formed, but that the parties had agreed to incorporate the pre-existing business known as Consolidated Services Group. It came to this conclusion based upon a number of facts, including the use of the corporate checking account and the fact that Salterio had signed the New England Coffee Agreement, which generated approximately 80 percent of the company's income, on behalf of the corporation, in his capacity as its president, and not in his personal capacity. The court held also that Salterio had violated a fiduciary duty—as a majority shareholder in a close corporation—to the company's other shareholders. And finally, the court ordered that the corporation be dissolved because of Salterio's fraudulent conduct and misuse of corporate assets. It appointed a receiver to wind down the business.[1]

Salterio had argued for a "reverse" piercing of the corporate veil. Usually used by parties attempting to break down the corporate shield against personal liability of shareholders in order to attach the shareholders' personal assets, in this case, Salterio asked the court to disregard the corporate form in order to prevent Lichtenstein from claiming rights as a shareholder. The court

---

1. *Lichtenstein v. Consolidated Services Group, Inc.*, 978 F. Supp. 1, 21 (1997).

noted that this equitable concept was generally used in the interest of justice to prevent harm to an innocent party. It did not believe that justice would be served to disregard the corporate form in this case. "The better rule would seem to be that a person who has voluntarily adopted the corporate form to engage in business is precluded from asking the court to disregard that form merely because the person has been disadvantaged by its use."

The trial court also found ample evidence to hold Salterio liable to the company and its shareholder, Lichtenstein, for fraud and misuse of corporate assets. For example, his apparent control over the business and his representation that there were no books or records because the corporation never operated could, in the court's opinion, reasonably be interpreted as dishonest in fact or the result of his reckless management of the company and his lack of business judgment. Further, in light of Salterio's treating the company as his sole proprietorship, including claiming the income and expenses of the corporation as business expenses on his personal income tax return, the court determined that any jury could reasonably find that Salterio's actions constituted misapplication and misuse of corporate assets.

On the other hand, the court failed to find any breach of fiduciary duty by the attorney Fryer. According to the court, there was no authority "under Maine law, for the proposition that a lawyer breaches his fiduciary duty to a former client and subjects himself to civil liability by rendering advice in a matter involving work done for a former client, to a client whose interest conflicts with the former client's."

The parties appealed, and Fryer moved for sanctions against Lichtenstein's attorney for pursuing "frivolous" claims against him. The trial court refused to consider this motion in light of the "suspicious" nature of Fryer's involvement in the matter. The court said, "Fryer's role would have been reasonably understood, in the beginning, as one of complicity with the activities of [Salterio] . . . in what appears to the court to be an effort to purloin the corporate opportunity."

The appellate court affirmed the judgments of the trial court against Salterio, as well as the order to dissolve the corporation. It also affirmed the dismissal of Fryer's motion for sanctions because Lichtenstein's claims were not "patently frivolous." According to the appellate court, Fryer's intermittent and arguably suspicious involvement by first advising Lichtenstein that the employment agreement was enforceable and that he would be sued for breach of his noncompete agreement and then turning around and advising him that there was no corporation, provided "sufficient basis" for a lawsuit against him, even if Lichtenstein ultimately failed to prevail.

Fryer represented a classic problem faced by an attorney for a small business: he started out representing all the partners in putting together agreements to form a company. Then he represented the company, in this case, as frequently happens, forming a close relationship with the president, until there is a point where there is confusion as to who the client really is. There are many attorneys who acquit themselves well in this type of situation, refusing to take a position when a dispute arises among the partners, and recognizing that it is time to step aside. But others, like Fryer, fail and fail miserably: when confronted with an honorable choice, they instead choose one client to the detriment of the others and behave in an unsavory manner that bears out the stereotype of the corrupt lawyer.

And as for Lichtenstein: he quite likely felt fairly brutalized by the experience. He had trusted several people: his colleague, Salterio, and later the attorney, Fryer, to protect his interests and he soon learned that not all is fair in friendship and business, particularly the competitive coffee business.

Coffee Break

How Coffee is Brewed: From Turkey to the Drip

Coffee came to Turkey from the former Ottoman province of Yemen, via Egypt. It was originally frowned upon, but coffee drinking quickly became viewed as a desirable custom. Today, as it has for centuries, coffee in Turkey is viewed as the ultimate sign of true hospitality. So famous is the Turkish coffee ritual that this manner of brewing coffee, popular throughout the Middle East, is referred to as "Turkish coffee." Coffee in Turkey is brewed in an *Ibrik*—a circular, straight-sided utensil, slightly narrower at the top than at the bottom, with a long handle that was originally useful for preparing coffee over a fire.

Turkish coffee is prepared by brewing finely pulverized coffee beans and sugar together with water. It is ordered according to the amount of sugar required: *az* (little), *orta* (medium), or *çok ekerli* (a lot).[1] Sometimes spices, such as cinnamon or cardamom, are added for additional fragrance. The resulting brew, served in tiny cups, is thicker and sweeter than the coffee to which most Americans and Europeans are accustomed. Ibriks can be found to brew one cup or several cups of Turkish coffee. The coffee is generally brewed in batches. To get the best drink, the Turkish coffee should not be consumed during the first two minutes; this is to allow the coffee grounds to settle to the bottom of the cup.

Some claim that the best coffee in Istanbul is found at Karukahvea Mehmet Efendi, in the Spice Bazaar, which is one of the oldest and most popular coffee shops. Visitors to the Spice Bazaar can attest to its popularity: one has to wait in line at any hour of the day to buy a packet of coffee. Turkish coffee is generally served in the afternoon, or preferably after dinner. In the morning, surprisingly, many Turks drink Nescafé.

The espresso machine was invented in Italy in the nineteenth century. "Espresso" means "made in the moment." It was initially a response to a busy society's desire for an "instant" coffee. The principle of espresso is simple: steam is forced through very finely ground dark roasted coffee that has been tamped down in a filter insert clamped into a machine. It takes less than a minute to brew and creates a dark, rich, thick coffee essence with a touch of hazelnut colored foam on top, called the *crema*. Some swear that this method produces the best coffee.

The first commercial espresso machine was invented in 1901 by an Italian, Luigi Bezzara. It was a complicated machine that required training to produce the desired result.[2] As improvements to the technology were made in the following decades, an espresso machine was developed that was capable of producing a large number of cups in a very short period of time. The result was the famous Italian coffee bar, where one can stop by and in less than two minutes be gulping down a demitasse of good, strong, hot coffee on one's way to work or to catch a train.

The percolator is the quintessential American method for preparing coffee. The design for the modern percolator was patented in 1889 by a farmer named Hanson Goodrich.[3] It soon became a staple in American kitchens and remained so until the 1980s, when the entry of the electric automatic drip filter method changed many Americans' habits. However, some will swear that the best coffee is made with a percolator. Others, once hooked on better-flavored specialty coffees brewed in coffee shops, will nevertheless admit that the brew produced by the percolator tastes overcooked. This is the case because the coffee is actually boiled. As water heats to a boil in a percolator, it is forced up a metal stem into a filter basket filled with coarsely ground coffee. The water passes through the coffee, drips back into the bottom of the pot, and then is forced back up to the top. It continues to recirculate in this manner until the desired strength is reached.

The electric drip method coffee maker has replaced the percolator in many American homes. The basic process for drip coffee is quite simple. Grounds are placed in a receptacle (the "drip basket") that is lined with a filter. Hot water is poured into the filter chamber and the infused brew drains into the server. The automatic drip coffee maker works by admitting water from a cold water reservoir into a flexible hose in the base

172

of the reservoir leading directly to a thin metal tube or heating chamber, where a heating element surrounding the metal tube heats the water. The heated water moves through the machine into a spray head, and onto the ground coffee, which is contained in a brew basket mounted below the spray head. The coffee passes through a filter and drips down into a carafe. Over the past few decades, various coffee companies have made modifications to improve on the brewing method or to simplify the process, but the basic concept remains the same. For many Americans, drip coffee is their preferred cup.

For the French, the best coffee is made with the French press coffee maker, and many coffee enthusiasts will agree. This elegant yet simple device is the subject of Chapter 20, and of a later Coffee Break.[4]

1. Barer-Stein, Thelma, *You Eat What You Are: People, Culture and Food Traditions*, Firefly Books, Canada, 1999, p. 432.

2. Pendergrast, p. 211.

3. Issued August 13, 1889, Patent Number 408707. The first known inventor of a prototype percolator was a New Englander, Benjamin Thompson, a prolific inventor, who might have rivaled Benjamin Franklin as a great American man of parts but for the fact that he fought on the wrong side in the American Revolution, and left for Europe when the Republic was formed. In 1784, he was knighted by King George III of England. He later went off to fight in Bavaria, becoming the Bavarian Major-General of Calvary and Privy Councilor of State, taking the title of Count Rumford of the Holy Roman Empire. *See*, "THE LIFE AND LEGEND OF COUNT RUMFORD" at http://www.middlesexcanal.org/docs/rumford.htm.

4. *See* Coffee Break, "Of Coffee and France: A Taste of Luxury."

Chapter Sixteen

The Coffee House Craze:
When Is There Too Much of a Good Thing?

Kent State Univ. v. University Coffee House,
10th Dist. No. 2AP-1100, 2003-Ohio-2950

n the 1990s, Stewart Lee Allen, a coffee enthusiast, took a road trip across the southern United States, from Oklahoma through Texas to Los Angeles, in search of the "perfect cup of coffee," or, more accurately, the perfect cup of "real American coffee."[1] Even then, to Stewart, this meant not an espresso or a cappuccino, but the dark heavy brew served in a roadside truck stop off Interstate 80 or what remains of Route 66.

For all the discussions of the quintessential American brew, however, in many metropolitan areas, by the late 1990s, the "American" cup was the coffee sold in the myriad of specialty coffee shops that had popped up in the last two decades of the twentieth century. In every college town throughout the country, besides the national coffee house choices such as Starbucks or Peets, there was at least one and sometimes there were several local shops, each competing for the caffeinated student clientele.

---

1. Allen, pp. 199-224.

Two things have always been critical to the success of these independent businesses: a warm, welcoming ambiance as a meeting and study place, and—what should be obvious—a good cup of coffee.

Kent State University, in the heart of Ohio, was no exception. In March 1994, Kent State (KSU) solicited bids from various food and beverage vendors to operate a new "Food Court" on the first floor of the university's Student Center in the area known as "The Hub." Prior to 1994, the Hub had only one eating place, a Wendy's restaurant. At the time of the bidding, other food locations in the Student Center included a candy counter in the hallway on the first floor, a cafeteria on the second floor, a formal dining room on the third floor, and the "Rathskeller" in the basement, which sold pizza and beer, and included a game room with pool tables.

The plans for the Food Court contemplated a maximum of eight food providers, each with a different menu or product line: KSU's Request for Proposal (RFP) contained the following description:

> "Proposals for the installation and operation of Fast Food Court Shops, by established national firms or organizations with extensive experience in a fast food restaurant operation, in the Kent Student Center, including but not limited to shops for hamburgers, pizza, Mexican/tacos, chicken, sub sandwiches/deli, oriental (Chinese) food, ice cream/yogurt/donuts, pretzels and coffee/pastry."

The "area" where the Food Court was to be located was specified as the first floor Hub, located in the Kent Student Center. The RFP also stated that "competition between the products among shops will be strongly discouraged." The university also specifically reserved the right to "contract for additional food operations whose main menu theme differs from that of existing Food Court Shops."

A local entrepreneur saw his opportunity to do as many others were doing at the time—open his own coffee shop. He attended an informational meeting where the university's representative answered questions and stated that the Rathskeller would continue to operate in the basement, selling pizza and beer. The entrepreneur then obtained a franchise from "Arabica," a coffee specialty business with a large number of franchised shops in Ohio, to open a gourmet coffee and pastry shop. Arabica likely appealed to him because it had an established known brand, but was less controlling than other franchisors—except for the coffee itself, he would be able to tailor his offering to the student community's tastes.[2] He submitted a bid for a coffee shop in the new Food Court.

His offer was accepted on August 31, 1994, and the parties entered into a 10-year lease for one of the eight units in the Food Court. The other vendors selected were McDonald's, Mama Ilardo's Pizza, Taco Bell, Subway, Mark Pi's, Friendly's, and Hot Sam's Pretzels.

The new Arabica coffee shop opened for business in September 1994, but sales were significantly lower than anticipated. The coffee shop owner talked with university representatives soon after opening because one of the other Food Court vendors had begun selling flavored coffees. In May of 1995, KSU agreed to lower Arabica's rent by half, from $66,000 to $30,000, and they also agreed to allow Arabica to operate a coffee cart in one of the classroom buildings.

In April 2000, KSU decided to change and expand its food

---

2. *See* http://coffee-franchises.brandexpansion.com/arabica-coffee-house.

service offerings in the Student Center. The candy counter was converted into a convenience store, Kent Market. And in January 2001, in a move to update its offerings, it replaced the old-fashioned Rathskeller on the lower level of the Student Center with "Jazzman's Cyber Café"—a coffee house serving specialty coffees, such as espresso and cappuccino, as well as offering Internet access. Two weeks before Jazzman's grand opening, the Kent Market began selling certain selections of Jazzman's coffee outside the Food Court area on the first floor. And, at this same time, the McDonald's in the Food Court began offering a selection of lower-priced espresso and cappuccino drinks.

Arabica's operator was incensed. He charged that KSU was violating its lease with Arabica by allowing McDonald's to offer espresso drinks and by allowing Kent Market to sell Jazzman's flavored coffees outside the Food Court. His lawyer met with KSU representatives to discuss these claimed lease violations and to demand a reduction in Arabica's rent. KSU refused. Arabica stopped paying rent on May 31, 2001, and KSU sued in the Ohio Court of Claims for breach of contract and to recover back rent in the amount of $37,000. Arabica filed a counterclaim against KSU for breach of Arabica's exclusive right to sell quality coffee throughout the Student Center under its lease.

The court of claims ruled in favor of KSU, concluding that Arabica had failed to prove the existence of any such exclusive right. It awarded damages to KSU. Arabica appealed.

Arabica argued on appeal that it had exclusive rights under the lease, which could have been proved by parol evidence—the oral or written statements and representations from the RFP and KSU representatives that "filled in the gaps" in the final written lease agreement—that the lower court had excluded. The court of claims had ruled that Arabica had the right to be the only specialty coffee vendor in the Food Court of the Hub, but not in the entire Student Center. The tenant wanted the court to consider the language in KSU's RFP that stated that "competition between like products among shops" would be "strongly discouraged." But the court concluded that the word "shops" only meant the eight shops located in the Food Court.

The appellate court confirmed the lower court's judgment. It noted that there was no specific language in the lease that prohibited KSU from leasing space in other areas of the Student Center for vendors of gourmet coffee. Arabica's counsel had pointed out that a number of other states, including next-door Pennsylvania, held a "modern" view, allowing a less strict interpretation of an agreement in order to accomplish "the intent of the parties." However, the Ohio court refused to follow this path, which it believed would lead to ambiguity in the rule. Under its interpretation, Ohio law mandated that "language of exclusive use clauses should be narrowly construed, and all doubts should be resolved against a possible construction that would increase the restriction upon the use of the real estate." It pointed out that had Arabica desired an exclusive right to sell specialty coffee throughout the entire Student Center, "it should have reserved that right in the express language of the contract." Absent that express right, the court refused to "imply such a provision."

Of course, what the owner of the Arabica shop could have argued was that he had relied on the representations of the university that the Rathskeller would stay. Given that assurance and also this small shop owner's likely negligible ability to negotiate better terms in the lease, he had only to hope that things would not change. That was, even in 1994, a naïve assumption in the dynamic world of coffee. But again, in 1994, who would have thought that the university would install a cyber café in its Student Center? Would anyone have guessed at the time that the Internet and social networking and the passion for specialty coffees together would gain such control over the coffee shop environment that, within less than 20 years, with wireless access and the ubiquitous laptop, staying connected while sipping one's latte would be the standard in the coffee house world?

The problem for the Arabica franchisee at KSU was that he could not foresee this new world. He was not blessed with a crystal ball and could not have known when he negotiated his lease the extent of the competitive pressures he would have to face in such a short time. Perhaps he was naïve, but then many others have been equally so. And the lesson is also that one can have the most wonderful ambiance, but where one has to compete in the end is in the quality of the coffee.

Coffee Break

The History of the Coffee Shop

"They reached the entry of Ahmed Abdul's coffee house [and] . . . descended to its strange space in the belly of the earth beneath Khan al-Khalili bazaar and sought out an empty alcove. . . The interior consisted of a spacious square courtyard . . . [with] a fountain in the center . . ..
The men smoked water pipes, drank tea and coffee, and chatted idly and interminably."[1]

The 1990s saw the rise of the coffee house as a "home-away-from-home." This was the ambiance that Starbucks shops sought to create, with comfortable easy chairs and side tables, newspapers, and soft music. I visited one such location on the North Side of Chicago on a winter's evening, in a neighborhood very near the Steppenwolf Theatre and Second City. It was a large place but so comfortably arranged it felt intimate. It was a Friday night and people were stopping in for a social interval, away from the cold. Some loners brought their laptops for work or surfing. Others came as couples or foursomes, to share a hot drink and good conversation before taking off for late dinners or other entertainment. Some came to stay longer. Several carried their Scrabble or other board games and installed themselves at strategically placed tables for an evening of social competition. Two men in a corner were playing cards. This, I thought, is the old general store from the nineteenth century, or it could have been an Americanized version of a café in France. As a student in Bordeaux in the early 1970s, I frequently stopped at the Café Montaigne in the heart of the old city. There, as in this Starbucks, groups of students came in for coffee and conversation, while at other tables older men played cards.

The coffee house came into existence at about the same time as coffee drinking left the religious sphere (where coffee was consumed in mosques before prayers), and became a secular activity. This new institution transformed social life throughout the Islamic world. Coffee houses supplied more than raw beans;

181

Coffee Break (continued)

they had the needed equipment and the expertise to prepare the brew and a convivial milieu in which to enjoy it. Ahmet Pasna, the governor of Egypt during the late sixteenth century, actually built coffee houses as a public works project, thereby garnering great political popularity. The social life of the coffee house has remained a part of Egypt since that time.[2] Today, shoppers at the Khan al-Khalili in Cairo, one of the biggest bazaars in the Middle East, can take a break at Fishawi's, which has been operating continuously day and night (24 hours) for at least the past 200 years.

In the mid-seventeenth century, Syrian traders introduced coffee to Istanbul, creating the city's first coffee houses.[3] Several of these traditional establishments, located near the banks of the Bosporus, remain today. (However, Istanbul also has more modern venues, including the ever-present Starbucks, which are popular with its populace.)

Coffee houses have always had a certain mystique. They were comfortable places where men could smoke and sip their coffee, and where they could share conversation and gossip. By the late seventeenth century, London was filled with coffee houses.[4] English wives railed against them because they kept the men away from home. They also worried about the suspected negative effects that too much coffee consumption had on their husbands' health. In 1674, a group of London housewives petitioned the mayor to ban "the hell brew" coffee in order to preserve their husbands' libido. The women did not succeed in their campaign.[5] Coffee houses were just too convenient as a place to congregate, to discuss current events, and to conduct business. Entire businesses grew out of English coffee shop meetings, including the British insurance industry.[6]

The coffee house also has an historic importance as a place where free thought, free conversation, and open discussion engendered more than one revolution. The good American patriots who threw the British tea into Boston Harbor in 1773, thus making Americans a nation of coffee drinkers, met and planned their act of defiance in a coffee house, the Green

Dragon.[7] Parisian cafes have had an equally important influence on French history and culture.

One of the earliest Parisian coffee shops that still serves many cups of coffee today is the famous Café Procope in Paris. Founded in 1686 by an Italian, Francesco Procopio, it was an immediate success, attracting a diverse clientele. It was there that the great French philosophers met to debate and discuss the latest events. Moliere and Voltaire were customers.[8] It is interesting that, whereas British coffee houses featured sober, serious businessmen, in the French coffee houses—and there were many in Paris at the time—the discussion turned more to the political. It was in the Café de Foy in the Palais Royal on July 12, 1789, that Camille Desmoulins leaped upon a table and urged the crowd that had gathered there to listen to the speeches to take up arms against the French aristocracy and to storm the Bastille.[9] And, amazingly, the people in the crowd did just that: they poured out of the coffee house into the streets and within a short time had managed to overthrow the French monarchy itself. Such was the power of coffee.

Today, it is just as likely that near the traditional Turkish coffee shop, for example, or across the way from the Deux

183

Coffee Break (continued)

Magots, in Paris, you will find a Starbucks. And what is all the more surprising is that the habitués of the Starbucks will not necessarily be American tourists, but just as likely the residents of the city. This is certainly the case in Paris, where young French students gather and socialize in a very animated Starbucks on the Boulevard St. Germain, while the tourists crowd into the Café de Flore nearby. It is hard to explain why Starbucks, as opposed to any other coffee shop, has achieved its global scale. It started as a small coffee roaster, much like Peets in Berkeley, but then it grew and grew, until there seemed to be a Starbucks on the corner of every commercial street and in every major city in the United States, and a Starbucks in major world centers. The surprising thing about Starbucks is its continued popularity. Even many who criticize Starbucks for its "bigness" and its "corporateness" will still go there for a reliable cup of coffee. And one does wonder if Starbucks had not been conceived and allowed to grow as it has whether good specialty coffee would be as available in the United States as it is today?

---

1. Mahfouz, Naguib, *Palace of Desire*, Anchor Books, 1991, Translated by William Maynard Hutchins (originally published in Arabic as *Qasr al-Shawq* in 1957), p. 68.

2. Barer-Stein, p. 118. For many men in Cairo, coffee houses became their second homes.

3. "Istanbul's coffee houses were the first truly secular settings for the sacred brew. Gone was any pretense of working oneself into religious ecstasy; men lounged and smoked and sipped." Allen, p. 102.

4. Allen, pp. 107, 127.

5. Allen, pp. 107-108.

6. Lloyd's of London (Lloyd's Coffeehouse). Other coffee shops early associated with British business were the Baltic Coffeehouse, the origin of the London Shipping Exchange, and the Jerusalem Café, the original home of the East India Company. Allen, pp. 129-130.

7. Kolpas, p. 22.

8. Wells, Patricia, *The Food Lover's Guide to Paris*, Fourth Edition, Workman Publishing, New York, 1999, pp. 141-142. According to Wells, Voltaire consumed forty daily cups of a blend of coffee and chocolate at the Procope, which some claim is the reason for his well-known wit. When Benjamin Franklin died in 1790, the Procope was draped entirely in black in his honor.

9. Schama, Simon, *Citizens: A Chronicle of the French Revolution*, Alfred A. Knopf, New York, 1989, p. 382.

Chapter Seventeen

Diluted Coffee:
The Importance of the Brand (Redux)

Starbucks Corp. v. Lundberg, 2005 U. S. Dist. LEXIS 32660 (2005); *Starbucks Corp. v. Wolfe's Borough Coffee, Inc.*, 477 F.3d 765 (2nd Cir. 2007); remanded, *Starbucks Corp. v. Wolfe's Borough Coffee, Inc.*, 2009 U.S. App. LEXIS 26300 (Dec. 3, 2009)

"The difference between a 'parody' and a 'knock-off' is the difference between fun and profit."[1]

Starbucks is the big coffee company that everyone loves to hate because it *is* big. But it also produces a reliable cup of coffee and many other coffee shops want to imitate it. Whenever Starbucks takes assertive steps to protect its well-known brand, it faces a war of negative comments posted in the blogosphere where these imitators prefer to wage their battles. "Trying the case" in the court of public opinion can influence a case, as Starbucks surprisingly learned in a recent battle to protect its famous name.

Starbucks first opened in Seattle in 1971, selling whole coffee beans and coffee supplies. The name of the shop was inventive, but not original, "borrowed" from the name of a character in Herman Melville's *Moby Dick*, as well as the character of the itin-

---

1. Deere & Co. v. MTD Prods., Inc., 41 F. 3d 39, 45 (2d Cir. 1994).

erant rainmaker in the play of the same name. From the day Starbucks first opened, it was a success.[2] By the mid-1990s, Starbucks stores were ubiquitous (1,000 stores including one in Tokyo by 1996)[3] and "the name Starbucks had become synonymous with fine coffee, hip hangouts, and an upscale image."[4] It had acquired this cachet not just because of good luck but through the hard work and dedication, as well as the smart business acumen, of its leaders. Accordingly, the company has not been pleased to see small coffee shop imitators attempting to grow their clientele through take-offs of its famous logo or name. On the other hand, Starbucks has had no choice, if it wanted to protect its brand, but to take on, through persuasion first and lawsuits second, those who deliberately used close imitations of its logo, trade dress, and name for their own marketing purposes. Starbucks has encountered mixed success in its efforts.

In October 2000, a woman named Samantha Lundberg acquired a coffee shop in the town of Astoria, Oregon, which had been operated under the name "Astoria Coffee House." In 2001, she changed the name of her shop to "Sambuck's Coffeehouse." Despite the similarity between the new name of her shop and Starbucks, she claimed that she was merely using her own name, "Sam," short for Samantha, and "Buck," which had been her maiden name (although she had not actually used this name since 1993 when she was married and taken her married name,

---

2. Pendergrast, p. 309.

3. Pendergrast, p. 376. Starbucks has been known to be uncompromisingly competitive as a company, moving into neighborhoods where other shops were located and using aggressive marketing techniques. Some residents of the Thousand Oaks neighborhood of Berkeley (birthplace of Peet's Coffee) were dismayed when Starbucks took over a desirable corner location from the beloved Ortman's Ice Cream parlor on upper Solano Avenue, just three doors down from a Peet's store. But, instead of driving Peet's out of business, more than a decade later, both stores—Peet's and Starbucks - have thrived, each with its own ambiance and its own clientele, while the nearby Jamba Juice store has closed.

4. Pendergrast, p. 376.

Lundberg, for all her personal and business affairs). Coinciden- tally, or so she claimed, the Sambuck's Coffeehouse had a green motif for its signage, similar to Starbucks' trade dress. At the time she changed the name of her business, there were more than 230 Starbucks' retail locations in the State of Oregon, including one that was less than a mile from Sambuck's Coffee- house.

In March 2002, an attorney from Starbucks contacted Lund- berg to advise her that her new store name infringed on Star- bucks' trademark and to ask her to change its name. She refused. No one was going to tell her she couldn't use her own name for her store. In fact, she produced a variety of souvenir items bear- ing the name of her coffee house—key chains, coffee travel mugs, as well as advertisements. Finally, after attempting to negotiate with Lundberg with no success, Starbucks filed suit against her in federal district court in Oregon, claiming trade- mark infringement and dilution.

The district court ruled in favor of Starbucks, finding that Lundberg's use of the term "Sambuck's" was likely to cause con- fusion among consumers who would likely see an affiliation between Sambuck's products and Starbucks, or who would assume a sponsorship by Starbucks of Lundberg's activities. The court ruled that Lundberg's use of the "Sambuck's" name was likely to dilute Starbucks' trademarks in violation of Oregon state law and that this infringed on Starbucks' registered trade- marks in violation of federal trademark law. Not only was there a "high degree" of similarity between the marks, but also both companies provided coffee-related products and services, and marketed these through stand-alone retail stores. Moreover, the two businesses competed in the same geographic region.

Lundberg had suggested that she had a right to use her "own name" as the name of her business. The court saw two problems with this defense. First, "Sam Buck" was not actually her name and had not been her name for more than a decade. Second, even if she had not abandoned her maiden name, "Buck," the similarity between her name and her mark would not have been a defense in this case. There is no right to use one's own name in a business where that name is also a strong mark belonging to another and such use would confuse the public.[5]

Lundberg presented a sympathetic case, at least to the blogging community who saw a small businesswoman trying to hold her own in the cutthroat world of coffee, challenged and defeated by Big Coffee. "What is the harm in allowing a single store to coexist, particularly in a little town in Oregon, with so many Starbucks stores in the area?" they asked. Would Starbucks really be hurt that much?

However, from a trademark law perspective, Starbucks did not have a choice. If a company is not vigilant in protecting its marks, then the mark becomes diluted. Trademark owners are aware, even if the general public is not, that words used to name common products, such as aspirin and zipper, were once well-known brands. A company with a familiar name cannot afford to be complacent under U.S. trademark law. Being less than vigilant is not an option. And the multitude of imitators who would seek to follow Lundberg could lead to a wholesale dilution of the famous Starbucks mark. The court record shows as well that Starbucks did not immediately sue Lundberg, but first tried to work with her, even offering her a cash payment, before taking her to court.

While some would see these efforts as a reasonable approach, others view them as "bullying tactics." And frequently

---

5. The Court cited as support for this ruling, *E&J Gallo Winery v. Gallo Cattle Co.*, 967 F. 2d 1280, 1288 (9th Cir. 1992); *discussed in* Robertson, C., *The Little Red Book of Wine Law*, Case 6, pp. 67-76.

those who are aggressive enough to intentionally "push the envelope" in imitating another's trademark are also those who resent being told that they have no right to infringe. This was the case for Lundberg. "I was in shock," she is quoted as saying, "I thought, is this real? I mean, they're attacking me?"[6]

And this was certainly the case for Jim Clarke, the owner of Wolfe's Borough Coffee and the Black Bear Micro Roastery, who admitted to deliberately taking on Starbucks when he developed a brand of coffee he called "Charbucks Blend" and later, "Mister Charbucks." He claimed it to be a "joking reference" that he made at the suggestion of a customer, "to what he considers an over-roasted brand." Clark did not believe that Starbucks would care. He was wrong. In August 1997, Starbucks called, asking him to desist. Clarke's wife, Annie, took the call and didn't like Starbucks' tone. According to Annie, Starbucks *demanded* that Wolfe's stop producing the Charbucks blend, instead of nicely *requesting* that they do so.[7]

According to news reports, "Clarke seems to have gotten caught up in the romantic notion of slaying a storefront savage—and one that's treated him in what he regards as an offhand manner." Clarke apparently rejected a settlement offer from Starbucks in 1998 that would have paid him $2,500 in exchange for dropping the "Charbucks" name.[8] And he has proved to be remarkably resilient—or some might say, stubborn—in his quest, making life difficult for Starbucks in court.

After what Starbucks described as a "prolonged but ulti-

6. Stossel, John and Goldberg, Alan B., "Starbucks vs. Sambucks Coffee: Beverage Giant Wants Shop Owner to Change Her Name," *ABC News online*, Dec. 9, 2005, found at http://abcnews.go.com/2020/GiveMeABreak/story?id=1390867.

7. Hyatt, Joshua, "Starbucks vs. Charbucks, One entrepreneur's vow: He won't get creamed by big coffee," *Fortune*, Small Business, December 1, 2003, http://money.cnn.com/magazines/fsb/fsb_archive/2003/12/01/359884/index.htm.

8. Hyatt.

mately unsuccessful attempt" to settle the matter, the company filed suit against Clarke and Wolfe's Borough in 2001. The case has endured for more than a decade. Starbucks sought an injunction against Wolfe's and Black Bear to force it to stop using the "Charbucks" name on the grounds that this use diluted the "Starbucks" trademark for coffee. A two-day trial was held in March 2005.

The Clarkes won the first round when a federal court judge ruled in December 2005 in favor of Wolfe's Borough, dismissing Starbucks' complaint and allowing the Clarkes to continue selling coffee with the "Charbucks" name. The trial court ruled that Starbucks had not proved either actual dilution to establish a violation of federal trademark laws or any likelihood of dilution to establish a violation of New York's trademark laws. The court also ruled that Starbucks had not proved trademark infringement or unfair competition because there was no likelihood that consumers would confuse the "Charbucks" mark for the "Starbucks" mark. The court's finding of no dilution was based on a recent U.S. Supreme Court decision, *Moseley v. Secret Catalogue, Inc.*,[9] which had interpreted the Federal Trademark Dilution Act (FTDA)[10] to require a showing of *actual* trademark dilution rather than the *likelihood* of dilution.

But the Clarkes' victory was short-lived. In 2006, while the case was on appeal, Congress amended the FTDA, in response to the *Moseley* case, to permit companies holding famous trademarks to prove only the likelihood of dilution, rather than actual damage to their brand.[11] Following this amendment, the appellate court determined that the revised statute applied to the Starbucks' matter even though the case had been filed

9. 537 U.S. 418, 433 (2003).
10. 15 U.S.C. §§1125(c), 1127.
11. 15 U.S.C. §1125(c)(1).

before the statute was amended because Starbucks was seeking an injunction against *future* acts and not damages for *past* infringement.[12]

The parties went back to the district court for round two. The lower court, in this second trial, ruled that, although the new law had allowed Starbucks to show a likelihood of dilution rather than actual dilution, Starbucks had still failed to demonstrate that likelihood. The trial court judge affirmed her 2005 finding that the marks were not similar because Wolfe's only used "Mister Charbucks" in connection with its own trade name, Black Bear. The marks, taken as a whole, were not confusingly similar. The court found that there was no dilution by "blurring" of the Starbucks trademark, which could occur when the public associates a trademark with someone else's goods or services, and such association "impairs the distinctiveness of the famous mark."

The district court found that even though Starbucks' mark was distinctive, and exclusively associated with its coffee, and that there was a high degree of recognition of the brand—all factors favoring Starbucks under the amended statute—it did not find the "Charbucks" mark to be very similar to the Starbucks mark. Although "Ch-arbucks" was similar to "St-arbucks" in sound and spelling, the court noted, the packaging was not like that of Starbucks' products; it was "different in imagery, color and format," with an image of a bear on the package.

Moreover, even though Wolfe's Borough *intended* to create an association with the Starbucks' mark, the court found that such intent did not mean that a likelihood of dilution or blurring resulted. According to the court, nothing in the record indicated that the intended association was likely to impair the distinc-

---

12. *Starbucks Corp. v. Wolfe's Borough Coffee, Inc.*, 477 F 3d 765, 766 (2d Cir. 2007) (per curium).

tiveness of Starbucks' mark. In fact, this intent, although a factor that should have weighed in favor of Starbucks, surprisingly, by the court's logic, weighed against the company. The court found that the distinctiveness of the character of Starbucks coffee was a factor in favor of Wolfe's and, in fact, it was "key" to the achievement of Clarke's stated goal, which was to signal to purchasers that the Charbucks coffee blend was "a very dark roast" not at all like other Black Bear coffee products.

The court concluded that "such an intended association, especially where, as here, defendant's mark is not substantially similar to plaintiffs, is not indicative of bad faith or of an association likely to cause dilution by blurring." Thus, ironically, as Wolfe's defense attorney later commented, the admitted intent to associate with the famous mark helped to demonstrate its distinctiveness.[13]

The court even went so far as to suggest that Wolfe's "use of a playful dissimilar mark" actually benefited Starbucks, by drawing attention to the dark roast but very different flavor of Starbucks' own coffee products. For this reason, Starbucks' mark was not diluted by "tarnishment" either.[14] Accordingly, even applying the lower standard of "likelihood" of dilution rather than "actual" dilution, the district court again found in favor of Wolfe's.

Starbucks again appealed.

On December 3, 2009, the appellate court once more rendered its decision. This time, the justices accepted most, but not all, of Wolfe's arguments and, except for the issue of whether

---

13. *See* http://www.KaufmanKahn.com/pdf/Starbucks-on-remand.pdf.

14. Dilution by tarnishment is "an association arising from the similarity between a mark . . .and a famous mark that harms the reputation of the famous mark." 15 U.S.C. §1125(c)(2)(C). A mark is tarnished, for example, when it is linked to products of shoddy quality, or is portrayed in an unseemly context, with the result that the public associates the lack of quality in the imitator's goods with the products of the owner of the famous mark.

Starbucks had demonstrated a likelihood of dilution by "blurring," it affirmed the district court's judgment. In considering the issue of "blurring" and considering the six factors examined by the district court, the appellate court concurred with the finding that the Charbucks marks were minimally similar to the Starbucks' marks. It also agreed with the district court that Charbucks marks did not dilute the Starbucks' marks through tarnishment.

The court concluded that Starbucks' survey showing an association of "Charbucks" with "Starbucks," even when coupled with a negative impression of the name "Charbucks," was insufficient to establish a likelihood of dilution by tarnishment. In fact, the court speculated, it could show the opposite, that "of the two 'bucks,' Starbucks is the 'un-charred' and more appealing product." Starbucks had argued that the term "Charbucks" was a pejorative term for Starbucks' dark roast and therefore created a negative association with Starbucks coffee. Although the court knew that the term had been used in that manner in the past in attacks on Starbucks, it did not believe that the Clarkes had that intent, but rather, that they were using the term for a line of coffee that was of a "high quality."

The appellate court nevertheless concluded that the district court had erred when it found no dilution from "blurring" because of the way in which the lower court had balanced the factors to be considered in making this determination under the FTDA, as well as in prior case law.[15] The lower court gave great-

---

15. The so-called "Polaroid" factors (*Polaroid Corp. v. Polaroid Elecs. Corp.*, 287 F. 2d 492 (2d Cir1961)): (1) strength of the trademark, (2) similarity of the marks, (3) proximity of the products and their competitiveness with one another, (4) evidence that the senior user may "bridge the gap" by developing a product for sale in the market of the alleged infringing product, (5) evidence of actual consumer confusion, (6) evidence that the imitative mark was adopted in bad faith, (7) respective quality of the products, and (8) sophistication of consumers in the relevant market.

est weight to only one of the FTDA factors, the first: whether there was similarity between the mark in question and the famous mark. Finding little to no similarity, the court had concluded that dilution by blurring had not been proven. The appellate court concluded that the district court erred to the extent it focused on the "absence of 'substantial similarity' . . . to dispose of Starbucks dilution claim," without taking into account other factors provided in the statute that would have weighed in favor of Starbucks. This error, in the appellate court's judgment, "likely affected its view of the importance of other factors in analyzing the blurring claim, which must ultimately focus on whether an association, arising from the similarity of the subject marks, 'impairs the distinctiveness of the famous mark.'"[16]

The appellate court also concluded that the district court erred in its consideration of other factors provided for in the FTDA, such as whether Wolfe's intended to create an association with Starbucks' mark. The lower court had found intent when Wolfe's deliberately chose the label "Charbucks" because of its association with the Starbucks brand, but had decided that this factor did not weigh in favor of Starbucks because the Clarkes did not act in bad faith. The appellate court noted that the "intent" factor in the FTDA did not "require the additional consideration of whether bad faith corresponded with that intent." Therefore, because the mark "Charbucks" was created with an intent to associate with the Starbucks mark, that factor weighed in favor of a finding of a likelihood of dilution, that is, in Starbucks' favor, not Wolfe's.

The district court also had determined that there was no "actual association" between the two marks in consumers' minds. But Starbucks had shown the results of a telephone sur-

---

16. 15 U.S.C. §1125(c)(2)(B).

vey where a third of those responding had answered "Starbucks" when asked what was the first thought that came into their minds when they heard the word "Charbucks." Because the district court had seen no evidence supporting actual *confusion* between the two marks (as opposed to an actual *association*), it had concluded that the factor did not weigh in favor of Starbucks. The appellate court ruled that this was an error: "the absence of actual or even a likelihood of confusion does not undermine evidence of trademark dilution."

Wolfe's had tried to argue that even if Charbucks diluted the Starbucks brand by blurring, it was meant to be a parody and was therefore exempt from infringement claims under the federal trademark statute, the so-called "parody exemption."[17] The appellate court rejected this argument because Wolfe's was using the brand to identify its own coffee, for profit, not to comment on or to criticize Starbucks coffee. It did not separate itself from coffee in order to make fun of it.

In light of these errors, the appellate court sent the case back yet again to the district court to consider whether Starbucks did, in fact, have a claim for trademark dilution due to "blurring." It is now round three and we wait to see what new surprises will develop in what has become a never ending saga between Starbucks, seeking to protect its brand, and its intrepid imitator.

---

17. 15 U.S.C. §1125(l).

Coffee Break

Italian Espresso and the Berkeley Experience

"Bad coffee equals expansionism, imperialism, and war; good coffee drips with civility and passivism and lassitude. I prove it. Quick—who makes the best coffee in the world?"

"The Italians?"

"And when was the last time the Italians won a war?"

"Hmm. What, A.D. 300?"

"And when did you Americans finally learn to make coffee?"

"Oh, I guess in the sixties sometime . . ."

"And when was the Vietnamese war?"[1]

The Italians have the perfect system for a quick cup of coffee. Go into any café, place your order, pay, and by the time you turn to the bar, your cup of espresso is ready and waiting. This is the case whether you frequent a trendy café in the heart of Milan or an Autogrille on the Autostrade. But you do need to know the system. When I was newly married and living in Europe with my husband, we took a train trip through Italy. This was in the late 1970s and Italy was then in the middle of one of its not infrequent "change crises." We had been living in France and did not realize this when we arrived in Italy. Thus we had not utilized one of the hoarding strategies we later learned to ensure we always had an ample supply of those difficult-to-find coins that were necessary to ride buses and, as we learned, to buy a cup of coffee. We never understood the origin of the crisis and the Italians we met seemed unfazed by the inconvenience.

In Florence, while waiting for our morning train to Rome, we stopped at the bar in the train station to buy a cappuccino. This was my first experience in an Italian bar. I walked straight to the counter and asked the barman for "due cappocini." He smiled broadly and served us two cups of frothy cappuccino. After enjoying our coffees, I walked over to the cashier to pay.

I handed the man behind the counter a large bill, all the lire that I had in my pocket, and told him "due cappocini." He handed back the bill, saying "spiccioli." I handed the bill back, telling him I had no change. He handed it back again. My Italian being limited, I could not make him understand that I was trying to pay for coffees that we had already consumed and he absolutely refused to take my money. So we had two cappuccinos in Florence on the house, made that much more delicious by our realization that they were the gift of a friendly Italian barman and his less than friendly colleague.

As the twentieth century drew to a close, many of those adventurers like me who had traveled to Europe as students came back and sought the same coffee-drinking experience that they had experienced while abroad in Italy. I came back from my year abroad with a small Italian stovetop espresso pot that I used on a hot plate in my dorm room. Some more adventurous than I founded their own coffee shops, such as Peets and Starbucks. I was lucky to move to Berkeley for law school, where I discovered Peets, by then a Berkeley institution. It had opened in 1966 on the corner of Vine and Walnut Streets, in a quiet North Berkeley neighborhood not far from the University of California campus. There was always a line outside the shop, made up of a diverse group of coffee aficionados all waiting to buy the wonderful dark-roasted coffee beans, as well as small clusters of Berkeley-ites—students, professors, aging hippies clad in their Birkenstocks—drinking the cups of coffee they had purchased at the small bar. There was no room to drink inside; everyone congregated on the street corner outside, to talk, to relax, and to enjoy their coffee in a leisurely manner. This was and remains the ultimate Berkeley experience. Long after Peet, the coffee shop has endured, now in several locations. But the ambiance and the crowd are much the same—perhaps more gentrified, but still Berkeley. For Peet's customers, the shop and its coffee are a morning ritual.

1. Conversation between Dr. Josef Joffee and Stewart Lee Allen, in Allen, p. 135.

Chapter Eighteen

Grounds for Divorce

Berardi's Fresh Roast, Inc. v. PMD Ents., Inc.,
Cuyahoga App. No. 90822, 2008-Ohio-5470

Michael Caruso and his wife, Angela Berardi-Caruso, founded a coffee business in the 1980s. Michael had been a biology and chemistry teacher living in Cincinnati, Ohio, with a passion for good coffee. The coffee shop was started initially as a side business—a home party company specializing in a wide variety of kitchen gadgets, which gradually grew into a retail outlet called "The Kitchenry." To generate foot traffic into their little store, the Carusos offered coffee and tea. Soon they had purchased a coffee roaster and were seriously in the business. By 1986, they were specialized in wholesale sales of freshly roasted coffee and had renamed their business Berardi's Fresh Roast, after Angela Caruso's Italian immigrant parents.[1]

Although the business started as a small family enterprise, with Michael roasting and Angela creating blends and selling coffee from a small retail store, it quickly grew into a nationally recognized specialty coffee seller. Michael had found his talent: establishing certain styles of roasting the beans to create unique

---

1. Meiser, Rebecca, "Coffee Clash: Angela Caruso Hired a Lawyer to Protect her Company. Instead, She Claims, He Helped His Father Take It Over," *Cleveland Scene*, August 31, 2005, http://www.clevescene.com/Cleveland/coffee-clash/content?oid=1491902.

flavors.

But this is not a business success story. Much as the Berardis shared a passion for coffee and were emotionally invested in a business they both loved, they eventually fell out of love with each other and, in 2000, they divorced.

As in many divorces, there is one item or asset that the husband and wife will fight over—a favorite painting, the family dog, antique silver. In the case of the Carusos, it was the family coffee business. For Angela, this was a business she loved, named for her elderly parents. For Michael, coffee and coffee roasting were his passions. Michael lost the initial battle. After a hard-fought negotiation, he agreed to be bought out. He also agreed to a noncompete agreement that prevented him from reentering the coffee industry for three years. This was to expire on April 19, 2003. But his acquiescence did not come cheaply. In return for his agreement, Angela agreed to pay him $930,000 in cash for his interest in the business. In addition, Berardi's agreed to make quarterly payments to Michael, which were identified as deferred compensation, for his "exemplary past performance with the company."

By the spring of 2002, Angela Berardi had transferred the coffee business to her divorce attorney and the couple's two adult sons, Michael and Dominic, realized that they had no future in Berardi's, contrary to what they had always assumed. Disappointed, they approached their father to convince him to return to the coffee business once his noncompetition agreement expired in April 2003. Caruso agreed and began to take steps in that direction.

In the fall of 2002, he approached lenders to investigate the availability of financing for the new venture. He also made inquiries about pricing and product availability from various vendors. In December 2002, he placed orders for roasting and other coffee-related equipment. In February 2003, he signed a lease for warehouse space and in April 2003, he took possession of the warehouse and equipped the facility. He set up a new business called PMD Enterprises, Inc., with the purpose of creating custom coffee blends to be sold under the name of "Caruso's Coffee."

On April 19, 2003, his noncompete agreement expired and he was open for business. West Point Market, a Berardi's customer, switched its business to Caruso's. Its president stated that he had changed because of Michael Caruso's reputation as a coffee roaster, because the coffee was less expensive that Berardi's, and because he preferred the taste of Caruso's coffee. Several of Berardi's employees also decided to leave and work instead for Caruso.

Berardi's filed suit against Michael Caruso, Caruso's Coffee, and the former employees, claiming tortious interference with Berardi's business relationships, breach of the noncompetition agreement, theft of trade secrets, deceptive trade practices, and the theft of Berardi's personal property. Caruso counterclaimed, demanding payment of $54,000 in deferred compensation payments that Berardi's had failed to make.

The trial court granted summary judgment in favor of Caruso on Berardi's claims and also granted Caruso's counterclaim for nonpayment of the deferred compensation amounts. Berardi's appealed, but the court made short shrift of all of the claims (with one minor exception).

Berardi's had claimed that Caruso had stolen Berardi's trade secrets by using Berardi's formulas to make Caruso's coffee blends. Caruso did not dispute that the formulas he had developed when he owned Berardi's now belonged to Berardi's. But he denied that he had used those same formulas in creating Caruso's various coffees.

Berardi's had two arguments in support of its contention. Its first was specifically in relation to a formula for coffee sold to West Point Market, a former Berardi client. Berardi's claimed ownership of the West Point formula. Caruso contended that this particular formula was owned by West Point because a West Point employee had contributed to the development of the formula with Caruso's ex-wife prior to the formation of Berardi's. According to Caruso, although Berardi's produced the coffee for West Point, it used West Point's proprietary formula. West Point's president also believed that West Point owned the formula but admitted to having had to contact Berardi's to obtain a copy of it when he switched his business to Caruso's. Because these facts were in dispute, the court determined that this question would have to be resolved at trial and could not be answered in a summary judgment motion.

Aside from this one formula, however, the court concluded that no other facts were in dispute regarding the creation of Caruso's other blends. Berardi's second argument in support of its contention that Caruso had stolen its trade secrets was due to a so-called "cheat sheet" that Caruso had developed. This sheet had three columns, listing Caruso's blends. The first was called "Past," the second, "Others," and the third, "Present." Caruso's employees testified that the cheat sheet was intended only for internal use. If a former Berardi's customer inquired whether Caruso's carried a coffee blend similar to one that Berardi's sold, then sales staff could recommend a comparable Caruso's blend. The court saw no evidence that contradicted this testimony. Brian Leneghan, an owner of Berardi's, contended that Caruso's employees were using the sheet as a sales tool to market Caruso's coffee blends as being the "same" as Berardi's, only cheaper. However, this testimony was based on hearsay. No customer had testified that this had actually occurred.

Caruso's also had submitted to the court the formulas for its blends and the comparable Berardi's blends as displayed on the cheat sheet and thus demonstrated that Caruso's blends consisted of different beans and percentages than Berardi's blends. Berardi's did not dispute this fact.

Finally, the company contended that Caruso's misappropriated its trade secrets by using Berardi's proprietary client lists. A client list can constitute a company's trade secret if the information "derives its economic value . . . from not being generally known and not readily ascertainable by proper means by other persons." Caruso's presented evidence that its client list had been developed by searching the Yellow Pages and the Internet, by customer referrals, and by making contact whenever Caruso or one of the employees was traveling. Although there may have been some overlap with Berardi's clients, there is no indication that Berardi's clients were specifically targeted, and the list contained no other information that could be proprietary, such as the type of coffee that client had purchased from Berardi's. Caruso's list only contained the client's name, address, and contact number.

But, Berardi's argued, Caruso and his employees were former Berardi's employees. This activated a rule called "inevitable disclosure," under which a threat of harm warranting injunctive relief existed when an employee with specialized knowledge commences employment with a competitor. Sorry, the court responded, this doctrine only applies when a former employee begins work with a competitor while the noncompete clause is still in effect. In this case, the court reminded Berardi's, the employees were engaged only after Caruso's noncompetition agreement had expired.

Berardi's also claimed unfair competition. The new owners contended that Caruso violated the noncompete by forming his business as well as by hiring employees and ordering equipment and supplies prior to the agreement's expiration. The court did not agree. Certainly, it conceded, Caruso had taken actions prior to the expiration date in preparation to compete. Berardi's argued that "preparation to compete" prior to the expiration of a noncompetition agreement was the same as competing. The court was not persuaded. It found that Caruso was not actively engaging in the coffee industry during that preliminary time. For example, he sent out a mass mailing to potential customers, but not before the expiration date. And, in fact, he testified that when potential customers contacted him prior to the expiration of the agreement, he frankly told them that he was not yet in business. "Preparing to compete," the court held, "does not equate to actively competing."

Berardi's finally contended on this issue that Michael Caruso had solicited Berardi's roaster for employment while the non-competition agreement was in effect and while this individual was still employed at Berardi's, but Caruso denied speaking with this individual until after April. This employee had, in fact, sought out Caruso's son, who was his cousin, in February 2003 (before the agreement expired) and he knew that his uncle was going back into the business. However, they did not discuss any future employment and he did not receive an offer of employment until the last weekend of April, after the expiration of the agreement.

Berardi's additionally claimed that Caruso's and its employees interfered with Berardi's customer relationships by inducing customers to terminate their business with Berardi's. "Tortious interference" is a legal concept that, to be proven, requires (1) the existence of a contract that (2) the wrongdoer knows about, and (3) that he intentionally seeks to cause one party to breach, (4) without justification, with (5) resulting damages. In Ohio, "fair competition" is considered a proper justification for interference when an existing contract can be terminated at any time without cause. Berardi's did not show that its customer contracts could not be terminated by the customers. Therefore, the court concluded that the fair competition justification for contract interference applied, unless Caruso had acted with "actual malice," that is, through unjustified, improper interference with the business, such as by disparaging Berardi's goods or services. The court found that when Caruso informed potential clients that his coffee tasted better than Berardi's and that it was less expensive, this was not actual malice, just fair competition. Caruso honestly believed that his coffee tasted better.

On the other side of the coin, Michael Caruso had demanded payment of $54,000 in deferred compensation. Berardi's contended that, because Michael Caruso had breached the noncompetition agreement, it did not owe the payments. The court found this argument to be specious for two reasons. First, the noncompete was irrelevant to those payments because they were owed to Caruso for past performance, recognizing his contribution to the past growth of the company and his past service. Any breach of the noncompetition agreement was beside the point. Second, the settlement agreement had been clear that these amounts were to be paid to Michael Caruso without any contingency.

Thus, except for the one question as to the ownership of the West Point blend, Michael Caruso and Caruso's won a substantial victory against Berardi's.

In many of these family-owned business disputes, the court case develops because of the acrimony and hostility between the two family members. In this case, it would not have been surprising to see Michael and Angela Caruso back in court due to events following their divorce. But in this case, the situation was entirely different and, in fact, made Michael and Angela effectively allies against Angela's avaricious divorce attorney and his family, who had managed to take over the Berardi's coffee business from Angela shortly after the divorce.

It is ironic that after the couple had fought so hard over who would be entitled to take sole control of the business that they had each worked so hard to grow, the business was taken over by someone outside of the family. After the divorce, it is safe to say that Angela did not fare as well as Michael. Michael had been obliged, unwillingly, to give up the business he had nurtured as well as the future ability to do what he loved— roast and blend coffee—bound as he was by the three-year noncompete. But he did have close to $1 million with which to console himself. And he continued for a while to receive the deferred compensation payments from the company, without having to do any further work. Angela got what she wanted: sole control of the business, but only for a short time. She had had to borrow the money that she needed to buy out Michael's interest. And, in the ensuing months after the divorce, she learned a lot about trust and the self-interest of others.

Her divorce lawyer, David Leneghan, had put together the paperwork for the sale of the business to Michael, including an agreement with a lender that the divorce court approved. However, after the settlement agreement was signed, Angela's loan fell through. Fortuitously, or so it seemed at the time, her lawyer was able to procure a loan from his father, Patrick Leneghan, a Cleveland businessman. The collateral for this loan was, unfortunately for Angela, the family business, Berardi's Fresh Roast.

The terms of this new loan were not favorable. One of the clauses of the agreement provided that, if she defaulted on the payments to her lawyer's father, she would be obliged to transfer ownership of the business to him. Angela Caruso claimed that

Patrick Leneghan gradually pushed her out of the business, cut her salary in half (which impeded her ability to repay the loan), and then fired her in 2002. He took over the business completely and brought in his son, Brian Leneghan, David's brother, to manage the business with him.[2]

It was at this time that Angela's sons approached their father to ask him to go back into business. When Michael Caruso reentered the coffee business in 2003, it was likely with Angela's blessing, as this move ensured their sons' futures. But she dreamed of getting back her own business. When Berardi's (under the Leneghan's management) sued Michael Caruso under the noncompete agreement, Angela Caruso brought a separate action against her lawyer, David Leneghan, for malpractice and fraud. In 2005, a jury awarded her $6.4 million.[3]

In the end, Angela Caruso learned a bitter lesson about coffee and greed, especially when an unscrupulous lawyer is involved. Basically, from her perspective, Michael Caruso walked out of divorce court with a million dollars and because of her self-interested lawyer, she walked out with a million headaches. He essentially had handed her coffee company to his father and she paid him $100,000 to do it.

It is indeed unfortunate that two people who both loved coffee and only wanted to share their enthusiasm with others should have been put through the coffee grinder, so to speak, when they encountered others who did not want to build a business on their own with care and enthusiasm but rather benefited from the couple's marital problems to take the fruit of their hard work away from them.

---

2. Meiser.

3. Bluestone, Andrew Lavoot, "$6 Million Legal Malpractice Verdict," New York Attorney Malpractice Blog, November 7, 2005, found at http://blog.bluestonelawfirm.com/legal-malpractice-news-6-million-legal-malpractice-verdict-html, citing an article by McCarty, James F. in The Plain Dealer Reporter.

The Kona Coffee Scandal

By the end of the twentieth century, American tastes had changed. Instead of convenience, consumers were now more frequently demanding quality. Rejecting the canned vegetables and frozen entrees, they now wanted fresh and natural, and were prepared to pay for the experience of consuming fine, gourmet foods. This trend was also evident in the coffee industry. Coffee consumers were no longer content to pop open a vacuum-sealed can to brew a cup of mediocre coffee. Convenience was no longer a quick cup at a local quick stop market. Ever on the go, the 1990s consumer demanded a freshly brewed cup from a nearby Starbucks, or one of its many local competitors. The gourmet trend favored local coffee roasters, selling specialty blends and freshly roasted whole beans. Customers were willing to pay twice or even three times the standard per pound price of coffee for a unique blend or a specialty coffee known for its high quality. One of these coffees was Kona, a high-quality coffee grown in Hawaii.

To coffee drinkers, "Kona" meant a mild, flavorful roast, with added cachet, and they were happy to pay more for this desirable bean. But in the mid-1990s, the Kona name suffered a serious setback, due not to any actions taken by the local Hawaiian producers but rather to one individual in California. In 1997, the U.S. government brought a criminal indictment against Michael Norton, a Berkeley coffee distributor, accusing him of passing off Central American coffee as premium Kona coffee from Hawaii.

In 1993, Norton, a local organic gardener, began marketing Kona beans under his Kona Kai Farms label to local gourmet coffee houses, including initially Peets and Starbucks, in Northern California. (These two later discontinued the brand because the coffee fared badly in blind comparison tastings with other Kona blends.[1]) Between 1993 and 1996, Norton made more than $14 million in profits from an illegal swap scheme, which had been very simple for him to execute. He imported mostly Panamanian

coffee beans selling at wholesale for approximately $2 per pound, through one of several food businesses that he operated, Nagoya Co., where his workers would remove the beans from the Panamanian distributors' bags and sort them. The beans would remain in the sorting bins until a new set of workers began their shift. These employees would bag the beans into Kona Kai Farms bags, which were labeled as 100 percent Kona beans from Hawaii. Kona beans were selling at the time for as much as $8 per pound. The employees were kept segregated into different shifts so that no one other than Norton was aware of the scheme. However, some of these employees eventually grew suspicious and one eventually approached the U.S. Customs Service, which began an inquiry.[2]

Norton was eventually sentenced to two and a half years in prison.[3]

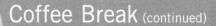

Coffee Break (continued)

One reason why Norton was able to pull off this scheme so easily was the immense trust that coffee consumers had in coffee labels, as well as the wide variations in the flavor of coffees that were labeled as Kona coffee. At the time of the scandal, most coffees carrying this label were actually blends. These blends varied greatly but a coffee could be diluted to contain as little as 2 percent Kona and could still be labeled as such.[4]

Product misrepresentation in the coffee business was not new, but in this case, because of the high profile of the investigation, the gourmet cachet that Kona coffee had garnered with consumers, and the highly regarded reputations of the coffee roasters who were duped into purchasing beans from Norton, the deceit resulted in causing very real harm to the Hawaiian coffee industry. The Kona farmers saw an immediate drop in demand for their product. They sued Norton and a number of the coffee roasters and received approximately $1 million as compensation for the damage to the Kona name. But this was a small sum, especially when spread over 650 Hawaiian coffee growers. However, this scandal also was the impetus for a coffee certification program in Hawaii, which took effect in 2001. Today, most Kona coffee in the market is certified under this program.[5]

---

1. Rubinstein, Steve, "Berkeley Man Settles Kona Coffee Suit," *San Francisco Chronicle*, Friday, October 1, 1999, A-21, found at http://sfgate.com/cgi-bin/article.cgi?f=/c/a/1999.

2. Fimrite, Peter, "Scalding Affidavit on Coffee Fraud Kona-gate grinds on, may spur regulation," *San Francisco Chronicle*, Wednesday, November 13, 1996, A-1, at http://sfgate.com/cgi-bin/article.cgi?f=/c/a/1996/11/13/MN59207.DTL.

3. "Berkeley Man in false java jam," *The Berkeley Daily Planet*, Monday March 5, 2001, at http://www.berkeleydaily.org/issue/2001-03-05/article/3737?headline=Berkeley-man-in-false-java-jam.

4. Castle, Timothy J., "The Kona Coffee Scandal Ends With More Questions Than Answers," *Tea and Coffee Trade Journal*, April 20, 2001, found at http://www.allbusiness.com/manufacturing/food-manufacturing-food-coffee-tea/784150-1.html.

5. Blanchard, Sarah, "Why Those Coffee Labels Matter: The Better the Bean, the Better the Brew," *Coffee Times*, http://www.coffeetimes.com/coffeelabels.html.

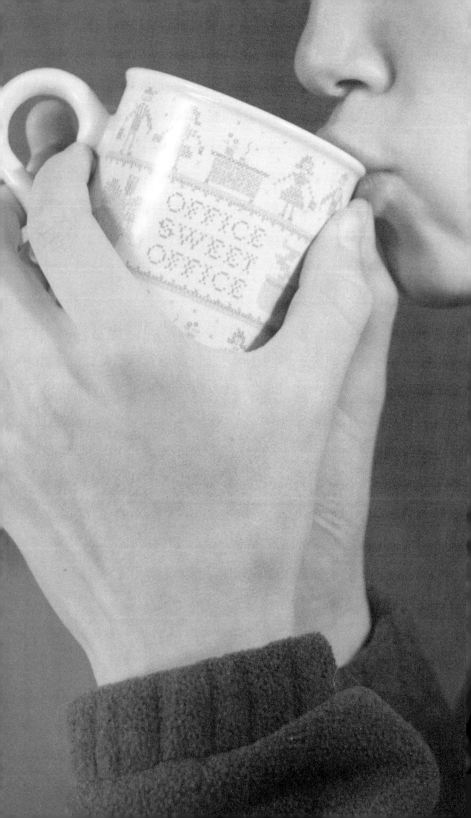

Chapter Nineteen

A Face-Off Against Nestlé:
The Use of an Image to Sell Coffee

Christoff v. Nestlé USA, Inc.,
47 Cal. 4th. 468 (2009)

In 1986, Russell Christoff, who was then a professional model, posed—gazing at a cup of coffee and drawing in the aroma—for a photo shoot arranged by Nestlé Canada, an affiliate of Nestlé USA. Christoff was paid $250 for his time and received a contract governing the use of his image, signed by his agent and by Nestlé Canada. The contract provided that if Nestlé Canada used the picture on a label it was designing for a brick of coffee,[1] Christoff would receive $2,000 (plus an agency commission). It also provided that the price of any other use of Christoff's image would require further negotiations. Without informing Christoff or his agent, and without paying him according to the contract, Nestlé Canada used Christoff's image on the coffee brick. He apparently never knew this, as he was living in California, not Canada, and did not see the packages in his local stores.

In 1997, Nestlé USA decided to redesign the label for its

---

1. A "brick pack" is ground coffee that is vacuum-packed in skin tight, laminated packages. Pendergrast, p. 344.

Taster's Choice® instant coffee. This turned out to be a fateful and expensive decision for the company. For the prior 30 years, the Taster's Choice label prominently featured a "taster," that is, the image of a person peering adoringly into a cup of steaming coffee. Nestlé wanted to keep the "taster" concept on its new label to retain continuity. Nestlé employees searched for the high-resolution artwork that met the necessary specifications, portraying the image of the original "taster," but were unable to do so; it had been misplaced during a corporate move. In their search, however, they found that Nestlé Canada had high-resolution artwork for a different taster, who turned out to be Christoff, and decided that this would satisfy the requirements. The company then decided to use the Christoff artwork because Christoff's image had a "distinguished" look and because this would provide continuity with the original Nestlé taster. Based on a discussion between employees of the two companies, and on the previous use of Christoff's image in Canada, Nestlé USA employees believed that they had the authority to use Christoff's image because it had been widely used in Canada. They never investigated the scope of the agreement that Nestlé Canada had made with Christoff and they never approached Christoff to obtain his consent to this new use.

Christoff's image was used in the redesigned Taster's Choice label beginning in 1998. Only a portion of Christoff's face was visible on the label and the picture was cropped just above the eyebrows. The redesigned label was used on newer Taster's Choice jars, including regular coffee, decaffeinated coffee, and various flavored coffees. Labels bearing Christoff's image were also produced in different languages to be sold internationally. For Mexico, alterations were made, adding sideburns, and his complexion was altered. Jars of coffee bearing Christoff's image were included in Nestlé's multiple advertising campaigns for Taster's

216

Choice, including on transit ads, coupons in newspapers, magazine advertisements, and Internet ads.

For 16 years after he had posed for the original Canadian label and for five years after Nestlé USA first introduced its redesigned Taster's Choice label using Christoff's image, Christoff was oblivious to Nestlé's ad campaign. His first tip-off came in May 2002, when a woman in a checkout line at a Home Depot store told him that he resembled the fellow on her coffee jar. In June of that year, while he was shopping in a Rite Aid store, he happened to see a can of Taster's Choice coffee.

In 2003, Christoff sued Nestlé USA, alleging that the company had appropriated his likeness to sell its coffee without his consent and seeking damages for unjust enrichment from the millions of labels on jars of coffee sold internationally for the preceding five years. This was six years following the introduction of the label but less than one year after his discovery.

California, like many states, has a statute (Civil Code Section 3344) that prohibits the misappropriation of a person's likeness.[2] This statute prohibits the use of another's likeness without consent for the advertising or sale of a product and provides for damages, which can include the profits from the sale of such products. Under California law, this type of action must be filed within two years of the person's discovery of the unauthorized

---

2. Cal. Civ. Code §3344 reads: "Any person who knowingly uses another's name, voice, signature, photograph, or likeness, in any manner, on or in products, merchandise, or goods or for the purpose of advertising or selling or soliciting purchases of products, merchandise, goods or services, without such person's prior consent . . . shall be liable for any damages sustained by the person or persons injured as a result thereof. In addition, in any action brought under this section, the person who violated the section shall be liable to the injured party or parties in an amount equal to the greater of seven hundred fifty dollars ($750) or the actual damages suffered by him or her as a result of the unauthorized use, and any profits from the unauthorized use that are attributable to the use and are not taken into account when computing the actual damages."

use, unless the aggrieved party should have known earlier of the use. This is called the "discovery rule."

Not content with the argument that Christoff should have discovered the use earlier than he did (which still would have made Nestlé liable for at least two years' worth of damages to Christoff), Nestlé's lawyers argued that California's "single publication" rule applied to its entire sales and marketing campaign using Christoff's image. Under this rule, a person has only *one* cause of action for a tort founded on a single publication (in this case the first label with his image).[3] Because Christoff had not filed his lawsuit within two years after Nestlé first "published" its label using his image, his entire cause of action against Nestlé was barred, they argued.

The trial court disagreed with this argument, concluding that the single publication rule applied only to defamation claims and, therefore, did not apply to Christoff's claims because they were based on his right of publicity. In addition, the jury decided that Christoff did not know of and could not have reasonably suspected this use of his likeness prior to seeing it in the Rite Aid store. They also found that Christoff's image had been used without his consent and awarded him more than $15 million in damages.

In 2003, Nestlé again redesigned the label for Taster's Choice, using another model, James Vaccaro, as the new "taster." Vaccaro was paid $150,000 for the use of his image for the next 10 years. The new label started circulating in May 2003 but jars of Taster's Choice with Christoff's likeness were still in Nestlé's inventory and would have been shipped to retailers after this date.

---

3. Cal. Civ. Code §3425.3 provides "No person shall have more than one cause of action for damages for libel, or slander or invasion of privacy or any other tort founded upon any single publication . . such as one issue of a newspaper or book or magazine."

Nestlé appealed the jury's multimillion dollar award.

The California court of appeal reversed, holding that Christoff's action was, in fact, time-barred because the single publication rule did apply.[4] If the rule had not applied, however, the appellate court found that Nestlé had used Christoff's image without his consent and that he had a right of publicity under Section 3344, even though he was not a celebrity. The court said "[n]o social purpose is served by having the defendant get free some aspect of the plaintiff that would have market value" and for which he would normally have been paid. Christoff had received no remuneration for this use. However, the appellate court was also troubled by the $15 million damage award, noting that Vaccaro had received $150,000 for the use of his image for 10 years. If the case had not been time-barred, the court would likely have reduced that award unless Christoff could have better demonstrated that Nestlé's profits on the sale of Taster's Choice coffee were attributable to the use of Christoff's image.

Christoff appealed to the California Supreme Court. At issue before the court was the actual reach of the single publication rule. This rule was customarily limited in its application to libelous comments in newspapers, magazines, and books. It seemed a stretch to argue that the right of publicity, which involved the misappropriation of a likeness (usually of famous persons), would come under the umbrella of a rule governing defamation. Are labels on commercial products sufficiently comparable to pages of publications which can linger in public sight for days or years?

The California Supreme Court agreed in principle that the single publication rule did apply to causes of action for unauthorized commercial use of a likeness, but the court was unsure

---

4. *Christoff v. Nestlé USA, Inc.*, 152 Cal. App. 4th (2d Dist. 2007).

whether Nestlé's unauthorized use of Christoff's image, including its production of the label, constituted a "single publication" within the meaning of the rule. Accordingly, it sent the case back to the trial court to determine the answer to this question.

Christoff had argued that the single publication rule should not apply to Nestlé's printing of a product label because it was not a single publication—a one-time occurrence—such as a daily newspaper, an edition of a book, an issue of a magazine, or a television broadcast. Nestlé, on the other side, countered that the rule was intended to apply to "multiple printings of the same publication."

The question before the court was: what is a "single integrated publication?" Whether the printing of a product label over a five-year period constitutes a single integrated publication within the meaning of the rule was an issue of first impression in California. No court had considered this question in this context before. The court observed that, in addition to producing the product label, Nestlé had also used Christoff's likeness in other forms, including transit ads, coupons in newspapers, magazine advertisements, and Internet ads. This raised a question whether each of these activities constituted a single but separate publication or whether the entire advertising campaign, along with the labels, should be considered a single integrated publication. In other words, did Nestlé's first use of Christoff's image on the first label trigger the statute of limitations for all subsequent uses in whatever form?

The court noted that the purpose of the single publication rule was to prevent indefinite and unending liability for a defamatory statement published in a newspaper or magazine. Without such a limitation, the general rule in defamation cases is that each time a defamatory statement is communicated to a third person, the statement is said to have been "published," giving rise to a separate cause of action. With mass communication, a single defamatory statement printed one time in a magazine article, for example, could be read by millions of readers over many years, depending on how long the magazine issue remained available in any location, such as in a library archive. The effect of the single publication rule is to make any single issue of a magazine a "single publication" for defamation purposes, no matter how many copies of the magazine were distributed and read. As the court observed, unlike product labels, publishing an issue of a magazine or newspaper or an edition of a book "was different because it was a discrete publishing event."

The court was troubled that a manufacturer could use the same product label over a period of years and yet be entitled to the same reassurance of limited liability, especially while the product label was still being produced. In book publishing, under the single publication rule, each new edition of the book counted as a separate publication, and the publisher would be liable for the defamatory statements in each of the editions produced until a correction was made. Without a better, more sufficient, factual record that explained how labels were produced and distributed, including when production began and ended, the court was reluctant to rule on this important issue. It sent the case back to the trial court to gather further evidence on this subject.

Thus, it remains a factual question whether the unauthorized use (in labels and advertisements) of one's likeness in California on a product is a single integrated publication, as Nestlé argued, or, as Christoff maintained, a repeating wrong. In her concurring opinion to this case, Justice Werdegar provided further deliberation around this question. She asked "whether *all* distribution of labels employing the original misappropriated image, whenever they occurred, should be deemed to constitute a single publication." In her opinion, the statute suggested that any reissue or

221

rebroadcast be treated as a separate publication even though no change had occurred in the contents from those in the original publication. She added, "I doubt defendant's entire five-year course of printing and distributing labels may be deemed a single publication simply because the labels were not substantially altered during that time."

This case has been closely watched by the entertainment and media industries, and product manufacturers (and not just those producing coffee), who sided with Nestlé in the litigation, as well as by the Screen Actors Guild, which submitted a friend-of-the-court brief in favor of Christoff. In their public statements, the attorneys for the parties expressed differing views. Christoff's attorney argued that it is one thing to publish a book or magazine or even to print a label that is libelous and quite another to appropriate—in essence, to take—a person's image, to place it on a label, to even change it in some instances (such as darkening his complexion for the Mexican consumer), and then to use it to make millions of dollars selling coffee, all without asking for permission, or offering to pay for this use.[5] Nestlé's attorney pointed out that if Christoff had asserted his right of publicity claim in a timely manner, Nestlé would have replaced his image immediately at a cost of $150,000.[6] This is, of course, not accurate (the $150,000 was only to pay a substitute model and did not accurately reflect the substantial cost of pulling product off retailers' shelves). But it is true that Nestlé would have had no defense at all if Christoff had brought his suit in the two-year period after the date Taster's Choice coffee with Nestlé's redesigned label had first shipped, and Nestlé would have likely

5. Dolan, Maura, "California Supreme Court Hears Case of Unwitting Taster's Choice Model," *Los Angeles Times* (online), June 4, 2009, http://articles.latimes.com/2009/jun/04/business/fiscoffee4.

6. McKee, Mike, "Calif. Supreme Court to Put Right of Publicity to a Taste Test," *law.com*, June 20, 2009, http://www.law.com.

had to pay Christoff some not insignificant sum as damages for the profits made from its unauthorized use during those 24 months. How fortuitous it was for Nestlé that Christoff apparently did not drink or buy instant coffee.

This case demonstrates that serious consequences can result from small, seemingly insignificant acts. For Christoff, it must have seemed as if he had won the lottery when the jury initially awarded him $15 million for a use of his likeness when he likely would have accepted a much smaller payment (perhaps $150,000 like Vaccaro) if he had only been asked. Afterwards, aggrieved and insulted, he wanted more. And it seems that Nestlé dodged an expensive bullet when it was able to make a very innovative argument and convince the California appellate courts of its merit, when taking a quick look at Christoff's original contract before launching an entire advertising campaign around his likeness would have alerted Nestlé's marketing group that they did not have the rights they needed to use his image. In the end, they were forced to rely on technical deficiencies in Christoff's case to deny him the damages that he sought for the real wrong that he suffered.

But even if Nestlé never has to pay a cent to Christoff, this case undoubtedly has proved to be very costly for the company because lawyers smart enough to think of and craft these types of arguments are not inexpensive. For the bystander to this case, it appears that it would have made better sense for Nestlé to offer Christoff some reasonable sum as compensation for the past use of his likeness and for Christoff to have bargained for a fair sum, rather than to have engaged in this ongoing wrangling. All parties could then have moved on with their lives long ago.

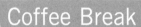

Coffee Break

The Ethics of Free WiFi: The Coffee Shop as Home Office

"It's nice to be able to buy groceries knowing that your pound of coffee is an actual pound. And actual coffee. And it makes the shopkeeper's job more relaxing if he can be confident that you'll pay for it, rather than slip it down your trousers. (And it makes your guests happier, knowing they won't be drinking trouser coffee.)"[1]

From the early days of coffee, coffee houses have always been locations for socializing and for doing business, whether in fifteenth century Cairo or eighteenth century England. People would come and spend the day, meeting and greeting friends and business colleagues. Who knows how many deals have been penciled onto paper napkins at Starbucks? Simone de Beauvoir and Jean-Paul Sartre held court in Les Deux Magots, a famous Left Bank coffee shop in Paris in the 1950s. And Hemingway spent his entire day in Paris cafes in the 1920s, writing his famous stories while nursing a single cup of coffee, because his apartment had no heat during the day. But it is useful to remember that Lloyd's of London may have started as a coffee house, but it failed as such and it was only its insurance business that kept it afloat.

Coffee shop owners have wisely been tolerant of the inclination of their patrons to want to linger over their coffee. Although they would prefer to sell many more cups of coffee, they also know that a coffee shop without patrons is one that will not succeed. A lively and friendly ambiance is a critical component to the success of the business. This has not changed even in the wired New Media age. When the Internet and its social networks were first introduced, many "brick and mortar" shops grew concerned that people would easily congregate online, in the comfort and privacy of their own homes. People would no longer have a reason to go out to find friends. This has not proved to be the case. Of course, many café owners were quick to recognize that patrons carrying laptop computers with wireless cards would appreciate having a place to plug in and connect, for free, while they enjoyed their coffee drinks. And it has proved to be a much appreciated convenience.

This phenomenon has provoked a challenge to coffee shop etiquette, however, particularly during the economic recession of the early twenty-first century, and as more people turn to their local cafes as their new home offices. "They come, they order, they plug in to the Internet. And they work and sit. And sit," noted a columnist in the San Francisco Chronicle in early 2010.[2] With rising unemployment in 2010, particularly in the finance and professional sectors, those who previously had offices but now found themselves jobless, yet needing greater and greater access to that wider world that would lead to their next employment opportunity, turned to coffee shops as an alternative office.

Or, having left large companies or law firms, self-employed entrepreneurs without the capital to establish a real office found coffee shops a welcome respite from the loneliness of working in their spare bedroom or garage. And with income short or nonexistent, an easy way to reduce housing costs is to cut off the home broadband or DSL service. For these people, the coffee shop, with its welcoming atmosphere, its free or minimal fee Wi-Fi, worked just fine as a new "home office" or "work cubicle." And it got them out of the house in the morning with a purpose.

But can it be such a good thing for the coffee shop owner? Certainly, it drives traffic. But with tables filled early in the day with customers who buy little—perhaps one cup of coffee or a latte—and stay through lunch, no space remains for mid-morning and after lunch drop-in customers who would just like a place to sit for a moment and enjoy their coffee. Coffee shop owners do not want to alienate customers who have been loyal patrons, but at the same time, they have costs—for coffee beans, for equipment, for rent, for staff—and they need paying customers to stay in business themselves.

All this leads to an important question: how much of the free Wi-Fi may a coffee shop patron take before it becomes a breach not just of coffee shop etiquette but of ethics? As ethics expert

Coffee Break (continued)

Randy Cohen opined, there is an "uneasy tension" between "consumerism and commerce."[3] It may be convenient to take advantage of a freebie, but ethically there is no difference between the person who fills his pockets at the "all you can eat" buffet for later meals, and the person who uses a coffee shop as a living room, without adequately compensating the shopkeeper. In either case, taking more than one's fair share is morally a form of theft.

On the other hand, coffee shop owners who offer free Wi-Fi and encourage its use—or rather don't discourage its overuse by imposing time limits or a fee for access—take a risk that some people will exploit their generosity. But the shop owner may not have been able to guess, when she installed the free access, the extent that demand would grow in such a short time. If only a few take advantage of the service, it is inconvenient for the café owner, but not a crisis. However, if every shop patron stayed all day occupying a table while buying only one small cup of coffee, then the shop would fail, which would be to the detriment of all. Thus the nonterrible free-loading behavior of one or two consumers can have terrible consequences if all behaved the same way. They would lose their favorite coffee shop.

One final thought that those who love free Wi-Fi should consider, however, as they sip their daily latte and surf the net: the "free Wi-Fi" comes at a cost. It is a nonsecure network and, while they are online, their confidential information is out there for the taking, by even more unscrupulous entrepreneurs. Data thieves have been known to drive by cafes with free Internet access, grabbing up all sorts of valuable information such as banking account passwords. Yes, it is true, there is no free lunch, and no free cup of coffee either.

---

1. Cohen, Randy, *The Good, The Bad and the Difference: How to Tell Right from Wrong in Everyday Situations*, Doubleday, New York, 2002, p. 29.

2. Seligman, Katherine, "Cafes' Crowded menu: caffeine, carbs, Wi-Fi: Hang-outs with Internet access struggle to fit walk-ins," *San Francisco Chronicle*, Friday, January 8, 2010, Section F, p. F1.

3. Cohen, p. 30.

Chapter Twenty

Coffee in Cyberspace:
The Importance of the Brand (Last Drop)

Chatam International, Inc. v. Bodum, Inc.,
157 F. Supp. 2d 549 (E.D. Pa. 2001)

Bodum is a well-regarded name in the coffee industry, particularly in Europe, for its innovative and stylish coffee makers. One of these is the Chambord, a model of an original French press coffee maker. In the early 1900s, the press pot, called in French a "cafeolette," became a popular means for making the filtered coffee the French loved. In the 1930s, Melior introduced a model with a stainless steel filter, a metal body, with a tempered glass beaker that fit inside the body. Bodum's predecessor, Bonjour Imports, bought the rights to that design and, in the early 1980s, introduced the "Cafetière Chambord," an elegant version of the coffee maker, named after the famous Renaissance castle, the Château de Chambord, in the Loire Valley of France. This castle had been built by King Francis I for his mistress and evoked luxury and taste.

Bodum acquired the rights to the Chambord coffee maker from Bonjour Imports and in May 1983, it registered the mark "Cafetière Chambord" for nonelectric coffee makers, noting that commercial use of this name for coffee makers had first occurred in 1980. In 1991, it registered "Chambord" for nonelectric coffee makers, also dating the first commercial use back to 1980. On November 6, 1996, PI Design A.G., an affiliate of Bodum, registered the domain name "chambord.com" with Network Solutions. The website was intended to advertise Bodum's Chambord line of coffee and tea makers, with a link to bodum.com, for the purchase of Bodum's line of housewares, including the Chambord coffee maker.

Chatam International sued Bodum in federal court in Pennsylvania for trademark infringement and dilution, and for violation of the Anticybersquatting Consumer Protection Act. Chatam sold a line of liqueurs and assorted food products under the trademark "Chambord." Chambord black raspberry liqueur was inspired by a unique liqueur produced in the Loire Valley of France during the late seventeenth century. It was said to have been introduced to King Louis XIV during one of his visits to the Château de Chambord. It was common during that time for digestifs and cognacs to be consumed at the conclusion of elegant meals. And, when coffee was introduced in France during that same time, the nobles took their liqueurs alongside their demitasses of after-dinner coffee.

At first blush, there seems to be a disconnect between a line of coffee makers and luxury liqueurs, with only a tenuous link between the two: the natural affinity between good coffee accompanied by a fine liqueur, and, of course, the fact that both products have utilized the name of the famous French castle to create an image of luxury and fine quality. But the thrust of Chatam's case was not so much consumer confusion on the shelf at the store, but rather in cyberspace. Chatam was upset because a potential liqueur aficionado would not be directed to Chatam's website for its line of liqueurs and fine candies when she typed in the name "chambord.com" but rather to Bodum's site where coffee makers were displayed. In other words, Chatam was perturbed that Bodum had arrived first to register the desirable domain name and didn't want to give up without a fight.

The Internet has changed the dynamic in trademark rights and the potential for infringement. In the 1990s, when the Internet was gaining ground as a means of doing business, companies holding famous trademarks were constantly stymied when they attempted to register the most common forms of their famous trademarks as domain names, only to find that someone else, with no rights at all to the mark, had arrived first and had acquired the right to use the domain name. This is much like the owner of a cabin in the woods who arrives for a holiday to discover a family of squatters occupying his vacation residence. The Internet equivalent is called "cyber squatting." To ensure the exclusive right to use its own mark as a domain name, the trademark owner found infringement lawsuits to be largely ineffective and thus frequently a ransom was paid to obtain a right to which the owner believed it should have been solely entitled in the first place.

In November 1999, Congress passed the Anticybersquatting Consumer Protection Act (ACPA).[1] Under this Act, it is illegal to register a domain name that is the subject of trademark protection. To establish a claim under ACPA, the trademark owner must show that the domain name was registered in bad faith. The statute provides various factors to be considered in determining whether the registration was actually in bad faith. Does the registrant have a trademark right in the domain name? Was there prior use by the registrant of the name for the bona fide offering of goods and services? Did the registrant intend to divert con-

---

1. 15 U.S.C. §1125(d).

sumers from the trademark owner's online location? Has it offered to sell the domain name for financial gain without having used or intended to use the domain name for the bona fide offering of goods or services? Did it give false or misleading information when registering the name? The statute provides a "safe harbor" for those who believe and have reasonable grounds to believe that the use of the domain name is a fair use or otherwise lawful.[2]

This was not the first time that Chatam had brought an action over the use of the "Chambord" mark for the French press coffee maker. Chatam had been selling a raspberry liqueur since 1975 under the mark "Chambord Liqueur Royale." In 1977, it registered this mark with the U.S. Patent and Trademark Office. In its application, it "expressly asserted no claim" to the individual word "Chambord." But in 1984, it registered the mark "Chambord" for liqueur and for milk chocolate and in 1986 and 1988, for fruit preserves and cake. Even before it registered the mark "Chambord" for liqueur and chocolate, and before Bodum acquired the rights to the French press coffee maker, Chatam brought a trademark infringement action against Bon Jour Imports.[3] It sought to prevent Bon Jour from using the name "Chambord" on its coffee makers, which Bon Jour had been doing since 1981. Eventually, the parties settled the lawsuit and a consent decree was entered. This decree prohibited Bon Jour from continuing to use "Chambord" for the sale of coffee, but specifically allowed it to continue to use the mark in connection with the sale of coffee makers.

In this new lawsuit, the district court rejected Chatam's anti-cyber-squatting claim against Bodum, finding that Bodum did not

---

2. 15 U.S.C. §1125(d)(1)(B)(ii).

3. *Chatam International v. Bon Jour Imports*, Civ. A. No. 81-5185 (E.D. Pa., March 11, 1982).

act in bad faith when it registered the domain name, chambord.com. It found also that Bodum had a valid, subsisting trademark, "Chambord." It had used this mark for an extended period of time to sell nonelectric coffee makers. Moreover, the court recognized that the consent decree authorized the use of the mark for that purpose. And Bodum had not registered other infringing domain names.

According to the court, although it was true that Bodum's use of the "Chambord" name was limited to a specific line of products, Chatam's use of the same name was also limited to certain products—liqueurs, chocolates, candy, and cakes. The court did observe that if Congress had wished to do so, it could have required in the ACPA that a website be shared for this kind of same-name situation, but it did not do this. Therefore, when two parties sell noncompeting products under the same mark, there is a race to the gate to determine who will obtain the most desirable domain name. In this case, Bodum was there first, and acquired "chambord.com"; Chatam had to settle for second-best, "chambordonline.com."

The court also rejected Chatam's trademark infringement claims. The main question in determining whether infringement had occurred in this case was whether Bodum's use of the "Chambord" mark to identify its coffee makers was likely to cause confusion as to the origin of such goods. Using a multifactor assessment[4], the only factor where the court thought there might be a close relationship in the minds of consumers was between coffee and liqueur as beverages. But, the court noted that the 1982 consent decree already constrained Bodum from selling coffee under the Chambord name and there was no evidence that Bodum intended to sell or market *coffee*, as distin-

---

4. *See* Coffee Break, "Diluted Coffee: A Trademark Primer."

guished from *coffee makers*, on the chambord.com site, or on any site to which this web page was linked.

Under the consent decree, the interdiction between liqueur and coffee was not extended to liqueur and coffee makers. "A consumer would be unlikely to associate a liqueur and a housewares product," the court opined. Moreover, it noted, the business styles and approaches used by the two companies were different. Chatam's advertising messages were designed to appeal to "romance and elegance." Bodum's emphasized "functionality and contemporary design." The court did not see any other areas where there could be a likelihood of confusion. The parties had been using the mark "Chambord" in parallel for more than 20 years without any evidence of actual confusion between the two.

Chatam argued that the Internet had dramatically changed things: it had removed Bodum's use of the "Chambord" mark from what was contemplated by the consent decree and resulted now in actual confusion. The court readily agreed that if the Internet is viewed as a single universe of trade and advertising media, with a prodigious commercial value of its own, these factors point toward product confusion. But, on the other hand, the court said, if "the Internet is seen simply as an overlay on the global marketplace, without materially affecting its existing divisions, these factors are either neutral or tilt the other way." In this case, the court was content to accept that the Internet was not the sole commercial outlet for either party but, instead, was in addition to broad advertising and sales activities in other media. The court was convinced that there was no likelihood of confusion where products have some overlap in channels of advertising and trade but primarily occupy different channels.

The court did express concern over whether Bodum's registration of "Chambord" as a domain name in an unrestricted generic top-level domain "created a substantial likelihood of non-pre-existing confusion." In other words, the court wondered what effect the initial and exclusive access to Bodum's products through chambord.com would have on the public and the marketplace and whether this would create a potential for dilution of Chatam's mark. Was there "initial interest confusion"? Infringement can be based upon confusion that creates initial consumer interest, even though no sale is finally completed as a result of the confusion. This is a great concern when products are in competition with each other. In those instances, consumers may be drawn to a product and identify it with a particular source without realizing until later that it came from elsewhere. This can be viewed as a variation of the practice of "bait and switch"—taking advantage of another's well-known name.

The court did not see these elements in the Chambord case, however. It concluded that "a consumer attempting to access an upscale liqueur product is unlikely to be dissuaded, or unnerved, by the sight of coffeemakers and other housewares, having first brought up the coffeemaker's screen . . . . Internet surfers are inured to the false starts and excursions awaiting them in this evolving medium."

Chatam had also claimed trademark dilution under the Federal Trademark Dilution Act of 1996 which was enacted to safeguard famous trademarks from attenuation resulting from unauthorized use. The court noted, however, that to show dilution, timing was important. When did Chambord become a famous mark as a liqueur vis-à-vis Bodum's first commercial promotion of the "Cafetière Chambord"? To prove dilution, Chatam had to show that Bodum's use of the mark for its coffee makers had to have occurred after the Chambord mark for liqueurs became famous. But Bodum had been using "Chambord" since 1980, and since 1982 through the consent decree, for its line of coffee makers, long before the brand for the Chambord liqueur had gained international recognition.

Chatam argued that the Internet registration and use of "chambord.com" constituted a new and different use from Bodum's previous use in commerce, which was limited to coffee makers, and that this new use arose after Chatam's mark became famous. The court was not convinced of the merit of this argument, noting that the statute speaks of "commercial use in commerce" without distinguishing between the types of use. It looks to the mark's fame at the time of the user's first commercial use, the court stated, "not when the first use occurs that the mark's owner finds objectionable." And, the court noted, the Internet is a "new universe of communication, not of use."

In the end, Bodum won, but the court did not perceive that either party had much to gain or lose in this case. It noted that "the loser, if any, in this cyberspace technology dispute is the public." It is hard to say, the court added, that "the time-honored entrepreneurial one-upsmanship of the first-to-the-trough" would really make that much of a difference to the sales of either party. Much like the Internet itself, the impacts are as yet an unexplored territory.

Coffee Break

Of Coffee and France: A Taste of Luxury

The French have been enamored with coffee since the days of King Louis XIV, when the beverage was first introduced to the Court. Initially, it was a drink for the nobility, much like the liqueurs that were consumed after sumptuous dinners. Even today, French coffee speaks of luxury, of "la vie en rose." Eventually, coffee became the beverage of the masses, even in France, but that did not prevent a certain "snobisme" among those who enjoyed the finer things in life—a good cup of freshly brewed coffee accompanied with a small digestif, such as the raspberry liqueur Chambord, featured in the *Chatam* case.[1]

It is no coincidence that both a liqueur producer and the maker of the French press coffee maker would each have selected the name "Chambord" for their respective products. A liqueur is all that is luxurious, elite. Likewise, the popular Bodum French press coffee maker has a certain elegance. The name "Chambord" is evocative of those same traits: an elegant, stately chateau. Look at a photo of the famous castle

Coffee Break (continued)

and note the simple lines, the reserve, and the lack of ostentation. It is classic. To select the name "Chambord" for a coffee maker is marketing genius, for it attributes to a piece of everyday equipment the same pride of place and taste that any French person feels about the Loire Valley and its famous royal palaces.

The French press is probably one of the most unique but effective of coffee makers. It has been known by a number of names—coffee plunger, press pot, coffee press, cafetière, cafetière à piston. In the early 1900s, it was known as a cafeolette. Its design is deceptively simple. It consists of a cylindrical carafe, usually made of glass. It has a filter made of either a fine wire or nylon mesh, which is attached to a plunger. There is a lid on top. To make coffee, all one needs is boiling water and coffee. This method of coffee-making produces a full-bodied and flavorful beverage. Ground coffee is placed in the filter, which is attached to a plunger. Boiling water is poured over the grounds and, using the plunger, one forces the hot water through the grounds to the bottom of the beaker or carafe. While the brew is steeping, the bulk of the coffee's flavor and oils are transferred to the water. All the coffee is in contact with the water for the same length of time, creating a balanced beverage.

A person drinking a cup of coffee made in this manner can imagine being in Paris among the most sophisticated of coffee drinkers. And, if one is feeling particularly kingly, one can also order a little liqueur, such as a Chambord, or perhaps a crème de menthe, or a glass of cognac. Note that the French are not the only society that appreciates a digestif with their after-dinner coffee. The Spanish, for example, enjoy *carajillos*, which is coffee and brandy combined together. But ask any French person, and he will tell you that in France, because they have the only true cognac (made in the region surrounding the town of Cognac, in southwestern France), as well as in his opinion, the best way of making a good coffee, it is all the more refined in France.

---

1. *See* Chapter 20.

Chapter Twenty-One

Fair Trade Coffee:
The Growers

El Salto, S.A. Escuintla Guatemala CA v. Psg Co. and Greenberg, 444 F.3d 477 (9th Cir. 1971)

A s the twentieth century drew to a close, various movements whose goal was to draw attention to the imbalance in the economics of the coffee trade gained a greater voice in the debate. But this was not a new development. For decades, efforts were made to raise the attention level so that coffee consumers could understand the true costs of their low-priced morning cup of joe, and the plight of the growers.

In the 1960s, the National Federation of Coffee Growers of Colombia began a very successful ad campaign in the United States, featuring Juan Valdez, a mustachioed idealized coffee grower, with his mule, extolling the virtues of his hand-picked beans. Unfortunately, even though much of Colombian coffee was produced by small family-owned businesses, most of the coffee imported into the United States from South and Latin America was not, and still is not, produced under such happy conditions. And even the Juan Valdezes in Colombia faced low coffee prices, which continued to fall to the end of that decade.[1] Besides being continually at risk to the vagaries of the weather,

---

1. Pendergrast, pp. 285-287.

pests, price volatility, and other uncertain economic conditions created by the boom-bust cycle of coffee production, growers also had to contend with unscrupulous buyers and outright fraud. Producers were vulnerable to the chicanery of traders and market manipulators and, to maintain their plantations, they were often dependent on loans from the brokers who also bought their coffee. The *El Salto* case is but one example.

El Salto was a Guatemalan company engaged in the production, processing, and marketing of raw and refined sugar and green coffee. El Salto had business dealings with Philip Greenberg, an Oregon man who acted as a coffee broker and trader, both on an individual basis and through his closely held company, Psg Co. In 1963, El Salto entered into several contracts with Greenberg and Psg to market its coffee in the United States. Initially, El Salto dealt with Greenberg individually. At the time El Salto and Greenberg began to work together, Greenberg loaned El Salto's affiliate, Orion Enterprises, $300,000 for equipment and other coffee plantation expenses. Greenberg later obtained a bank loan for this same amount.

In August 1963, Greenberg formed Psg with himself as sole shareholder and officer. In April 1965, Psg and El Salto executed a sales contract that obliged Psg to purchase a minimum of 6,000 bags of El Salto's coffee from the 1965-1966 crop year. This agreement designated Psg as both the buyer and the "sole and exclusive" agent for El Salto in the United States. Under this agreement, El Salto was to pay a commission to Psg equal to 2-½ percent of the sale price of the coffee sold under the contract. In August 1965, El Salto and Psg signed a new agreement even more favorable to Psg that designated Psg as the exclusive sales agent for El Salto's coffee exports for the crop years 1965-1966 through and including 1968-1969. El Salto agreed to pay a 2.5 percent commission on coffee sales and guaranteed Psg a minimum annual commission of $25,000 per year for services rendered by Psg to El Salto.

Business relations at first were amicable until El Salto asked to be paid for the coffee it had shipped to Psg's account. After the August contract was signed, Psg negotiated eight sales of El Salto coffee to American purchasers. Psg refused to forward $100,000 in receipts from these sales to El Salto, claiming that it was entitled to withhold them under the April 1965 contract. Finally, El Salto sued both Greenberg and Psg in federal district court in Oregon, demanding payment, and asking the court to hold Greenberg personally liable for Psg's obligations to El Salto.

At the trial, the jury found that the August 1965 contract superseded and nullified the April 1965 agreement, that Psg had unlawfully retained $105,286 in coffee contracts, and that Greenberg had unjustifiably retained $2,187 on one of the coffee sales. The jury also found that Greenberg had breached his obligations to El Salto as its agent but that he should not be held personally liable for Psg's debts. Judgment was granted in favor of El Salto for damages and the amount earned from the coffee sales that had been unlawfully withheld by Psg and Greenberg.

The district court also held that Psg had violated Section 2(c) of the Robinson-Patman Act by claiming agency commissions under the August contract.[2] Under the facts established at trial, Psg had acted both as a coffee buyer and at the same time as a broker, claiming commissions from El Salto on the same sale.

Both parties appealed.

Psg claimed that it had been entitled to withhold payment of the proceeds from the coffee sales in order to pay down the

---

2. 15 U.S.C. §13(c). Section 2(c) prohibited parties to a sales contract from granting or receiving a commission, brokerage fee, or any allowance or discount in lieu of any such fees, except for services actually rendered in connection with the sale or purchase of goods.

$300,000 loan that Greenberg had made to El Salto's affiliate several years earlier. The April contract provided:

> Payment for coffee to apply against $300,000 advance made by Psg to El Salto, until such advance and interest due has been liquidated. Balance of funds after liquidation of $300,000 advance, less commission and expenses, to be remitted to El Salto upon completion of contract.

El Salto contended that the $300,000 advance had been paid back in full. According to the testimony of its officer, the reference to the advance had been inserted into the April 1965 contract by Greenberg in order to facilitate his loan from an Oregon bank (for the proceeds he had earlier advanced to fund El Salto's equipment purchases). According to testimony by both parties, no one denied that these loans (both Greenberg's loan to El Salto and the bank loan to Greenberg) had been paid off before Psg claimed any right of setoff as a justification for its failure to pay El Salto amounts owed for coffee sales.

Psg argued that all this testimony, even if undisputed, should have been excluded at trial because it constituted parol evidence, oral statements not included in the written contract that were superseded by the contract terms. The appellate court disagreed. It found that the contractual language in question simply provided for the manner in which amounts due under the contract were to be applied. El Salto's additional oral evidence at trial did not vary the terms of, or contradict, this agreement. El Salto simply claimed (and the jury found) that no unpaid balance on the loan remained against which payments from coffee sales could be set off.

Psg contended that the language in question not only provided for the disposition of sums due, but also constituted an undisputable acknowledgement by El Salto of a then-existing indebtedness. But the court determined that the contract language was far too imprecise to accommodate such a construction. It noted that Oregon law allowed extrinsic evidence to be introduced whenever there was an ambiguity, as here.

Once this confusion was clarified, however, El Salto faced a much bigger hurdle. It was able to convince a judge and a jury, as well as an appellate court, that Psg owed it over $100,000, but it could not actually get paid that sum if Psg did not have the money, as seemed to be the case.

El Salto had asked the trial court (and raised this request again on appeal) to "pierce the corporate veil" of Psg and hold its sole shareholder, Greenberg, personally liable for Psg's debt to El Salto for the coffee sales proceeds. First, it argued, it had dealt with Greenberg personally and had relied on him on an individual basis long before Psg was formed. To El Salto, Psg was Greenberg and Greenberg was Psg. Second, El Salto contended that Greenberg had organized Psg solely for tax purposes and to shield himself from liability for his own unscrupulous actions. As the sole officer and shareholder of Psg, Greenberg was its alter ego and should be liable for acts that he undertook, in whichever capacity. As support for this argument, El Salto pointed out that Greenberg had failed to keep separate books for his personal income and expenses and those of the corporation.

But the appellate court was not persuaded. The justices did not view these facts as being sufficient to warrant going so far as to strip away the corporate structure under which Greenberg conducted business and had dealt with El Salto. They also noted that El Salto had not shown that Psg was an "obviously undercapitalized corporation." In other words, it was unfortunate that Psg did not have the funds to pay El Salto what it owed but the court would not require Greenberg to make El Salto whole out of his personal funds. In American jurisprudence, no matter the ethical implications, absent significant fraud, as opposed to mere unsavory dealings, courts have tended to respect the corporate entity.

Even before the Fair Trade movement took hold, basic rules of equity demanded that parties treat fairly those with whom they engage in trade. There is a long history of unfair business dealings in the coffee industry. El Salto may have been vindicated in its claim, but it gained nothing. It won the case but ultimately—if Psg had no funds, which seemed to be the case—it lost the larger fight to earn fair compensation for the coffee beans it had shipped to the United States to be sold. And, by hiding behind his corporate shell, Philip Greenberg was able to make money through his dealings with a less sophisticated coffee grower, violate antitrust laws without consequence, deprive this grower of the value of his coffee, and then walk away with impunity.

Coffee Break

Fair Trade

The Netherlands was an early and a major player in the coffee trade, which was one of the principal factors in the spread of colonialism. In the seventeenth century, the Dutch smuggled coffee tree saplings from Yemen and transported them to their colonies in Indonesia. They planted them and began to grow coffee, in particular on the island of Java. Later, they started large coffee plantations in Sumatra and Bali. The Dutch became the leading coffee traders in Europe. As a result of the policies pursued by the Dutch and the tribal leaders who collaborated with them, the local people were forced to stop growing the rice, fruit, and vegetables they needed to sustain themselves, and instead turned the land over to the production of coffee. This brought about a horrific famine, which caused many deaths. The Dutch finally abandoned this policy and allowed the local people to plant food crops alongside the coffee.

Max Havelaar: Or the Coffee Auctions of the Dutch Trading Company, a novel written by a former official in the Dutch East Indian Civil Service under the pen name Multatuli, first published in 1860,[1] tells the story of Max Havelaar, a Dutch civil servant. Havelaar was a young idealist who wished to end the ill treatment and oppression of the native Javanese caused by the corrupt coffee trade. The novel aroused controversy when it was first published in the Netherlands, because of its depiction of Dutch coffee dealers. But it had great appeal with the Dutch populace that only grew over the twentieth century: Max Havelaar became a folk hero.

In recognition of the role that this novel played in the popular imagination as the Dutch considered the role that their nation had played in the history of coffee, the name was adopted by the Fair Trade movement as a symbol of their goals. In the 1980s, when coffee prices, already descending, fell sharply, a group of Dutch social service organizations and churches joined together and formed the Max Havelaar Foundation in 1988 to promote the

247

Coffee Break (continued)

trade in, and consumption of, coffee products that would be certified as "Fair Trade."

The Dutch were not alone. Fair Trade started as an outgrowth of various social movements aimed at improving labor and environmental standards in developing nations. For centuries, growers have been the victims of the volatile coffee market. Part of the problem has been the lack of transparency, both for the grower and the consumer. Because coffee, for the most part, is grown on plantations in distant countries in, for example, Africa or South America, it is not possible for even the most socially conscious consumer to buy directly from the grower, as she might buy vegetables at a local farmer's market. Much of the price that is paid for a cup of coffee at the consumer level is not seen at all by the grower: it is reflected in the layers of middlemen who are involved in the transport of coffee from the plantation to the cup.

The grower, whether in Africa or South America, deals with a broker, who earns a commission by arranging to sell the grower's beans to an exporter. The exporter in turn pays the grower and then sells the coffee to an importer, with his profit margin added in. The importer adds his profit margin to the price offered the exporter and then sells the green coffee at that price plus shipping costs to the roaster. The roaster sells the coffee either to a food wholesaler (such as Folgers) or to a coffee shop proprietor, who will then increase the price again in order to cover her rent, taxes, and employment costs. In short, it is a long way from the tree to the cup with many an opportunity for price abuse and inequity built in.

Even though the inequities have existed for generations, the 1980s to 1990s generated a true coffee crisis, when prices paid to growers imploded. In response to very real hardships faced by growers, churches, initially—which were already providing sanctuary for laborers migrating north to escape the violence in Guatemala, Nicaragua, and El Salvador—and then other concerned groups, sought to create an alternate economy to the one that they viewed as oppressive to small farmers.

In the early 2000s, the depression in world coffee prices created a significant crisis for growers. In Vietnam, by then the world's third largest coffee producer after Brazil and Colombia, the price obtained for green coffee beans paid back to the growers less than 60 percent of their production costs.[2]

Fair Trade is a market-based approach that involves certifying and labeling products that meet certain standards. Fair Trade principles apply to a number of commodities, but particularly coffee, if for no other reason than that coffee is the most heavily traded commodity after oil. The Fair Trade certification process enables consumers to identify and reward producers by paying a higher price for their coffee (relative to uncertified products), compensating them fairly, while achieving certain goals in improved labor conditions and environmental sustainability.

Today, several nonprofit organizations oversee certification and labeling for coffee, licensing the use of the "Fair Trade" trademark in each major market. The oldest and best known of these organizations is the Max Havelaar Foundation. In the United States, Fair Trade certification is organized by Transfair USA, created in 1998.[3] The Fair Trade logo on Fair Trade-certified products signifies guaranteed minimum prices to the growers for their coffee, long-term trading relationships, acceptable working conditions, and environmentally sound protection. Since the first Fair Trade organization was founded in the Netherlands in 1988, it has taken a profitable niche in Europe's coffee business, accounting for 5 percent of total sales.[4]

One of the first and foremost principles of the Fair Trade movement for coffee is a guaranteed minimum price for farmers for their beans no matter what the current market prices, to prevent farmers from losing money on their crops. Fair Trade groups work with democratically run cooperatives of small farmers, who receive credit—up to 60 percent of the price of the coffee—up front before they actually deliver the coffee in order to enable them to invest back into their farms.

Another issue that also gained attention toward the end of the twentieth century was the destruction of wide swaths

Coffee Break (continued)

of rain forests and the environmental degradation caused by large coffee plantations. The second half of the century saw a shift in the way that coffee was grown and produced, brought on by the rapid increase in coffee production and the surge in consumer demand for specialty coffees. To meet this growing demand, the coffee industry shifted from its reliance on small coffee producers (the Juan Valdez of the coffee commercials) to industrial cultivation on larger plantations. Traditionally, coffee is grown under a canopy of shade trees. With the changes in production to boost coffee exports, coffee farmers converted from shade- to sun-grown coffee, cutting down shade trees to grow coffee in the open. Coffee varieties that thrived in the sun started to replace traditional coffees.

Coffee grown in the sun was promoted for two reasons. One was the increased demand for coffee that created incentives to dramatically increase coffee production. More sun trees can be planted per acre and each plant produces as much as three times more coffee than a plant grown in the shade. The other reason was to prevent the spread of a fungus called coffee rust that was destroying traditional coffee plantings. This rust thrives in shaded humid environments. The fear of coffee rust also led to increased use of chemical pesticides and fertilizers on coffee plantations.

Opposing the trend toward industrialized coffee farming in recent years has been the growing consumer demand for food products produced using sustainable practices. This demand has greatly promoted the Fair Trade coffee movement. As an added benefit, many coffee connoisseurs claim that sustainably grown shade coffee tastes better than sun-grown, mass-produced coffee. This is probably because coffee grown by these traditional methods takes longer to mature, and a bean that has matured slowly has a sweeter taste.

In recent years, Fair Trade organizations have been criticized because they have entered into relationships with large coffee retailers, such as Starbucks and Dunkin' Donuts, licensing to them the right to use the "Fair Trade Certified" label on coffee sold in their stores. Concerns have been raised that this has enabled these companies to engage in so-called "greenwashing," the practice of using Fair Trade as a cover to enhance their public image for sustainability while drawing attention away from the real abuses in the coffee trade.[5] However, many praise these same companies for the steps they are taking.[6] It would seem unreasonable to expect large multinational organizations to completely switch their sources of supply to solely Fair Trade-certified products. And there is some concern whether the Fair Trade market could become large enough to achieve a real amelioration in standards in developing nations.[7] Nevertheless, sales of Fair Trade-certified coffee have increased substantially in the United States in the last few years.[8]

Other companies have taken a different approach, working with organizations other than the Fair Trade Organization FLO to obtain a certification for sustainable practices. One of these is the Sara Lee Corporation, which obtained Utz certification for certain of its Douwe Egberts' products.[9] Another is Kraft Foods, which, along with Lyons in Britain and Lavazza, Italy's biggest coffee maker, have established relationships with the Rainforest Alliance, a sustainability organization established in the late 1980s with the goal of halting rainforest destruction.

The principal way these organizations differ from the Fair Trade organizations is in the price paid for coffee. The Fair Trade organizations guarantee a minimum price to the growers, which is generally higher than the market price because it is based on a reasonable return to the growers for their investment in their sustainable plantations rather than the vagaries of the commodities market. Critics of Fair Trade argue that the minimum price guarantee under the Fair Trade model exacerbates the problem of globally depressed coffee prices. It draws growers into the market attracted by an artificially high price, which in turn leads to excess coffee supply.[10] Organizations such as the Rainforest Alliance offer no minimum guaranteed price. And some will argue that price, rather than sustainability,

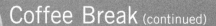

Coffee Break (continued)

is the real reason why large food companies have shown a willingness to work with this organization rather than the Fair Trade groups. Rainforest Alliance coffee is less expensive than Fair Trade Certified coffee. Whatever the arguments, pro or con, it is nevertheless certain that as long as consumers demand Fair Trade coffee, producers will find ways to provide it, while still making a profit on their product offerings.

---

1. Multatuli, *Max Havelaar*, Translated by Roy Edwards, Penguin Books, 1987.

2. Purvis, Andrew, "Is Global Business Hijacking the Fair Trade Bandwagon?" *The Observer*, Sunday, Jan. 29, 2006, at http://www.guardian.co.uk/lifeandstyle/2006/jan/29/foodanddrink.fairtrade.

3. In 1998, Max Havelaar, Transfair, and a number of other separate organizations formed an international umbrella organization, Fairtrade Labeling Organizations International (FLO) creating a uniform fair trade logo. Weihe, Ted, "Cooperative Fair Trade Coffee: The U.S. Experience," U.S. Overseas Cooperative Development Council, Presentation to COPAC Conference on Fair Trade Coffee, Jan. 21, 2005, in Berlin, Germany, found at http://www.copac.coop/about/2005/weihe/pdf.

4. Collier, Robert, "Coffee with conscience: Fair Trade offers farmers a better deal, Network ensures cooperative farmers get paid higher price," *San Francisco Chronicle*, Sunday, May 20, 2001, http://www.sfgate.com/cgi-bin/article.cgi?f=/c/a/2001/05/20/MN196612.DTL.

5. Hiscox, Michael, "Fair Trade and Globalization," Harvard University, Department of Government, February 23, 2007, p. 6, found at http://www.wcfia.harvard.edu/sites/default/files/Hiscox_Fair.pdf.

6. Hiscox, p. 6.

7. Hiscox., p. 7.

8. Hiscox., p. 8.

9. *See* Chapter 22: "Can You Mandate Fair Trade?"

10. McAllister, Sean, "Who is the Fairest of them All?" *The Guardian*, Wed. Nov. 24, 2004 at http://www.guardian.co.uk/lifeandstyle/2004/nov/24/foodanddrink.shopping1.

Chapter Twenty-Two

Can You Mandate Fair Trade?

*Douwe Egberts Coffee Systems Netherlands B. V.
v. The Province of Groningen*, Case 97093/KGZA
07-320, Groningen District Court (Nov. 2007)

*"Coffee brewed without the bitterness
of injustice just tastes better."*[1]

As the Fair Trade movement has progressed, pressure has been placed on large corporations (such as Starbucks) to offer Fair Trade-certified coffee among their product offerings[2], as well as on governments to encourage Fair Trade by imposing certification as a "must have" into their purchasing requirements. Some have pressed further. In 2002, a ballot measure in the city of Berkeley, California, would have required that all coffee served in Berkeley be organic or certified Fair Trade. The measure—which effectively pitted growers in the developing world against small coffee shop owners in Berkeley—was

---

1. Deborah Jones, Global Exchange, a nonprofit that has promoted Fair Trade since 1999, quoted in Murmann, Mark, and Weir, Laila, "Coffee Measure Tests Berkeley's Taste for Fair Trade," Election 2002, The UC Berkeley Graduate School of Journalism, November 6, 2002, http://journalism.berkeley.edu/projects/election2002/stories/000111/html.

2. "Purchasing Fair Trade Coffee Gives People a Simple, Everyday Way to Support Living Wages for Farmers in the Developing World," PRESS RELEASE, Global Exchange, September 22, 2000, http://www.globalexchange.org/campaigns/fairtrade/coffee/pressrelease092200.html.

opposed by nearly every restaurant and café in the town and lost overwhelmingly at the polls. The mayor supported having the city purchase Fair Trade coffee only but questioned whether a local government could dictate the buying decisions of virtually every business in town that served coffee.[3] Even on a narrower scale, however, can such a certification be mandated as part of a competitive bidding process?

Some governments have felt constrained by competitive bidding regulations from making a Fair Trade certification a requirement. In fact, in the European Union (EU), one legal guidance issued several years ago suggested that, although Fair Trade options can be welcomed, a bid cannot be rejected or considered to be noncompliant simply because it did not include desired Fair Trade options.[4] This is because, according to the guidance, specifications framed in terms of "fair" and "ethically traded" as requirements do not adequately define characteristics or performance as required by EU rules.

This was the problem faced by the Province of Groningen in the Netherlands several years ago. The province issued an invitation to bid for vending machines in government offices, which included coffee supplies. By the time bids were closed, five had been received. Douwe Egberts, the largest Dutch coffee company, was not among the finalists. It filed suit to terminate the procurement process and to require that the bids be redone. The company argued that specifications in the Groningen bid package violated EU law because they were discriminatory and too vague.

The specifications in question included the following:

The coffee ingredient currently used is 100% Arabica of supreme quality. In addition, coffee and tea must be Max

---

3. Murmann and Weir, Election 2002.
4. http://www.ogc.gov.uk/documents/Guidance_on_Fair_and_Ethical_Trading.pdf.

Havelaar and EKO certified. It is a requirement that the qualities remain of this high standard. . . . You are required to demonstrate that your products are allowed to bear both quality marks. . . .

The Max Havelaar Foundation awarded the international Fair Trade quality mark under the name of "Fair Trade Max Havelaar" to promote Fair Trade conditions in the Netherlands. Any bids that did not comply with this specification were effectively eliminated.

As one of the oldest and the largest coffee company in the Netherlands, Douwe Egberts had long been the coffee supplier of choice throughout the country. Although a subsidiary of the global consumer products conglomerate Sara Lee Corporation, since 1978, the company had long roots in Dutch history. Douwe Egberts was founded in 1753 by Egbert Douwes and his wife, Akke Thysses. They began selling coffee, tea, and tobacco in their small shop, De Witte Os (The White Ox), in Joure, a small village in the Netherlands. Originally Egbert Douwes only sold his product locally. However his son, Douwe Egberts, who entered the business around 1780, built up a national reputation by supplying coffee and tea to shop owners throughout the country, spreading the fame of the Douwe Egberts brand. Gradually, the company grew to become the Dutch market leader for coffee.[5] By the 1950s, the company was responsible for over 50 percent of coffee exported from the Netherlands.[6]

In the Groningen bidding, Douwe Egberts was not able to certify that its coffee would be Max Havelaar or EKO labeled.[7]

---

5. Douwe Egbert's Official Website: http://www.douwe-egberts.gr/gren/Retail/Who WeAre/OurCompany.

6. Pendergrast, p. 269.

7. EKO certification issued by Skal for organic products sold in the Netherlands is an assurance that the agricultural product carrying the certification has been produced by organic methods. It is allowed on products containing more than 95% organic ingredients. http://www.skal.nl/English/EKOQualitymark/tabid/109/Default.aspx.

The fact that Douwe Egberts lacked the Max Havelaar label was due to its own lack of action. As the largest coffee company in the Netherlands, the company assumed that it would be first choice among coffee purchasers, by the strength of its brand alone, and therefore it failed to anticipate and appreciate the growing sustainability and Fair Trade movements. Thus, when first approached in the 1980s by the social organizations that were trying to establish a certification program when the Fair Trade movement was first gaining traction, the company did not initially respond. The organizations then approached a number of smaller companies that were competitors of Douwe Egberts to gain support for their movement. In 1988, this group launched the Max Havelaar Quality Mark for coffee.[8]

In the bid that it submitted to the Province of Groningen, Douwe Egberts argued that, although the coffee it was proposing to provide lacked the Max Havelaar certification, it would be Utz certified, which it argued was the equivalent.[9] At the time of the bidding, Douwe Egberts had submitted a number of written questions, asking, perhaps wishfully, whether the Max Havelaar

---

8. Pendergrast, pp. 354-355.

9. "Utz certified" or "Utz Certified Good Inside" are marks for an industry-led certification program, which claims to be the largest coffee certified in the world. http://www.utzcertified.org/index.php?pageID=101. It was founded by Ahold Coffee Company, a large Dutch coffee company as Utz Kapeh which means "good coffee" in the Mayan language QuichÚ, to ensure that the company was not purchasing coffee from producers who were using child labor. An office for the organization was opened in Guatemala City in 1999. In 2002 the head office was opened in The Netherlands. Its standards for certification are considered to somewhat less stringent than the Max Havelaar Fair Trade requirements particularly in that it offers producers no minimum or guaranteed price for their crop. Utz certified producer organizations are therefore vulnerable to the volatility of the coffee market. "Utz certified" also does not have clear requirements with regard to the remuneration of hired labor; only national laws must be followed. The program also lacks crop pre-financing and producer support. *See*, Fox, Tim, "The Coffee System: What Standard, What Means? 'Fair Trade' and 'Utz'", Graduate School of International Relations and Pacific Studies, University of California, San Diego, Prepared for Professor Peter Gourevitch, Support from Panta Rhea Foundation, Edited by Jennifer Cheng, MPIA 2008, Corporate Social Responsibility, Spring 2007 P. 62, http://irps.ucsd.edu/assets/020/8416.pdf.

certification criterion was a "want" or a mandatory requirement. Groningen responded that it was a "knock-out" requirement. When asked whether the province would consider Utz- certified coffee to be the equivalent to Max Havelaar-certified coffee, the province stated its view that the basic standards and objectives of Utz-certified were not as stringent as those of Max Havelaar and therefore the two certifications were not equivalent.

Douwe Egberts then asked the province to change its requirement for coffee from "Coffee: Max Havelaar and EKO" to "Coffee: sustainably produced and certified." But the province refused because it wanted to pursue "only the highest possible sustainability" and it believed that the Max Havelaar certification indicated to the producers which requirements should be met. However, recognizing the possibility that other quality marks could meet the basic premises for sustainability, the province then revised the bid requirements to spell out what it was requiring: 1) a warranty that the coffee would be purchased directly from small farmer cooperatives, 2) a cost-effective minimum price (to ensure that the costs for socially and environmentally friendly production were covered), 3) an assurance that, if the world market price exceeded the guaranteed price, the world market price would be paid, 4) prefinancing for coffee farmers (that is, assurances that, if desired, the growers would receive a percentage of the selling price before shipment, so that they could make necessary investments), and 5) long-term trade relationship between the coffee supplier and the growers.

In its suit, Douwe Egberts asked that the province be required to start over with its coffee procurement program, that is, to issue a new bid package that had neither the Max Havelaar certification requirement nor specific conditions imposed for how sustainability had to be obtained. According to Douwe Egberts, by imposing these conditions, the province had excluded other quality marks granted by independent certifying institutions, which constituted discrimination against suppliers who qualified for those other certifications.

Douwe Egberts also claimed that the province's insistence on having Fair Trade certification as a "knock-out" criterion (instead of a "nice-to-have") was not legitimate because the certification requirement was not critical to the goal of the bid package—to provide quality coffee for its "hot beverage" facilities. According to Douwe Egberts, the Utz-certified quality mark, which it had obtained for its coffee, was equivalent to the Max Havelaar certification with regard to sustainability. Douwe Egberts also contended that the additional requirements the province had imposed were ambiguous, allowing for multiple interpretations, and therefore illegitimate.

The province disagreed. In its reply brief, it stated its belief that it had complied with all mandates of the applicable procurement statutes. It also noted that, at both the national and the European Community level, there was a strong preference for integrating Fair Trade principles into procurement policies and it had acted accordingly when it set up the requirements for its coffee purchase. It was not true that only Max Havelaar-certified coffee had to be supplied: the requirement, as clarified by the province in its reply to Douwe Egberts, was only that the coffee to be supplied comply with the quality requirements that the province had set out in the clarification it had issued before bids were submitted. Douwe Egberts could have taken these clarifying statements into account when preparing its bid. Moreover, these requirements—to which Douwe Egberts had objected—were critical to the procurement objective, quality coffee, because they all related to the sustainability of the coffee to be supplied. Further, they were not so specific as to favor or eliminate any particular company, so as to be, in other words, discriminatory, as Douwe Egberts charged. The province also pointed out that Douwe Egberts deliberately chose not to comply with the other basic requirements set out in the bid package with regard to sustainability. According to the province, the environmental aspects of the Utz certification were not the only goal the province sought to achieve when it mandated Fair Trade coffee; there were social aspects also that were part of Groningen's requirements that differed from the standards for Utz certification.

The Max Havelaar Foundation was allowed to intervene into the case. In its brief, it pointed out that it was not discriminatory—or favoring only one or two suppliers—to mandate Fair Trade conditions in a procurement context. The foundation noted that, in the Netherlands, there were approximately 20 potential coffee suppliers with certifications that complied with the basic premises that the Province of Groningen set out. It was both lawfully permitted and socially desirable to ask suppliers to offer products that met the basic principles for Fair Trade.

The court ruled in favor of the province. When it issued its clarification, removing the "Max Havelaar" criterion and replacing it with a detailed description of the principles to which the coffee supplier had to agree to adhere, the province did not amend the procurement requirements or change them, as Douwe Egberts alleged, which would have invalidated the competitive bid process. Rather, it had merely rephrased the standards that the province expected to be met, in order to clarify them.

For the court, the central question was whether the province was entitled to use basic Fair Trade principles as required standards in a public procurement context. The court ruled that it could do so; nothing in the EU or Dutch procurement regulations precluded the imposition of additional requirements. The principles that the province defined as "must haves" were, according

261

to the court, sufficiently clear, and adequately related to the object of the procurement process: to obtain quality coffee. Moreover, nothing in the province's requirements was discriminatory, the court ruled, even if the number of prospective bidders was reduced somewhat. As long as the award criteria were objective, indiscriminately applicable to all offers, and related to the product being procured, the process was evenhanded. The fact that there were at least 20 qualified suppliers in the Netherlands alone, as the Max Havelaar Foundation had noted, as well as others in other parts of Europe, belied Douwe Egbert's contention that the bid process discriminated against it. Moreover, Douwe Egberts itself had the option, had it chosen to do so, to supply coffee that met Groningen's basic requirements. But it chose not to do so.

And finally, the court said, as long as there was no unequal treatment or restriction of the free movement of goods, as there was not here, the province was entitled to establish policies to promote sustainable, economic, and social development of emerging economies. The criteria in the province's bid package had the additional effect of furthering both EU and Dutch policy "to pursue sustainability and positively influence social and environmental standards."

The court ordered Douwe Egberts, as the losing party, to pay not only the province's costs of the proceedings, but also those incurred by the Max Havelaar Foundation. Bitter coffee for Douwe Egberts.

About the Author

Carol Robertson has been a practicing attorney for 30 years, including as a partner at a major San Francisco law firm and as corporate counsel with San Francisco Bay Area companies. In the course of her practice, Ms. Robertson has had the opportunity to represent restaurateurs, food and beverage producers, and retailers in their general business matters. She has taught French at the high school and college levels, and holds a BA and an MA in French Literature. She interrupted her studies toward her PhD in order to attend law school at the University of California at Berkeley (Boalt Hall School of Law), where she graduated in the top 10 percent of her class in 1980.

She has been a frequent speaker at professional seminars, workshops, conferences and conventions throughout the United States and Canada, on various business and legal subjects, and has taught English at the Law and Business School and at the College of Sciences at the Université de Pau, France. Ms. Robertson has been an adjunct professor at John F. Kennedy University in Pleasant Hill, California in the School of Management and in the Law School, where she has taught courses in Business Law, Business Ethics and Negotiation Techniques.

Ms. Robertson has been a coffee enthusiast since her college days. She enjoys traveling to coffee-loving countries, including Egypt, Turkey and throughout Western Europe. As a college student, she spent a year at the Université de Bordeaux, in France, where she earned a Diplôme Supérieur d'Études Françaises, and from where she returned with her first stove-top espresso coffee maker. She has returned many times to France and Italy since that initial sojourn, frequently bringing home in her suitcases new equipment for brewing coffee. With her personal collection of coffee makers, she is able to share with friends on a moment's notice an espresso, a French café filtre or even a Turkish coffee, and she can't say which she prefers. Not that she has to stay home to enjoy coffee—Ms. Robertson lives in Berkeley, home of the original Peets, where any number of coffee shops, including a Starbucks, are just a short walk away. As she says, when one is in the mood for a good cup of coffee, it is nice to be able to sit down and take pleasure in the moment.

Index

K

Kaffeeklatsch, 68
Keefe, Martin, 164–66
Kellogg, John Hartley, 131
Kent State University (KSU), 176–80
Kent State University v. University Coffee House (2003), 175–80
    See also lease for coffee shop
Kenya, 77
Khali-Beg edict, 144
Khan al-Khalili (Cairo, Egypt), 181, 182
The Kitchenry (Cincinnati, Ohio), 201
Kona coffee, 210–12
Kona Kai Farms, 210, 211
Konditorei, 68
Kraft Foods, 251

L

labeling
    See also advertising; branding
    ingredients and adulteration, 25, 29–30
    Kona coffee, 212
    warning labels, 132, 154–55
Lanham Act of 1946, 86, 87
Latin America, 78, 136, 147, 241
    See also specific countries
Lavazza, 251
lease for coffee shop, 176–80
    exclusive use clause, 179
    parol evidence, 178–79
Leneghan, Brian, 204, 209
Leneghan, David, 208, 209
Leneghan, Patrick, 208–9
Lichtenstein, Arnold, 163–70
Lichtenstein v. Consolidated Services Group, Inc. (1999), 163–70
    See also minority shareholders
Liebeck v. McDonald's Restaurants (1994), 159–61
likelihood of confusion, 58, 59
    Lapp Factors to determine, 89
    private-label sales, 82–85
    and trademark protection, 86, 87
Lion brand coffee, 29
liqueurs, 230–36, 237
Little, George, 3–8

Little v. Barreme (1804), 3–8
    See also "Flying Fish" case
Lloyd, Edward, 14, 16
Lloyd's of London, 14–16, 224
Lloyd's Register, 16
Louis XIV (king of France), xii, 9, 230, 237
Louis XV (king of France), 9, 10
Louis Ender, Inc. v. General Foods Corp. (1972), 91–97
    See also trademark protection
Lundberg, Samantha, 188–91
Lyons, 251

M

Manhattan Coffee Co., 71–75
maritime insurance, 12–23
    access to information, 15–16
    American colonies, 16–17
    brokering, 14
    fraud, 15
    insurance companies, emergence of, 17, 182
    Lloyd's of London, 14–16
    rating criteria for "seaworthy" vessels, 17–20
    "running policies," 18, 20
    underwriting, 15–16, 17
    uniform rating system, 17
market control, 41–49
    See also antitrust law
marketing. *See* advertising
Marsalli, Charles, 55–59
Marsalli's Blue Ribbon Coffee Co., 57–58
Marsalli's Blue Ribbon Coffee Co. v. Blue Ribbon Products Co. (1958), 55–59
    See also branding
Marshall, John, 7
Martinique, 3, 10
Mary W. case, 18–20
    See also maritime insurance
Max Havelaar: Or the Coffee Auctions of the Dutch Trading Company (Multatuli), 247
Max Havelaar Foundation, 247, 249
    certification for Fair Trade, 257–62
"Maxim" trademark, 91–97
Maxwell House, 42, 51, 81, 92, 99, 108

crisis in 1980s, 147, 247, 248
crisis in early 2000s, 249
and ICAs, 146–47
minimum resale prices, 44–45
price wars, effect of, 29
valorization plan, 35–36, 37, 145
private-label sales, 72, 73, 81–85
likelihood of confusion, 82–85
product liability
flawed design, 155–58
hotness of coffee, 151–58
warning, necessity of, 154–55
Prohibition period and coffee
sales, 43
Prussia, xii
Psg Co., 242–46
publicity, right of, 218, 219, 222
put options, 121

Q

quality vs. profitability, 55–59, 99
"Quasi-War" with France, 5, 8
quotas on coffee imports, 135–48

R

Rainforest Alliance, 251–52
Reagan, Ronald, 137
reckless misrepresentation, 117–19
Red Can Coffee. *See* Hills Bros.
Red Can Coffee
religious rituals, coffee's use in, xi, 98
resale pricing, 45–49
restraint of trade. *See* antitrust law
Rio No. 7 coffee, 36
roasters, patents for, 98, 104
roasting, 26–27, 34, 35, 50, 52, 201
Robinson-Patman Act §2(c), 243
robusta coffee, 52, 61, 77, 99, 105
Rosenberg, Bill, 127
Royal Crown Coffee, 59
Ruddy, John, 113–19

S

Salterio, John, 163–70
Sambuck's Coffeehouse (Astoria,
Oregon), 188–91
Sara Lee Corporation, 251, 257
scienter, 115–16
sea loans, 13–14

Securities Exchange Act Rule 10b-5,
116, 117
seizure
of foreign warehoused coffee, 37
of ship cargoes, 4–8
self-service grocery stores, 43, 50
Sherman Antitrust Act, 36, 37, 45
ships
See also maritime insurance
rating criteria as "seaworthy,"
17–20
seizure in Caribbean, 4–8
side effects of coffee drinking, 130
Sielcken, Hermann, 36–38
single publication rule, 218–22
Sixth Amendment, 143
slave trade, 21–23
smuggling, xii, 9–11, 78, 108,
135–43, 147, 247
South America, 78, 136, 241
See also specific countries
Soviet Union, 136, 137, 146
Spain, 238
Spice Bazaar (Turkey), 171
Sri Lanka, 9
Starbucks, 100, 181, 182, 184, 199, 210
Fair Trade, 250, 255
trademark protection, 187–97
Starbucks Corp. v. Lundberg
(2005), 187–91
See also trademark protection
*Starbucks Corp. v. Wolfe's Borough
Coffee, Inc.* (2007 & 2009), 191–97
See also trademark protection
substitutes, 34, 131, 145
sugar market, 28–29
Sultan of Cairo, 144
Sun Insurance Company, 18–19
sustainability as criteria for Fair
Trade, 250, 251, 259–61

T

Taft, William Howard, 36
takings, 32–33
Talbot, Silas, 8
Talleyrand, 5
tarnishment and trademark
protection, 88, 194

taste. *See* flavor

Taster's Choice labeling, 216–17, 222

Tata Coffee, 78

tax deduction for expenses, when allowed, 74–76

Teamsters Union, 65

Theodor Wille & Co., 36

Thompson, Benjamin, 173

tortious interference with business relationships, 203, 206–7

"tourist coffee," 137, 146

trade dress, defined, 86

Trademark Act. *See* Lanham Act of 1946

trademark protection
blurring, 88, 193, 195–96
consent agreements, 86, 92–97
definition of trademark, 86
dilution, 87–88, 188–90, 191–93, 235–36
domain names and cyber squatting, 231–36
famous marks, 87–88
infringement, 82–85, 87, 188–90, 192, 233–34
intent and bad faith, 196
license of trademark, 86
parody exception, 197
tarnishment, 88, 194
and unfair competition, 57–59, 86, 95–96, 192

trade secrets, 203–5
cheat sheet of blends, 204
inevitable disclosure, 205
noncompete agreements, 202, 205
proprietary client lists, 205

Transfair USA, 249

trespass, 7–8

"triangular route," 21

Turkish coffee and coffee houses, 132–33, 145, 171–73
See also Constantinople/ Istanbul cafes

U

Uganda, 77

underwriting, 14, 15–16, 17

unfair business dealings, 246

unfair competition
See also antitrust law; trade secrets
and noncompete agreements, 205–6
and trademark protection, 86, 95–96, 192

union organizing, 63–67
election petition, 65
interference with union activity, 66
union authorization card, 65

United Nations coffee conference (1962), 136

United States v. See name of opposing party

Utz certified coffee, 251, 258

V

Vaccaro, James, 218

vacuum packaging, 44, 50, 51, 103

valorization plan, 35–36, 37, 145

Vietnam, 78, 249

voting trust agreements, 165, 168

W

wagon men, 63–64

warehousing of coffee, 37–38

warning labels, 132, 154–55

washed coffee, 61

Werdegar, Justice (California), 221

West Point Market, 203, 204

wet processing, 60–61

White, James, 30, 31

"white frosts," 109

WiFi in coffee shops, 224–26

Woolson Spice Co., 29, 30, 33

World War I and instant coffee, 98

World War II and instant coffee, 99

Wright (coffee trader), 13, 17–20

X

XYZ affair, 5

Y

Yemen, xi, xvi, 78, 171, 247

Yuban, 104–5

Z

zipper, dilution of trademark, 87, 190